# Humanizing Pedagogies with Multilingual Learners

Help ensure your multilingual students have access to equitable, humanizing teaching and learning in all the content areas. This comprehensive resource bridges theory into practice with applicable, easy-to-understand instructional methods for K-12 teachers who may not have a background in TESOL, ESL, or bilingual education.

Each chapter uses a three-part learning cycle to help you translate theory into practice: Explore, Make It Work, and Share. In Explore, the authors provide research, ideas, and resources to support your work with multilingual students. In Make It Work, you are given options to take the ideas from Explore and apply them to your practice. And in Share, you're encouraged to think about the ways to share your knowledge in informal or formal professional learning spaces. As you work through the learning cycle for each module, you'll gain important takeaways on topics such as the larger social context, a positive orientation to your students, humanizing assessments, grouping students, uncovering and addressing language demand, developing conceptual understandings, developing literacy, and fostering authentic talk.

The book's hands-on approach to pedagogy will leave you feeling ready and empowered to reach each of your multilingual students more effectively as you strive for equity and justice in the classroom and beyond.

**Kara Mitchell Viesca**, Professor of Teaching, Learning and Teacher Education at the University of Nebraska-Lincoln, focuses her scholarship on advancing equity in the policy and practice of educator development, particularly for teachers of multilingual learners.

**Nancy L. Commins**, Clinical Professor Emerita at the University of Colorado Denver, has focused her decades of teaching, scholarship, and service to connecting theory to practice and creating educational environments that build on and expand the cognitive, linguistic, and cultural assets that all children – especially multilingual learners – bring with them.

# *Equity and Social Justice in Education Series*
Paul C. Gorski, Series Editor

Routledge's Equity and Social Justice in Education series is a publishing home for books that apply critical and transformative equity and social justice theories to the work of on-the-ground educators. Books in the series describe meaningful solutions to the racism, white supremacy, economic injustice, sexism, heterosexism, transphobia, ableism, neoliberalism, and other oppressive conditions that pervade schools and school districts.

**Identity-Conscious Practice in Action**
Shaping Equitable Schools and Classrooms
*Liza Talusan*

**Social Studies for a Better World, Second Edition**
A Guide for Elementary Educators
*Noreen Naseem Rodríguez and Katy Swalwell*

**Teaching Storytelling in Classrooms and Communities**
Amplifying Student Voices and Inspiring Social Change
*Maru Gonzalez, Michael Kokozos, and Christy Byrd*

**Igniting Real Change for Multilingual Learners**
Equity and Advocacy in Action
*Carly Spina*

**Anti-Oppressive Universal Design for Teachers**
Building Equitable Classrooms
*Diana Ma*

**Integrating Educator Well-Being, Growth, and Evaluation**
Four Foundations for Leaders
*Lori Cohen and Elizabeth Denevi*

**Humanizing Pedagogies with Multilingual Learners**
Transforming Teaching in Content Areas
*Kara Mitchell Viesca and Nancy L. Commins*

# Humanizing Pedagogies with Multilingual Learners
## Transforming Teaching in the Content Areas

Kara Mitchell Viesca and Nancy L. Commins

Routledge
Taylor & Francis Group
NEW YORK AND LONDON

Designed cover image: Shutterstock

First published 2026
by Routledge
605 Third Avenue, New York, NY 10158

and by Routledge
4 Park Square, Milton Park, Abingdon, Oxon, OX14 4RN

*Routledge is an imprint of the Taylor & Francis Group, an informa business*

© 2026 Kara Mitchell Viesca and Nancy L. Commins

The right of Kara Mitchell Viesca and Nancy L. Commins to be identified as authors of this work has been asserted in accordance with sections 77 and 78 of the Copyright, Designs and Patents Act 1988.

All rights reserved. No part of this book may be reprinted or reproduced or utilised in any form or by any electronic, mechanical, or other means, now known or hereafter invented, including photocopying and recording, or in any information storage or retrieval system, without permission in writing from the publishers.

*Trademark notice*: Product or corporate names may be trademarks or registered trademarks, and are used only for identification and explanation without intent to infringe.

ISBN: 978-1-032-67018-8 (pbk)
ISBN: 978-1-032-67219-9 (ebk)

DOI: 10.4324/9781032672199

Typeset in Palatino
by SPi Technologies India Pvt Ltd (Straive)

# Contents

*Acknowledgements* . . . . . . . . . . . . . . . . . . . . . . . . . . . . . . . . viii
*Meet the Authors* . . . . . . . . . . . . . . . . . . . . . . . . . . . . . . . . . . ix

Introduction . . . . . . . . . . . . . . . . . . . . . . . . . . . . . . . . . . . . . . . 1

**Section I  Context** . . . . . . . . . . . . . . . . . . . . . . . . . . . . . . . . . 23

1  **Immigration, Migration, and Language Policies** . . . . . . . . 25
   Complexity Thinking and Critical Reflection Questions:
   *How do the racial and linguistic identities and migration histories of my multilingual learners from different backgrounds affect how I interact with and teach them? What impacts do systemic racism and linguicism have on my classroom, my students, their families, and communities?*

2  **Dominant Cultural Narratives** . . . . . . . . . . . . . . . . . . . . . . . 45
   Complexity Thinking and Critical Reflection Questions: *What impacts do perceptions of difference held by me, my students, their families, and communities have on our classroom community? What do I need to do for differences to be positive and productive rather than a source of harm and marginalization for multilingual students and their families?*

3  **Toward a Multilingual Classroom Ecology** . . . . . . . . . . . . 65
   Complexity Thinking and Critical Reflection Questions: *How do policies and current practices impact our (me, my students, their families, their communities) perceptions of varied language practices and our willingness to engage in communication across differences? How can I open my classroom as a space where varied language practices (languages, dialects, and registers) are utilized for the purposes of teaching, learning, and effective communication?*

**Section II   Orientations** .................................87

**4 Co-Constructing Learning Communities**...............89
   Complexity Thinking and Critical Reflection
   Questions: *How can I orient myself and my students toward interconnectedness and openness to build a strong community where we can collaboratively solve problems, disrupt inequitable issues, and create a sense of belonging? What systems, policies, and practices impact my ability to establish these kinds of relationships with students and families?*

**5 Humanizing Assessments**...........................111
   Complexity Thinking and Critical Reflection
   Questions: *How can I use assessment to create a complete and complex picture of my students? How is assessment data used to sort, label, and promote deficit narratives of multilingual students? What roles do or should families play in the assessment of my students? How do curiosity and creativity contribute to humanizing my assessment practices?*

**6 Pluralism in Practice**..............................133
   Complexity Thinking and Critical Reflection
   Questions: *What role does pluralism play in your practice? In terms of control in the classroom, what is important to you? Where might you be able to give up some of it? Where might you struggle to offer students agency and shared responsibility in the classroom? Why?*

**Section III    Pedagogy** ...........................155

**7 Meaningful Collaboration** .........................157
   Complexity Thinking and Critical Reflection
   Questions: *What tensions and complexities need to be addressed in my classroom for collaboration to be meaningful, equitable, and just? What opportunities exist and what barriers do I have to overcome for me to work as a collaborator in student learning?*

8  **Grouping in a Multilingual Multitasking Classroom**...180
   Complexity Thinking and Critical Reflection
   Questions: *Whom do students typically get to work with in my classroom? Across their whole school day? What markers of identity get attended to in determining such grouping? How can I group and regroup with multilingualism in mind? What other factors need attention to ensure that inequities are not perpetuated as my students work together in different groups?*

9  **Authentic Language Practices** .....................201
   Complexity Thinking and Critical Reflection
   Questions: *What do I currently do to promote student agency, meaning-making, and a commitment to equity in the use of different language practices? How can I address the complexities of using a variety of language practices to humanize the languaging in my classroom?*

10 **Deepening Conceptual Understandings** ..............223
   Complexity Thinking and Critical Reflection
   Questions: *Do I treat students as complex multiplicities with a variety of important life experiences that can inform their growth and development? Do I do so even if those perspectives and experiences are different from my own or the knowledge that is valued at school? Is there space in my curriculum and instruction for ideas, perspectives, and life experiences that students bring from a variety of cultural and linguistic backgrounds? Do I sufficiently decenter whiteness and monolingualism to make space for different ways of knowing and being in my classroom?*

   *References*.............................................248

# Acknowledgements

The ideas in this book come from years of extensive collaboration with dozens of incredible scholars across the world. To everyone who worked on the eCALLMS, ICMEE, OPETAN, and INNODI projects—thank you! We love you and this book would not exist without you! Thank you also to Rebecca Field for your early engagements with this book and our ideas. Your collaboration was deeply valued and impactful! To every teacher, student, and family and community member we have interacted with, thank you for helping us to be better teachers. And gratitude to Sonia Szeton for transforming our ideas about the Conceptual Reservoir into the beautiful image in Module 10.

**From Kara:** Thank you to Nancy, not just for co-authoring this book with me but also for being such a strong, consistent, and positive force for good in my personal and professional life. I cannot imagine who I would be without your kind patience and the considerable wisdom you graciously share. I also want to thank my mentors, friends, family members, students, and colleagues who daily push me to see the world more expansively and situate myself within it as a force for justice. You know who you are and I love and appreciate each of you so much. And finally, to Gama—amor de mi vida—no part of me exists that hasn't been made better from getting to live in partnership with you. Words are insufficient to express my gratitude for the support and care you have offered (over many years) that made this book possible.

**From Nancy:** Without Kara, her energy, brilliant mind, and persistence, we wouldn't be writing a dedication. I am so grateful to have her friendship and wisdom in my life. I extend my deep gratitude to friends and family who have encouraged me along the way: Alex and Kate, whose presence in my life is a daily gift; Aida, who keeps me calm; and especially Ken, whose unwavering support and enduring love get me through each day.

# Meet the Authors

**Kara** is passionate about people, teaching, and learning—essentially the core ideas of this book. She grew up as a monolingual speaker of English, but owing to an impactful high school German teacher, had an opportunity to spend her first year after high school as an exchange student in Germany. The contrast between experiencing the world monolingually and then experiencing it bilingually created profound insights that have guided her life and career path. She taught middle school German, English as a Second Language (ESL), and English Language Arts in Virginia and California. She also taught English in the graduate school at Peking University in Beijing China for a year and volunteered as an English teacher at a home for orphaned children in Mexico for a summer. Through all these experiences, she developed many questions that led her to earning a PhD and becoming an educational researcher and teacher educator. Her scholarship focuses on advancing equity in the policy and practice of educator development, especially for teachers of multilingual learners. She has led $4.6 million in federal grants intended to improve the practice of teachers of multilingual learners and conducted research in classroom across the US and several western/northern European countries which have led to dozens of publications in myriad academic journals. Early in her doctoral work, Kara began a journey of unlearning and deconstructing from whiteness and white supremacy that continues to this day. Also early in her doctoral work, Kara met her now husband and became part of a vibrant, caring, and supportive family, the Viescas (originally from Mexico), where she is continuing to use and improve her Spanish. Therefore, across her personal and professional endeavors, Kara seeks to engage in multilingual racial justice efforts targeted at creating the world that should be—an equitable, just, peaceful, and caring one—where multilingual community thriving is the norm.

**Nancy** has experienced tremendous joy working as an educator of multilingual learners. Aided by the various languages and dialects that make up her linguistic repertoire, her work with students, teachers, and families from diverse linguistic and cultural backgrounds has taken many different shapes. She has been a classroom teacher, university professor, program director, school district administrator, and independent consultant assisting schools and districts in their efforts to improve instruction for multilingual learners. In 2017, she retired from the University of Colorado Denver, where she helped lead the teacher education program representing Culturally and Linguistically Diverse Education. She is co-author of two previous books—*Linguistic Diversity and Teaching* (Lawrence Erlbaum) and *Restructuring Schools for Linguistic Diversity: Linking Decision Making to Effective Programs* (Teachers College Press)—as well as many articles and book chapters. She spent the 2011–2012 school year as a Fulbright Scholar at the University of Turku, Finland. Her research and teaching focused on preparing teachers to work with a student population that was becoming more racially, linguistically, and religiously diverse with the goal of immigrant integration. Her work in Finland continued for seven more years as a Visiting Professor and Senior Fellow. In those capacities, Nancy and her colleagues developed a professional endorsement for teaching multilingual learners and continued to conduct research. They received a grant from the Ministry of Education to develop and provide professional learning for faculty at seven of eight universities that prepare new teachers. This was in response to changes in the Finnish national curriculum which expects that all teachers be both linguistically and culturally responsive to their students. Officially 'retired,' Nancy as Clinical Professor Emeritus remains active in promoting humanizing teaching practices and community building while spending a lot of time gardening, walking, reading, and listening to live music surrounded by a loving family and amazing friends. She is always guided by these intentions: Be kind, listen more, fight oppression.

# Introduction

Picture a second-grade classroom in the midwestern US, led by an experienced teacher and composed mainly of multilingual students. It has a calm, caring feel to it as around the room children are working in groups, some of them with an adult, others collaborating with their peers. Across the different groups, students and adults are using English and languages other than English. They are engaging with texts that relate to students' lives and cultural practices outside of school. There is total inclusion of learners with disabilities. Students take on leadership roles and engage each other as they successfully collaborate without the supervision of an adult. Not everyone is involved in the same activities or even the same language, yet all students are deeply engaged in meaningful learning across an hour-long time span, illustrating strong thinking skills, creativity (one group is performing puppet shows for each other), and expansive language practices. A fantasy? No. A made-up vignette? No. This is what a group of experienced multilingual scholars from the US, Finland, and Germany recently observed as part of joint research they were conducting. Some declared it the best teaching they had ever witnessed. All felt it represented the essence of humanizing pedagogy.

We both have seen versions of this classroom where students are engaged, motivated, and learning across elementary and secondary grades. We ourselves try to engage in this kind of teaching at multiple grade levels and with adults. What underlies creating such classrooms is not just the technical act of teaching. To achieve this kind of teaching with multilingual learners, various factors and processes, including a deep commitment to equity and justice, need to be attended to. In this introduction, we begin an exploration of knowledges and skills, processes, and lenses that underlie teaching multilingual students that is humanizing. Our hope is that together we can help all multilingual students access the kind of teaching and learning experienced by the second graders in the classroom described above.

## Humanizing Pedagogies

The notion of humanizing pedagogies has a long history in our field. It is often traced back to Paulo Freire (1994), who in the 1970s worked with minoritized groups in Brazil and illustrated how education, when humanizing, can be a liberatory praxis for freedom from oppression. Many scholars, us included, have been impacted by Freire's work and furthered his ideas in a variety of ways.

We have also been influenced by Lilia Bartolomé (1994), who wrote about the need for us to move beyond what she termed a "methods fetish" and toward a humanizing pedagogy. Bartolomé argued that focusing solely on technical aspects of teaching (e.g., strategies), something that is very common in the field of teaching multilingual learners, will never create the kind of learning opportunities that students deserve. She called for teachers to develop ideological clarity and to create pedagogies that humanize students and attend to inequitable power relationships. In 2013, Maria Del Carmen Salazar published an extensive review of the research literature documenting the principles and practices of humanizing pedagogies from contexts around the globe. The tenets she offered as key focus on the interconnected nature of humanizing practices as well as the need for holistic attention to all aspects of individual and collective humanity. She specifically noted the need for critical reflection and action.

Recent work on culture and language in pedagogical practice, while not explicitly referring to humanizing pedagogies, has impacted our perspectives as well. For instance, Samy Alim, Django Paris, and Casey Wong's (2020) exploration of culturally sustaining pedagogies promotes pluralist practices that connect students' core identities with the learning processes they experience in school. To achieve this kind of pluralism, we must decenter whiteness. The dominant ways of seeing, doing, and being in the world are typically connected to the cultural practices of White people constructed through and for the purpose of sustaining white supremacy. Such practices have to be decentered in order for space to be created for other cultural and linguistic practices and ideas to also be engaged with meaningfully. As whiteness is decentered, the other aspects of culturally sustaining pedagogies that Alim and colleagues call for can be attended to. These include the reality that culture is complex and that the purpose of teaching and learning should be for sustaining lives and reviving souls. They also call for the creation of socially just, pluralistic societies and for loving critique and critical reflexivity.

Gail Prasad and Marie-Paule Lory (2020) also have provided important insights into our view of humanizing pedagogies in their work defining "plurilingual allies" or how teachers can act in ways that support the variety of language uses and backgrounds that multilingual students bring to the classroom. They suggest that as teachers we take steps to acknowledge linguistic privilege, develop a multilingual awareness, disrupt monolingualism as a norm, develop a practice of multilingual listening, engage in linguistic risk-taking, seek out opportunities to work with people from minoritized backgrounds (linguistic, cultural, and social), and advocate for linguistic reconciliation and social justice.

Humanizing pedagogies embrace all aspects of every human in the learning community and create the context for each person to be and become the best, most desired version of themselves (for short, we will refer to this as self-actualization). If we are striving for justice and equity, it is important that self-actualization be something that can happen for each person in the classroom, not just for some. Therefore, we must ensure that one person's (or group's) self-actualization does not come at the cost of another's. We need to also account for and contribute to this opportunity for each other and with each other. In classrooms, this looks like collaborative problem-solving when conflict arises, restorative practices to repair harm, and democratic decision-making to account for the varying needs and wishes of all members of the learning community.

This vision of justice and equity aligns with and is informed by the work from prominent abolitionists like Kelly Hayes and Mariame Kaba (2023) and Patrisse Cullors (2022) as well as from Indigenous scholars such as Leanne Betasamosake Simpson (2017) and Robin Wall Kimmerer (2013). Combined their work generates a comprehensive vision of what is possible, as well as the avenues to get there, grounded in a reverence and respect for all life. In our view, equity and justice are achieved when each individual and community/group gets to live their most desired life in authenticity and as cherished members of a larger community. This is possible when an abolitionist perspective of accountability is put into place that focuses on transformative consequences versus punishment. For instance, instead of teacher-designed classroom behavior reward systems based on punishing students for misbehaviors, co-constructed classroom community agreements can articulate expected behaviors as well as consequences for not sticking with the collaboratively determined agreements. When students play a role in co-creating classroom agreements and expectations as well as the kinds of transformative consequences that support community members in living up to shared expectations, a very different kind of learning space can be constructed.

We have found that the current and future teachers we work with want to create the kind of classroom where everyone can be and become the best, most-desired version of themselves. What they are often not prepared for is how hard it is to make this vision of justice and equity a reality, even with the best intentions given the societal barriers we face. It is complex and difficult work, which is why we wrote this book—to articulate both the challenges and possibilities while we conceptualize and operationalize our work in a way that this vision can actually be put into practice in more classrooms. Throughout the book, we offer a roadmap that moves from the abstract and distant to what humanizing teaching and learning can or should look like in classrooms with multilingual students. Since we ourselves are teachers and this book is being written for people like us (current and future teachers), our emphasis will be on the work we all need to do together for equity and justice to be achieved.

To us, teaching is both an art and a science where we collaborate with students, families, communities and our colleagues to foster growth. Our success depends on our ability to expertly weave together our knowledge and skills with those of the other members of the learning community. Therefore, we conceptualize humanizing pedagogies through the metaphor of collaboratively weaving a colorful tapestry.

In community weaving projects, each weaver brings tangible resources and useful skills to ensure the success of the project. The most memorable tapestries are distinct for how they weave together different kinds of materials and colors, including all the resources the community members offered for their production. Thoughtful coordination, collaboration, ongoing communication, and learning from one another's strengths are all necessary in order to ensure a long-lasting final product. This tapestry is most vibrant when it is co-created with other members of the community who will actually use it.

Similarly, humanizing pedagogies with multilingual learners require strong communication, collaboration, and inclusive practices. Our research suggests that the knowledge and skills we need to engage in humanizing pedagogies with multilingual learners fall into three large domains: *context, orientations,* and *pedagogy*. As we seek to weave a colorful, community tapestry, the distinctions among *context, orientation,* and *pedagogy* are less important than what is created when all are brought together. Each domain is attended to across this book, in the hopes we can all grow our knowledge and skills in each area while we also weave what we know and can do together with our students and their families to create humanizing pedagogies.

In addition to knowledge and skills (our own and those of our students and their communities) which represent the raw materials we need to collaboratively weave a tapestry, we need to attend to the processes we use to weave them together across a whole community. This is complex and at times can be challenging, especially when we are striving for equity and justice. Two important processes are needed to do this work: critical reflection and complexity thinking. These are essential for finding solutions to perplexing issues and growing our creativity to co-construct equitable and just humanizing pedagogies. Throughout this book, we go deeper into each domain and how they manifest themselves through three different lenses: intrapersonal, interpersonal, and systemic.

## Knowledge and Skills

The three domains of knowledge and skills that frame this book—*context*, *orientations*, and *pedagogy*—emerged from a 2019 literature review published with several colleagues (Viesca et al., 2019). The individual modules will provide an in-depth exploration of each as they are the bedrock that teachers of multilingual students need in order to create great teaching and learning opportunities across all content areas. We begin here with a brief exploration of how we conceptualize these ideas.

### Context

In 2024, Vice President Kamala Harris went viral for pointing out the importance of context, repeating a saying she learned from her mother. Harris recalled how her mother would ask, "You think you just fell out of a coconut tree?" and then would explain, "You exist in the context of all in which you live and what came before you." This reality isn't always obvious or emphasized in our society. For example, recently on the news, in a discussion of a major international event, the newscaster said, "It just happens that..." and went on to describe a political majority in a region that was using their power in a particular way. The use of that phrase, "It just happens that...," was striking as it suggests that the power of this political majority was a natural occurrence, something that just happened, versus the reality of deliberate political maneuverings grounded in historically created contexts that impact contemporary policies and practices.

Similarly, it is not unusual to treat the composition of classroom communities as if they just fell out of a coconut tree or as something that "just happens" as a natural occurrence. However, that is not the case. There are historical, political, and social factors that impact our and our students' presence in classrooms. This is perhaps most obvious with multilingual populations who are also often closely linked to immigration and migration. It doesn't take much to see how a war in Ukraine means an uptick in Ukrainian students in US schools or the opening of a meatpacking plant leads to an increase in immigrant families in the surrounding area. The contextual factors that impact who is in our classrooms also affect how we all interact with one another. Further, the context in which we live and what came before us also helps determine the kinds of resources we have access to, the ideas that are privileged, and the social and economic hierarchies that students, families, and communities experience in society.

Throughout our teaching careers, we have used the mantras "Nothing is neutral" and "Teaching is a political act." Misunderstandings and harmful practices can arise when we don't recognize that the context of our classrooms includes history, policy, current events, as well as other social and economic factors. It is important that, as teachers, we continually pay attention to the context in which we and our students live as well as what came before us. These myriad facets deeply impact the kinds of relationships we can have among the humans in our classrooms as well the ideas and knowledge we explore and engage with through our collaborative learning.

When we first talk with teachers about context, they quickly point to the physical environment in their classrooms and suggest the value of displaying multilingual posters and word walls. And, yes, these are good things to do. But the knowledge and skills we build around context are so much more than changing the physical space of our classrooms. We need to attend to policy, history, economics, public sentiments, cultural narratives, expectations, resources, vibes, experiences, relationships, and so forth.

It is particularly important to attend to the historical and contemporary practices that have created social hierarchies and how they are replicated in our classrooms and community. These complex hierarchies vary and encompass a variety of social identities and material realities typically organized around race, language, class, gender, sexual orientation, religion, culture, and ability. They impact what happens in our classroom at the intra- and inter-personal level as well as systemically.

For instance, two students who speak the same language and are in the same classroom might come from rivaling ethnic communities that have long been in conflict and bring aspects of that conflict to school. Or perhaps in a classroom led by a female teacher, a male student from an overtly patriarchal religious background tells the teacher that he doesn't have to do what she says because she is a woman. Or what about the third-grade student who recently totally withdrew from learning and is struggling to get through each day after their father was deported when his place of work was raided by immigration officials?

None of these situations "just happen" nor do the social hierarchies, policies, or histories that create and sustain them. Theses challenging classroom circumstances (all real) come from decisions that people made (either historically or contemporarily) and are further influenced by our institutions and cultural practices, all of which are impacted by oppressive systems like white supremacy, heteropatriarchy, ableism, and classism. We may not have been part of the creation of the social hierarchies, oppressions, histories, or policies impacting our classrooms, but we certainly hold responsibility for their continuation or disruption. If we don't understand the historical, political, and broader social context that surrounds our students, their families, and our classrooms, we run the risk of perpetuating inequities associated with them. It is not possible for one book to engage with every relevant contextual factor for humanizing pedagogies with multilingual students, but we will explore a few important ones throughout this book.

## Orientations

We think of orientations broadly as the ideas, ideologies, beliefs, attitudes, dispositions, perspectives, values, philosophies, and theories that determine the direction our decisions and practices move in. Just as we orient our bodies or our car toward a destination, our ideas and perspectives can orient our decision-making in classrooms.

We have often seen schools and classrooms that are oriented toward control and domination. We've seen lots of educational spaces that are oriented toward "one size fits all," insisting that all students have to do the same thing at the same time to demonstrate the same learning on the same assessment in the same language. We often see orientations that put productivity over people when teachers either choose or are forced to put curriculum pacing guides over poignant teachable moments where students can connect with each other and/or important ideas. Similarly, we often see orientations where policy is privileged over people as educators choose to implement policies that harm rather than take agency to either change the policies or simply ignore them and make the choices that are best for the well-being of the people involved. In our own research, we have documented how schools are overwhelmingly oriented toward English as all that matters, difference as deficit, race evasion, and the myth of meritocracy.

But let's imagine instead what schools and classrooms could look like if they were oriented toward things like openness— where teaching and learning embrace multiple knowledges with grace. Building on that openness could include an orientation toward interconnectedness where teaching and learning produce belonging. Adding in an orientation toward agency would create teaching and learning grounded in self-determination. What happens if teaching and learning are oriented toward shared responsibility where collaborative accountability guides decision-making and power-sharing? What would our classrooms look like if we were oriented toward curiosity and teaching/learning that focus on growth, exploration, and inquiry? Can we imagine classrooms oriented toward creativity where teaching and learning generate possibilities and transformation?

Hopefully, the benefit of these kinds of orientations resonates and you can see the possibilities of working with such orientations in your own practice. We are happy to report that such orientations guiding school and classroom decisions are not just a lofty idea; we've seen them in practice to incredible positive effect. We visited a school where most of the student population was multilingual, and the orientations described above were guiding individual and collaborative decision-making. We observed classes, spoke with students, teachers, and administrators, and found that there was a great deal of shared responsibility and agency. Students held elected positions and regular whole-school assemblies functioned as townhall meetings to discuss issues and solve problems. Students participated in and led decision-making around the artwork to hang in the building, quotes to represent their learning, and even the remodel of their library. Creativity and curiosity were constantly fostered through a school-wide commitment to experiential learning and inquiry. Lessons and units were organized around inquiry questions rather than learning objectives, which opened up the possibility for a variety of authentic learning journeys with multiple outcomes. Further, we saw openness and interconnectedness where differences were openly discussed and embraced for what they positively contribute to a learning community. We saw students discussing and thinking about the impact of their actions and ideas on others, especially those who were different from themselves. The outcome was a disruption of the typical cultural scripts where teaching is performed as monitoring and learning is performed as compliance. Teaching and learning opportunities at this school focused on growth through exploration and inquiry and were generating transformative possibilities from what *is* to what *should or could be*. The emphasis shifted from mastery to growth, from memorization to exploration, and from standardization to generative difference. We suggest that other educators can make these shifts as well by attending to the orientations guiding their work and moving toward openness, interconnectedness, agency, shared responsibility, creativity, and curiosity.

Across the modules of this text, we explore these orientations in order to build skills and knowledge about how they can enhance our ability to create humanizing pedagogies with multilingual students. Additionally, we encourage you to think about and name other orientations that are meaningful to you and have guided your own work with multilingual students as well.

## Pedagogy

Pedagogy is the day-to-day teaching and learning that occurs in classrooms. We view pedagogy as the integration of both practice and theory, which cannot be separated from either the larger context or teachers' orientations. While we have seen them in place, the orientations described above are not always seen in schools and classrooms. More typically, educators' orientations underlie a context where teaching is performed as monitoring and learning is viewed as compliance. For instance, teachers often make assignments (from a text or lecture) and then expect students to master the assignment individually. Often students are expected to recite facts either in writing or orally using standard English and classrooms are dominated by whole-class instruction, typically only in English. In secondary classrooms especially, lecture typically dominates, grounded in what Freire called the "banking" model of education—where the teacher deposits knowledge into students or there is a heavy emphasis on direct instruction or telling students things. Many pedagogical approaches position the teacher as the person who holds all the power in the classroom. Further, many pedagogies operationalize accountability as punishment and continually expect everyone to do the same thing at the same time. These practices and perspectives on pedagogy are uninspiring for most educators and certainly not sufficiently robust to support today's students in becoming the kinds of critical thinkers, innovative problem-solvers, flexible collaborators, and effective communicators necessary to take on the challenges of our world now and in the future. Yet these pedagogies are found in many classrooms today and are neither humanizing nor effective.

Our colleague and friend Annela Teemant (2024) has articulated a vision of what an equitable and just pedagogy could look like based on decades of her own and others' research. She asks us to imagine classrooms where teachers and students worked together on real products and real problems. Where classroom activities are language-rich and designed to develop higher-order thinking as well as full multilingual linguistic repertoires. Where learning activities are meaningful and related to students' lives, experiences, interests, and language practices. She supports teachers challenging students to apply their learning in complex ways to meaningfully solve real problems, especially those related to injustice and inequity. Such teaching is dialogic and small group–centric rather than whole-class, lecture-based. At the core of her vision is multitasking—different students doing different learning activities at the same time—as the norm rather than monotasking where everyone is doing the same thing at the same time. In these classrooms, all students have learned to work well with all other students and are the leaders of their own learning and the learning of others. Further, students have agency to make choices about their learning.

Truthfully, this doesn't have to be imagined. We have strong theoretical and empirical research that illustrates how to do these things as well as the dramatically positive outcomes of enacting these kinds of humanizing pedagogies (e.g., Tharp et al., 2000; Teemant & Hausman, 2013). We have visited such classrooms and implemented these pedagogies. We have witnessed the dramatic impact on learning, connection, and well-being that result. Having a foundation from which to build these kinds of pedagogical practices is the main focus of this text and addressed in every module.

## Processes: Critical Reflection and Complexity Thinking

There are two important processes that teachers interested in equity and social justice must become comfortable in applying. They are critical reflection and complexity thinking—the processes necessary to collaboratively weave the knowledge and skills described above into humanizing pedagogies. Here we briefly explore these processes to lay a foundation for the critical reflection and complexity thinking questions that appear in every module.

Critical reflection allows us to examine our practice to be better from one day to the next. By critical we do not mean "essential" or "negative"; rather, we draw on the thinking of critical theorists who explore power relations and attend to how to achieve more equity and justice. We have designed a process of ongoing reflection across each module that centers students and how they and our teaching are affected by issues of power, inequity, and injustice. Critical reflection asks who has power and who doesn't across the various situations we engage in. Critical reflection challenges mainstream assumptions and dominant narratives to explore other ways of seeing and being in the world than those we already are familiar with. We can always ask ourselves, what other possibilities or perceptions exist?

For instance, a student might not be speaking in class. We can jump to conclusions about that student and decide that they are shy or non-verbal or that their English just isn't good enough yet and leave them in their silence. Or we can ask what other possibilities or perceptions might be in play? Through critical reflection and investigation, we might learn that the student is willing and able to talk in certain circumstances where they feel safe, can use their full linguistic repertoire, and can draw on their cultural understandings of the world. By discovering these things, we can then create the ongoing possibility for the student's engagement rather than leaving the student to remain in silence.

In addition to this kind of critical reflection, the equity and social justice work at the center of humanizing pedagogies requires a thought process that can embrace contradictions, ambiguities, multiple perspectives, and points of view. That is complexity thinking. For many of us, this kind of thinking requires shifts in how we typically approach the world. Kathryn Strom and Kara Viesca (2021) offer multiple shifts that can be put into place to embrace complexity in teaching and learning. For instance, one shift is moving from *either/or* perspectives that can create artificial binaries and be simplistic as well as ignore various nuances and complexities to an *and, and, and* perspective. An example of this is moving from seeing students as *either* speaking *or* not speaking English to embracing the complexities of their full linguistic repertoire. A student can speak some English *and* lots of Urdu *and* have limited formal schooling experiences *and* be a very creative thinker *and*... so on and so forth.

Along similar lines, another shift is from seeing individuals to seeing multiplicities. We are all composed of multiple identities, positionalities, relationships, cultures, languages, and so forth. For instance, a student who is new to English, labeled "English Learner" by the district, is often seen in essentialist ways that do not account for their multiplicities. That student isn't just learning English, they are also a multilingual learner living a multicultural, multilingual life with many linguistic and cultural assets and repertoires. When we attend to those multiplicities, we can allow our students to tell us who they are rather than just seeing them as stereotypes, labels, or as representatives of surface features like their culture, race, ethnicity, or nationality. As multiplicities ourselves, we also have our failures, flaws, and imperfections. Thinking through all of these complexities is important to fully embrace our humanity as well as that of our students as we engage in humanizing pedagogies.

A popular contemporary complexity theorist Rosi Braidotti often defines "we" as "we-who-are-not-one-and-the-same-but-are-in-this-together" (Braidotti, 2022, p. 8). This illustrates another shift from neutral and universal to everything as situated and political. In this book, we, as authors, use the term "we" frequently because we believe we are writing to our peers, our colleagues, and our friends who are on a similar learning journey. However, we are also not one and the same. Nancy and Kara in some ways have many similarities (White, cisgender female, and multilingual academics) *and* we are different in many others (geography, generation, religious backgrounds, and so forth). We work in different contexts and have different privileges and challenges. We have each made unique contributions to the things we claim in this book as ours together. Sometimes, using the term "we" suggests neutrality and universality—that we are all the same. However, especially for those who have historically been marginalized and exempted from meaningful participation in various forms of "we," it is anything but neutral and universal. In reality, everything we do as human beings and educators is both situated and political. There is no such thing as neutrality when we live and work in a society that was historically constructed and is contemporarily perpetuated around inequality for racially minoritized people, women, the poor, the differently abled, LGBTQ+ people, and so forth. Those historical constructions of inequity live on today, so there is no such thing as neutrality or universality of experience, perspective, or privilege. Through critical reflection and complexity thinking, we can grapple with this reality in ways that are humanizing and affirming for our students, families, and communities.

## Lenses

As mentioned above, we have found that most pre- and in-service teachers are ready to jump on board with a "let's-all-get-along-and-be-in-harmony" vision for equity and justice in classrooms (in other words, a vision of justice and equity grounded in self-actualization in reciprocity, as described earlier). However, we have also found that it is a lot harder to do the deeply transformative work of removing barriers to equity and justice that always exist in ourselves, in our interactions with others, and across the larger socio-political systems we all live, work, and exist within. The processes of critical reflection and complexity thinking can help us do that work which is enhanced when we recognize that change must happen at different levels all at once. For this reason, we name three different but related lenses—*intrapersonal, interpersonal, and systemic*—that we can use to examine both what is and where we might go next as we pursue justice and equity.

At the *intrapersonal* level, we all have work to do to remove barriers to equity and justice (and will for the entirety of our lives). For instance, we all have biases and are impacted by the dominant cultural narratives that are part of society. Our biases can make us jump to conclusions about intellectual abilities when we hear someone speaking English with what we perceive as an accent. Dominant cultural narratives that circulate in our society can lead us to view the parents of our students as uncaring or uncommitted, our students of color as behavior challenges, and our White students as children just being children. Further, owing to multiple negative aspects of modern life, many of us have experienced trauma and developed survival techniques that can impact how we see ourselves, how we see others, and how we perceive our positions and roles in society. When we have unhealed trauma, our ability to reason through challenging situations (like student misbehavior in classrooms) can be impacted. All of this is quite complex and will be explored further in our modules. However, the point we would like to make here is that every person, regardless of background, educational attainment, and history with trauma, has opportunities for intrapersonal growth to learn more about themselves and the way they see themselves and others. The opportunities for learning at this level are deep, endless, and vital for equity and justice to be achieved. Here are some questions that can help us apply the intrapersonal lens in our work:

- What do I uniquely bring to the world (or this specific situation)? How do I talk to myself about as well as understand my strengths and opportunities for growth?
- How do various aspects of my identity and life experiences affect what I see and how I act? In what ways might my perspective be limited? How can I expand my perspectives of myself and others, particularly to better understand power and privilege?
- How do I carry trauma and pain? What techniques do I use to self-regulate and/or give myself kindness and grace during challenging times or when I personally fall short? What techniques do I use to push myself toward growth to limit the trauma and pain I create for others?

Next is the *interpersonal* lens. When we critically reflect and engage in complexity thinking through this lens, we turn our attention to the impact of our actions, words, beliefs, and behaviors on those around us. We need to pay attention to how power and privilege are operating in our everyday interactions while we build strong, humanizing relationships. In order to see and engage with students, families, and colleagues as fully human, we have to draw from what we learn about ourselves and our perspectives from an intrapersonal lens to carefully consider the contexts we work in and the impact of our interactions from an interpersonal lens. Here are some questions we can ask to work through the interpersonal lens:

- How do I typically build relationships? Am I aware of power dynamics when I interact with others? Am I aware of the impact my actions, words, beliefs, behaviors, and so forth have on others? How do I try to address them?
- How do I respond to challenging situations? What assumptions do I make when there is a conflict or difference of opinion/perspective? How do I repair harm I may have caused?
- How do I respond when I've been harmed? How do I protect myself? How do I find healing?

The final lens is *systemic*. While not always visible or obvious, the systems (educational, economic, political, cultural, linguistic, and so forth) that govern our daily lives deeply impact us at the intrapersonal and interpersonal level. Often, we can see how we need to do work on ourselves (intrapersonal) and in the ways we communicate and engage with those around us (interpersonal). It can be harder for us to see how systems are working and impacting us at both levels. Yet they are. Essentially, we both shape the systems we live and work within while we also are shaped by them.

The institutions/systems that organize our daily modern life have deep histories and are not natural occurrences that are inevitable. The systems that organize modern life were created by people for people and are perpetuated or disrupted by the ways we choose to live (both through our intra- and interpersonal actions). We and others have both sought to understand what has happened historically and what is happening currently in schools, communities, and classrooms for multilingual students. Because of this research, we can document how systems of racial capitalism, white supremacy, ableism, and the heteropatriarchy have played consistent and powerful roles in shaping all of modern life, including schools and typical approaches to teaching and learning. It is not within the scope of this book to explore and document all that history; however, it is important to attend to systemic issues to address injustice and to achieve equity. Here are some questions we all can ask ourselves:

- How do systems produce power, privilege, opportunity and/or inequity for me, my students, our families, and our communities?
- How do systems like white supremacy, heteropatriarchy, and ableism impact what I know, believe, and can do as a teacher of multilingual learners?
- What am I doing that perpetuates inequitable systems? What am I doing that disrupts inequitable systems and their impacts?
- What can I do inside and outside the classroom to account for external systemic pressures?

Self-actualization in reciprocity, our vision for justice and equity as well as the outcome of engaging in humanizing pedagogies, is not possible without attention to removing the barriers that do exist at each level (intra- and interpersonal as well as systemic). Further, what we find particularly important is how the intra- and interpersonal interact with and are woven together with the systemic. All three impact one another and all three together need to be attended to for humanizing pedagogies as well as equity and justice to be achieved.

## Book Organization

We have organized the resources in this book around both our research and the successes we have had as teachers. It's also grounded in over a decade of designing and offering online professional learning for teachers. It's possible that you have been one of the thousands of teachers across the US who have engaged with our work online and found benefit in it. It's also possible that our approach is entirely new to you—so we want to share the thinking behind it and the logistics of how you can best make use of this book.

As researchers and teacher educators, we spend a great deal of our time generating and reading research, but we will never be the expert in *your* classroom that *you* are. We deeply respect what you know and bring to the learning opportunities in this book. And as such, we have developed this book to provide you with maximum flexibility to take thoughtful agency in your learning while you also collaborate (as possible) with colleagues and/or peers to support the learning of those around you as well. This approach is important for us. Engaging in humanizing pedagogies with multilingual learners in our current test-based accountability-centric, inequitable, racist, linguicist, ableist, and overly standardized contexts will never be achieved through a quick-tips-and-strategies approach, especially one that focuses on language teaching strategies alone. Therefore, we are inviting you on an inquiry-grounded learning journey that you can and should be in charge of.

We have designed 10 modules and divided them into three sections: Context (Section 1), Orientations (Section 2), and Pedagogy (Section 3). Each module has been developed around important critical reflection and complexity thinking questions that illustrate the kind of learning you will engage with inside that module. We have ordered the modules 1 through 10 in what we think is a thoughtful progression that introduces and revisits certain ideas and provides meaningful ways to grow. However, one of our modules may cover a topic you already feel you know a lot about. Or you may have a pressing issue in your classroom that a later module might help you with. Please feel free to choose how you will engage with the modules, in which order, and with whom so that you can design the most thoughtful learning journey that will be beneficial to you today and into the future.

Once you have selected a module to work through, we ask you to start with an initial reflection, capturing your thinking regarding the module's critical reflection and complexity thinking questions. We encourage you to focus on the various issues that might be standing in the way of equity and justice being achieved in your classroom. You might also want to link your reflection to components of humanizing pedagogies discussed above (knowledge and skills, processes, and lenses).

After you reflect, you will engage in the three-part learning cycle that was so successful in our online professional development work: **Explore**, **Make It Work**, and **Share**. In the process, you will design and implement your own authentic response to the module critical reflection and complexity thinking question(s) based on your own experiences and contexts. In the **Explore** section, we provide information to you. We draw direct connections between research and theories to the things that do or could happen in your classroom while attending to the various complexities at play. We provide ideas and resources to engage with in ways that are meaningful to your work with multilingual students in your current or future classroom.

The next part of our three-part learning cycle is where you can act on the information in what we call **Make-It-Work** activities. In this section of the module, you are given several options to take the ideas from the **Explore** section and literally *make them work* in your practice. Each module has four options. The first three revolve around the lenses discussed above: intrapersonal, interpersonal, and systemic. We provide you with clear guidance to accomplish these tasks. The fourth option is "You make it work," where you can either take the ideas we have offered and tweak them to fit your local context and learning wishes or totally design your own learning opportunity based on what would be most meaningful to you. Once you have completed your selected **Make-It-Work** opportunity, we recommend you revisit the module critical reflection and complexity thinking question(s) and your initial reflection. Then draft a new reflection to answer the module's question(s) given what you have discovered.

**Share** is the final component of our three-part learning cycle based on research regarding the value of collaboration in teacher learning. We encourage you to think widely about the ways your engagement with this book can impact your practice as well as that of others. For the greatest benefit, we hope that your learning journey can occur within existing collaborative learning structures or create informal ones with one or more colleagues. This might be in spaces like a professional learning community (PLC) or a formal class structure. You can also work with one (or more) colleague(s) as you choose. The goal of sharing is to engage with the learning in this book in collaboration with colleagues and/or peers to discuss ideas, experiences, questions, and potential further inquiries to expand each other's learning experiences. If you are reading this book on your own, you can still find ways to share your learning to solidify and grow your ideas and practice. **Share** doesn't have to happen only with other people reading the book; you can share via hallway conversations, lunch chats in the faculty lounge, grade-level meetings, and so forth.

At the center of the learning approach for this book is you. You are the driver of your own learning across these modules. You can choose which modules to do, the order you do them in, and the people you discuss them with (e.g., your PLC, your class peers, and your colleagues). You can even choose to do multiple **Make-It-Work** options and spend extended time on one module. You may find value in re-doing a module after some time has passed as it could surface different insights and opportunities at different timepoints in your career. In this way, we believe that the resources we have developed in this book can assist you in striving for equity and justice as you create humanizing pedagogies with multilingual learners across varying contexts and over time.

If you are ready to get started, we recommend that you review the Table of Contents and examine the varying critical reflection and complexity thinking question(s) for each module. Then select where you would like to begin. If you don't have strong feelings about starting with any specific module, then turn to Section 1 and get started with Module 1.

Thank you for joining us on this learning journey. May we all work toward justice and equity through engaging in humanizing pedagogies with multilingual learners in all our classrooms!

# Section I
## Context

# 1

# Immigration, Migration, and Language Policies

Our classrooms are uniquely shaped by individual and collective histories as well as current realities around immigration, migration, and language policy. As educators, we need to understand the complex interplay of these histories and current realities in order to truly know our students as well as engage in humanizing pedagogies with them.

To begin our exploration, consider the following questions for complexity thinking and critical reflection: *How do the racial and linguistic identities and migration histories of my multilingual learners from different backgrounds affect how I interact with and teach them? What impacts do systemic racism and linguicism have on my classroom, my students, their families, and communities?* Be sure to keep your initial reflection, notes, and ideas so you can revisit them during the Make it Work and Share sections of the module.

 **Explore**

As teachers, we've worked with students from all over the world. Some of our students have spoken languages we never heard of until we met them. Others speak language(s) we ourselves know.

Some have spent their whole lives in the US, others have more recently arrived. Some view their arrival with great enthusiasm, and others with much less. There are as many different motivations and experiences as there are students in our classrooms, each one with their own unique history and relationship to various aspects of immigration, migration, and language policy. Engaging in humanizing pedagogies with multilingual learners necessitates our understanding of the historical context of immigration, migration, and language policy. It also requires attention to the relationships between that history and current realities especially regarding the lives of our students and their communities and families.

To fully understand the history of migration in the US and elsewhere requires confronting difficult truths and disrupting myths that are ingrained in our national narratives. People have immigrated and migrated throughout history for various reasons, but the level of displacement and movement we are seeing today is unprecedented. According to the UNHCR (the UN Refugee Agency) (2024), we are currently witnessing the highest levels of human displacement on record. Halfway through 2024, owing to conflict, persecution, poverty, climate change crises, and human rights violations, 122.6 million people—approximately 1 in every 67 people across the world—have been forcibly displaced. Millions of others are stateless or without a nationality, severely limiting their access to basic rights like education, health care, employment, and freedom of movement. These population shifts have implications for teachers everywhere as the arrival of newcomers often increases xenophobia and nationalism, issues that are growing across the globe. These issues directly impact our students, their identities, their education, and their futures very personally.

## Historical and Contemporary Contexts of Immigration and Migration in the US

In this section, we focus on the US context as it is not possible to explore the history of immigration and migration for all the nations of potential readers of this book. So, for readers working and living in countries outside the US, we invite you to build the same kinds of understandings about your own context that is provided here for readers in the US.

Just as there are many different histories and experiences with immigration and migration in our classrooms, the history of migration in the US is complex and can be viewed from multiple and often conflicting perspectives. It is frequently said that we are a "nation of immigrants" since most people currently living in the US have ancestry that traces back to other countries of origin. This dominant narrative centers on White European immigrants arriving at Ellis Island. For some, the associated images conjure up patriotic sentiments and pride set to Neil Diamond's song, "Coming to America" as a heart-warming soundtrack. While such feel-good narratives do reflect the experience of some, they are not the reality for many. US history around immigration also includes Native American genocide, the stealing of African people to sell and enslave on US soil, and other discriminatory, exclusionary, and oppressive policies and practices aimed mostly at non-White populations.

In order to build strong relationships with students and families as well as within our classroom learning communities, it is important to recognize that there is no single immigrant experience. Some families still hold on to idyllic stories that have been passed down through generations about overcoming adversity and realizing the "American dream." Other families are struggling to make ends meet and/or face a variety of issues of oppression and discrimination limiting access to quality jobs, health care, education, housing, and so forth. Many immigrants today and in the past have faced hostility, nativism, xenophobia, racism, and oppression.

Nowadays, people arrive in cars, boats, or planes as well as on foot, sometimes after thousands of miles of dangerous travel. Immigrants arrive with different statuses and documentation or, at times, lack thereof. Some have come with families and others alone, including many minors who were not accompanied by an adult they know or trust. Some have secured visas for work or residency, and some come as tourists and then stay. Some hold official refugee status—meaning they have been displaced from their homes by war or natural disaster and have been heavily vetted and granted special status by the United Nations. Others come seeking political asylum because their lives are at risk due to political or criminal violence in their home communities. Many people around the world see the US as offering economic opportunities, civil liberties, and legal freedoms not available in their home countries despite the adversities they know they may face.

These histories and contemporary experiences don't just impact students and families outside the classroom. They also impact how we as teachers see them, how they see us (and schools in general) as well as how students in our classrooms see each other. Together this impacts the relationships and opportunities for learning we can have.

The current US immigration system tends to dehumanize those seeking to immigrate and mire them in a complicated and dysfunctional bureaucracy. There has not been a comprehensive update to US immigration laws in decades, resulting in incredible backlogs in addressing applications and paperwork for people seeking to immigrate through the so-called "front door." Even with proper documentation, high financial fees and extensive waiting periods, up to over 20 years, are the norm. This means that for many seeking to immigrate, there is no "front door." Some students in our classrooms have no legal pathway to citizenship because they were brought to the US as minors without documentation. These major legal challenges and issues are unlikely to be meaningfully attended to soon due to the political divisiveness of this issue and the overall inability of our two major political parties to work together to find solutions related to immigration.

It is outside the scope of this module to comprehensively explore everything related to immigration and migration in the US. However, two broad and intertwined topics—race and language—are particularly relevant in the context of immigration, migration, language policy, and our work engaging in humanizing pedagogies in classrooms. Both language and race have been used historically and today to dehumanize multilingual students and their families, impacting opportunity, power, and privilege as well as their positionality in society.

## Race: A Brief Historical View

Race has long played a major but often under-acknowledged role in immigration and migration patterns and policies throughout our history. For instance, in 1619, when enslaved Africans were first brought to this continent, they were treated brutally and denied the rights and privileges of their enslavers. Thus began the creation of the concept of race and its use in society to oppress and deny rights and freedoms to countless human beings across history. While slavery had long existed in the world, the concept of race had not until it was created to justify the enslavement of Africans in a new country where all men were supposedly created equal.

The concept of race and racial categories was eventually tied to citizenship. In 1790, just seven years after the end of the Revolutionary War, the Naturalization Act was passed, restricting citizenship to free Whites, and codifying that citizenship was officially denied those who had been taken from Africa and brought to the US in bondage. Citizenship at that time was also denied to the Indigenous communities whose lands were being stolen and occupied. The genocide of Indigenous populations as well as the erasure of Indigenous languages, lack of access to citizenship, and denial of sovereignty on tribal lands are central to US history.

Racially minoritized people have consistently been treated poorly in the US, especially in the context of immigration and migration. For instance, in 1848, after the US annexed Texas and declared war on Mexico, the Treaty of Guadalupe Hidalgo was signed. In this situation, the border moved, not the people. The treaty promised to protect the land, language, and culture of the people who were living in the impacted areas (what today we call California, Texas, Utah, New Mexico, Arizona, Nevada, and parts of Colorado and Wyoming). The people were also given the right to become US citizens if they decided to stay. However, Congress refused to pass one key article in the treaty, meaning that promised protections were not realized. The rights to their ancestral lands as well as their culture and language, similar to the many treaties with Native American communities, were not recognized. Instead, the people who had been on the land for generations had to prove in court, and in English, that they had rights to their own land.

Also in the 1840s, large numbers of Chinese immigrants started coming to the west coast to work in mining, agriculture, and building the Transcontinental Railroad. In 1850, however, the California legislature passed the Foreign Miners Tax, which required Chinese and Latin American gold miners to pay special taxes that were not required of their European counterparts. In 1878, the US Supreme Court ruled that Chinese individuals were ineligible for naturalized citizenship; and in 1882, Congress passed the Chinese Exclusion Act that prohibited Chinese immigration for 10 years. It was renewed in 1892, made permanent in 1902, but repealed in 1943.

Since citizenship was tied to race, several court cases were brought to test the definition of "White." For instance, in 1923, a Japanese businessman, Takao Ozawa, petitioned the Supreme Court for naturalization by arguing that his skin was as White as any so-called "Caucasian." However, the court ruled that he was of the "Mongolian" race and thus did not qualify for naturalization.

Key features of all these policies and practices are othering and dehumanization which suggest that some people are less than because of their race—a label/category that was usually determined by skin color or national origin. As teachers of multilingual learners, we need to grapple with the complexity of this history and acknowledge that the notions of the American Dream and ability to assimilate (like a melting pot) are both true for some (especially those in White bodies) and not on offer for others (particularly those in racially minoritized bodies). Often, White people who immigrate quickly become unmarked and seen as truly "American" while, even after generations, those families living in and positively contributing to the US with racially minoritized bodies are continually marked as "other."

Our laws no longer officially grant citizenship status based on race; however, it still plays a major role in how newcomers are welcomed into and treated within US society. No matter how long racially minoritized families have been in the country, how well they speak English, or how engaged they are in the community, many still regularly face situations suggesting that they do not actually belong. This was certainly the case for the thousands of US citizens of Japanese descent who were placed into internment camps during World War II, losing their homes, possessions, and livelihoods in the process. This was also true when not too long ago, the president of the US told four Congresswomen of Color to go back to their countries. Three of the four women were born in the US and the fourth was a naturalized citizen, meeting the requirements to be a US congressional representative.

We've heard countless stories (which are increasing in frequency) from friends, family, students, co-workers, and so forth, all US citizens, describing various situations where because of their racial minoritization, they were told either directly or indirectly to "go home" or that they do not belong. This is the racialized reality that full assimilation in the US is on offer only for immigrants who are phenotypically White. If having a White body is the unspoken criterion for full citizenship, racially minoritized people will never be able to melt in or assimilate.

For these reasons (and more that will be explored in future modules), we reject the "melting pot" metaphor regarding immigrants and their roles as contributors in the US and prefer the more positive (though still overly simple) metaphor of the US as a "salad bowl." The most delicious salads have diverse flavors, vegetables, fruits, seeds, nuts, legumes, and so forth. None of these components need to lose their essence in order to contribute to the quality and deliciousness of the salad. In fact, when one feature is eliminated, the salad becomes decidedly less flavorful. If immigrants coming to the US are not expected to assimilate and disappear into the pot, they can maintain aspects of their identities, cultural practices, and language as well as contribute to a more extraordinary whole. While we would not argue this is happening today, it is a future we are working toward.

## The Impact of Racialized Immigration Histories Today

For many recent immigrants, their race or skin color did not enter into how there were viewed or treated in their home countries.

The ways they are racialized in the US is a totally new experience that is both confusing and hurtful. We've heard countless stories from multilingual students and their families of exclusion, discrimination, stereotyping, and overtly racist behaviors. These range from being questioned about their right to be present in a space (like a social event, an educational institution, or even a church), to inequitable treatment in coffee shops and grocery stores, to frequently hearing racial slurs and demands that they return home. The reality of how immigrants are viewed through racial lenses deeply impacts their experiences both inside and outside the classroom. Students have reported to us about being ignored by teachers or viewed as less capable. We've visited schools where multilingual programs and classes are in the worst classrooms with insufficient resources to support students and teachers in effective learning. Research has consistently shown that multilingual learners are under-represented in high-level classes and gifted programs and over-represented in basic skills classes and often erroneously placed in special education. The racializing of immigration in the US certainly plays a role in the kinds of learning opportunities afforded multilingual learners who are overwhelming students of color.

These complex histories and current realities affect multilingual students' and families' access to wealth, housing, employment, citizenship, health care, food, and transportation. They frame all their interaction with institutions like education and the government. We must critically reflect and think complexly about these historical and contemporary issues as we seek to disrupt the inequities and injustices they create in classrooms, schools, and society in general. A good place to start is through an inquiry into the historical and contemporary opportunities and roadblocks experienced by multilingual communities locally. As we explore local histories, we can and should draw connections to opportunities and issues that still exist today.

Sometimes teachers we work with want to immediately do these inquiries with their students, something we definitely encourage with a word of caution. We recommend avoiding asking all students to research their family's specific immigration history. This raises sensitive issues for students and families—from families experiencing separation due to migration, adoption and/or foster care, to the reality of some families' experiences with immigration being linked to Indigenous genocide or forced enslavement. We need to be thoughtful about how we create learning opportunities related to immigration and migration in order for our work to be inclusive and foster belonging.

One approach is to work with students to identify a local community of interest to research and learn more about. This might be a community that they or someone they care about belongs to. Or it could be a community that they simply would like to learn more about. These investigations are particularly beneficial when multiple local ethnic, racial, religious, and linguistic communities receive attention across the inquiries conducted by our learning community. We must work with students to avoid replicating stereotypes as well as problematic assumptions and deficit narratives. Centering and elevating the voices and perspectives of the community itself are good places to start.

Research should focus on how the community sees itself, the values it holds, the definitions it has of success. We can invite people to our classes to share their history, contributions, culture, and language either in person or using digital technologies (like Zoom or pre-recorded videos). On our own or with our students, we can visit or participate in events sponsored by local museums or cultural institutions as well as take advantage of their online resources or learning opportunities.

Through this work, we can grow with our students as we connect history to contemporary life in our local community. We can proactively engage our students in conversations about the history of race and immigration and how racialization happens today. All of us can benefit from deepening our abilities in this area through study, collaboration, healing, and practice. If you would benefit from additional support to develop the skills to have thoughtful conversations about race and equity in your classroom, a great place to start is with the impactful learning opportunities offered through the Equity Literacy Institute (https://www.equityliteracy.org/).

## Language Diversity and Loss

Language diversity has always been a feature of life in the US and globally. However, not all languages have been or are treated equally. Some are held in high esteem while others are treated as less than—constructing a tangible linguistic hierarchy that impacts our social interactions and the ability for a language to thrive. Historically, "old world" languages often disappeared in families within a couple of generations (Portes & Hao, 1998). One reason frequently noted why immigrants leave their languages behind is the desire of parents to save their children from the discrimination they themselves faced as speakers of those languages. As a society, we at times glorify how quickly previous generations of immigrants learned English and assimilated, but we ignore what this tragic loss represents socially, culturally, psychologically, and economically. The loss of intimacy and connection in familial relationships that occurs when certain languages and the people who use them are treated as inferior results in an unnecessary breakdown of stability in some immigrant communities. We have to ask why, with all we know about the benefits of multilingualism, is the loss of immigrant languages something we exalt?

We often hear about heroized past immigrants quickly learning English, typically accompanied by questions about why today's immigrants can't do the same. Such sentiments seldom delve into how or in what context immigrant ancestors used English. We wonder how these exalted immigrant ancestors would score on the English language proficiency tests our students take today, such as WIDA Access or ELPA21. In fact, there is no evidence that people are learning English at slower rates now than in the past. There have always been immigrants in the US who have kept their languages while still participating in the larger society. Individuals and groups have run businesses, taught school, performed in the theater, and much more in languages other than English, drawing on their abilities as well as connecting with and supporting other members of their language community. This history is often overlooked in the glorified assimilationist narratives of immigrants in the past.

We also have to wonder whether those immigrants who so quickly learned the language used only English. Did they also engage in various public and private activities in other languages. Based on our own experiences as multilingual individuals and decades of working with multilingual students, families, and communities, we know it is quite likely that they used all the language resources available to them as they established their life in the US. Myths about past immigrants using only English have helped to create the false narrative that English is *all* that matters in the education of multilingual students. Gaining proficiency in English is certainly important, but many other things matter in their education as well.

The labels we use also impact our perceptions of our students. Across the country, multilingual students are often referred to as "English learners" (or ELs for short). By labeling students this way, we acknowledge only a small part of who they are and focus their educational journey almost exclusively on English learning. For many multilingual students, their perceived or real English "deficiency" is the focus of their education until they are no longer labeled "English learners." Then students' language profiles are no longer considered at all. Former "English learners" are typically treated as if they were monolingual English speakers, ignoring their full capabilities and identities as multilingual. The way schools treat English as all that matters also contributes to students' losing the facility they once had in languages other than English.

We need to move away from the idea that English is all that matters and create a long-term, comprehensive multilingual educational journey. This is why we advocate that educators use the term "multilingual learners" for students who live their daily lives using two or more languages because their multilingualism is a major part of who they are and their lived realities. Further, their multilingualism is a major asset for the learning and thinking they can do in schools and should not be overlooked, regardless of their level of English proficiency.

Language loss is both a historical and contemporary reality for Indigenous communities in the US and beyond. The US has an extensive history of actively seeking to erase Indigenous linguistic and cultural practices. This reality is often completely missing in conversations around immigration and migration but totally relevant in the context of honoring and embracing multilingualism. The language-loss crisis in Indigenous communities began with colonialization but continues into modern-day practices as well. The recent use (into the late 20th century) of boarding schools to deculturize Indigenous communities and remove children from the linguistic practices of their families and communities directly impacts many people alive today and has had devastating consequences on Indigenous language and cultural practices.

As educators, we have an important role to play in disrupting this history of language loss and creating a multilingual future. In every class we have taught, we've worked with students who are multilingual as well as students who are just one or two generations away from the loss of their family's heritage language(s). These students never speak about that loss of language with happiness or gratitude but as significant and tragic. We cannot easily reclaim the languages that have already been lost, though important efforts toward revitalization can be supported and grown. Additionally, our practices, messages, and engagements with multilingual students and their families can help prevent language loss in the future if we actively support language maintenance and growth.

## Language Policy

There are both explicit and implicit language policies that are part of the ecosystem that affect the lives of multilingual students and their families. While we may not be aware of them, specific language policies have historically and currently been imposed directly or indirectly. Overt or official language policies openly dictate language practices in schools, classrooms, and public places. Implicit or covert policies, though not codified, also determine the language and social practices expected in our classrooms.

On March 1, 2025, an executive order was signed designating English as the official language of the country. Many are surprised to learn that the US has never had an official language until this point. Historians suggest that the colonial settlers who founded the US deliberately chose not to designate an official language. There are different perspectives as to why this happened. Some argue that having an official language would have impeded garnering wide support for the revolution and shut out people because of the language they spoke. Other historians suggest that there wasn't a need to have an official language because English was already so dominant. The recent presidential order declaring English the official language, changes little, as we have long been functioning as a society as if it already were.

Educational language policies are situated in societal norms and dominant beliefs while they are also impacted by different power relationships among and across language groups. Throughout US history, there has been an ongoing use of restrictive language policies toward groups our society has sought to control. At the same time, multilingualism and language opportunity have been embraced for those who already enjoy various levels of social power, most consistently those in White bodies with economic capital.

Wiley (2004) conducted a historical analysis of educational language policies by language groups. He illustrated how language policies have been used as instruments of social control, with different groups during different eras receiving differing treatment. These differences are clearly linked to the broader status of those groups in society at that time, especially due to race. For instance, during the period of 1740 to 1845, "compulsory ignorance laws" set legal limitations to the language rights and limited the educational opportunities for enslaved African Americans. Mission schools were created to promote English among Native American populations. Yet, during this same era, multiple midwestern states passed laws ensuring that German/English bilingual schools could thrive.

When global politics shifted, even those with economic power and white privilege suffered from linguistic discrimination. In the early 20th century, particularly during World War I, previously accepted instruction in German began to be banned. A majority of states then passed laws that officially designated English as the language of instruction. This restricted the use of "foreign" languages in public schools during that time. However, in the aftermath of World War I, the Supreme Court decided in *Meyer v. Nebraska* (1923) to overturn a Nebraska law from 1919 that banned instruction in German. Several similar cases, including one regarding the use of Japanese in private schools in Hawaii, were decided during the 1920s. These decisions allowed for more flexibility in the use of languages other than English in classrooms, but it was still an era of official deculturalization and language disruption for Native American communities. This continued well into the 1990s when the Native American Languages Preservation Act, a largely symbolic measure, was passed.

A current effort to recognize and promote bilingualism and biliteracy illustrates the way that language policies continue to intertwine race and other issues of inequity. The Seal of Biliteracy was developed to "highlight the linguistic assets of English Learners" by officially recognizing their bilingualism even if it wasn't acquired in school (Aguirre & Chou, 2024, p. 17). It is currently granted in all 50 states and the District of Columbia. According to the most recent data available, only 38% of students earning the Seal of Biliteracy were ever labeled "English Learners." And only 8% of the awards are going to Heritage Speakers of languages other than English. This means that the overwhelming majority of the students receiving the Seal of Biliteracy are from English-speaking backgrounds who have become bilingual and biliterate in another language by the time they graduated from high school, not the group the Seal was intended to elevate.

These disparities result in part from the criteria that have been created for earning the Seal of Biliteracy. Subtirelu et al. (2019) found that students labeled "English Learners" had to provide more sources of evidence of their English language abilities than their English-speaking peers. Further, they had to attain a higher level of English proficiency than students learning languages other than English had to attain in those languages in order to earn the Seal. In addition, the tests that determine proficiency in languages other than English were designed to capture the kind of language learning that occurs in world language classrooms, not necessarily the language practices of students in their homes and communities. When monolingualism and whiteness guide our decision-making, policies and practices inevitably will privilege English monolingual students, most of whom are White, even while we attempt to honor and celebrate bilingualism for students from language-minority communities.

Our classroom policy-making is also influenced by federal level policies. For instance, in 1974, the *Lau v. Nichols* Supreme Court case determined that educating bilingual learners in a language they did not understand was not an equal educational opportunity. Therefore, schools had to offer language supports and remedies to ensure that students could have a high-quality education even if they didn't yet know English. This launched an era of expanded bilingual education policies. Some states mandated bilingual instruction in schools where there were 20 or more students speaking the same language other than English.

In 1981, the case *Casteñeda v. Pickard* established criteria for acceptable program remedies under *Lau*. This standard is still in use by the Department of Justice in evaluating programs for multilingual learners. It requires that school districts attend to three things to ensure that they are taking appropriate actions to overcome language barriers: (1) Programs must be informed by an educational theory that is recognized by experts in the field as sound. (2) The actual practices in use must be a reasonable reflection of the educational theory that has been adopted. (3) And, after a trial period, the success of the program in helping students overcome language barriers must be illustrated. These are important standards for all teachers to know about and use to hold schools and districts accountable. We have worked with many districts and schools that have not yet met these standards. Being aware of what is happening in our settings is part of our responsibility as equity-minded teachers of multilingual learners.

Another major impact on educational language policies was the passage of No Child Left Behind (NCLB) legislation in 2001. NCLB dramatically increased testing requirements in English and created incentives for higher test performance. While there was no explicit ban on teaching in languages other than English, school- and district-level language policies rapidly shifted. The most troubling was that because only test results in English counted for accountability purposes, instruction in languages other than English was significantly reduced, even in bilingual programs across the US (Menken, 2010). This is despite the vast body of research that shows the far superior long-term impact on both English development and grade-level content knowledge from quality bilingual education approaches (let alone the impact on home language maintenance). Additionally, because the results from tests given in languages other than English didn't count in rating schools, many districts that did maintain bilingual programming stopped using such tests. The decision to do so meant that teachers and families did not receive valuable information about students' learning.

In the late 1990s and early 2000s, some high-profile restrictive educational language policies were put in place in California, Massachusetts, and Arizona as a result of statewide ballot initiatives. Fortunately, those policies have been overturned or modified. This has opened up more instructional possibilities for multiple languages to be used in classrooms in those states. This means that in most communities across the country today we can proactively co-construct our own classroom-level language policies together, something we advocate that all students and teachers do collaboratively.

While not a language policy per se, the Supreme Court decision in *Plyer v. Doe* (1981) is one that all educators working with multilingual learners should know about. In that case, the Supreme Court ruled that public school personnel in the US are not allowed to withhold educational opportunities for children on the basis of immigration status. What this means is that public school personnel are not allowed to ask students or their families for information regarding their immigration status, documentation of citizenship, or social security numbers. In our experience, this rule is violated on a daily basis in school offices across the country, making students and families unnecessarily vulnerable to discrimination and loss of safety. By being aware of this policy, we can help ensure that our schools and districts comply with it.

Co-creating policies and practices with students and families to allow for agency, shared responsibility, creativity, and curiosity across all teaching and learning activities is an important way we can center and elevate multilingualism. We once taught a middle school English as a Second language class with students who were still quite new to learning English where we openly discussed the value of using all of the linguistic resources that students had to support their learning. In this class, students taught each other words and phrases from their languages and were also deliberately grouped to be able to use their languages to support each other in their learning. It was very easy to know if students were on-task, regardless of the language they were using, due to the work they produced as well as from reading their body language. Developing supportive multilingual language policies with students and families is something we should all be doing in our classrooms and schools.

## Make It Work

In the Explore section, we discussed important ideas regarding immigration, migration, and language policies and how they impact our work and relationships in classrooms. Now is your chance to play with these ideas and make them work in your practice! Below we have provided some options of how you can do that, thinking about the intrapersonal, interpersonal, and systemic levels of engagement. Any of these could (and potentially should) be done just by yourself but also could be accomplished through learning activities with your students. As you choose an option, keep in mind the module's critical reflection and complexity thinking questions: *How do the racial and linguistic identities and migration histories of my multilingual learners from different backgrounds affect how I interact with and teach them? What impacts do systemic racism and linguicism have on my classroom, my students, their families and communities?* We encourage you to revisit the components of humanizing pedagogies from the introduction and think about the implications of what you learned from engaging in this module in relation to context, orientations, and pedagogy. When you have completed your Make It Work activity, reflect on your findings to share them with your colleagues.

## Make it Work Options

### Intrapersonal: Language Autobiography
Purpose: To explore how your own language trajectory has shaped your life experiences, perspectives, and expectations.

Start from the beginning of your life and map out your experiences with different language(s) and how those experiences have impacted how you view language(s), language usage, and speakers of various of languages. Things to consider include the following: the role that language plays in your identity, how you view people who speak languages or dialects that are different from yours, the languages you view positively and those you view negatively, how comfortable you are in the presence of languages other than English, the reasons for your comfort or discomfort, the messages you might be sending to your students and their families about their multilingualism, and the experiences that will help you feel more comfortable around languages other than English. Most importantly, consider what you need to do within yourself to be someone who can sustain multilingualism in your classroom and community. Are there wounds that need healing? Emotional barriers that need attending to? Biases around different language practices that need to be addressed? Based on what you learn from this exploration, consider how you can develop and/or maintain a strong sense of yourself as a language user. What else can you do to understand and embrace your own linguistic identity and strengths? Then, from this place of strength, describe how you can/will help your students conduct their own language autobiographies and develop a strong sense of themselves and their strengths as language users.

### Interpersonal: Community of Interest Exploration

Purpose: To build understandings, connections, and equitable relationships with local communities regarding their histories and current experiences.

Consider the various racial, linguistic, ethnic, and religious groups in your local community. Identify one of these groups to better understand and invest some time, care, and energy into getting to know them. It is especially valuable to spend time getting to know one or more communities your students belong to. As you learn about the community, be sure to pay attention to their history locally, focusing on how the community defines itself and what it values about itself. Take note of who the leaders are and were, what contributions members of the community have made, what barriers they have overcome, any cultural and linguistic assets they bring to the broader local community, and the values and vision of success the community holds and is striving for today. Based on what you learn, reflect on the power dynamics and relationships between this community and your school and classroom. Is there a balance or imbalance of power with this community? Also, use the information you learn to build relationships with members of the community, seeking to include their perspectives and experiences in the classroom through inviting leaders to visit, making community materials and resources available to students, participating in community events, and so forth. Reflect on these experiences in terms of how your learning can inform your interpersonal actions and relationships with students, families, and community members. We encourage you to consider the "platinum" rule and treat others the way *they* would like to be treated (over the "golden" rule of do unto others as you would have others do unto you). What has your learning about the history and current situation of a local community helped you understand about how to caringly interact with members of that community in your classroom, school, and broader society? Be sure to put that learning into practice!

## Systemic: Language Policy Exploration and Development

Purpose: To build an awareness of language policies at various levels and attend to their impact in your classrooms.

Investigate current language policies at various levels, including in your classroom, at your school, in your district, and at the state level. Explore the official and unofficial policies that relate to how language is used in instruction and assessment. Consider how these overt and implicit policies impact your ability to sustain multilingualism in your practices. Note how different types of multilingualism might be getting treated differently (e.g., the multilingualism of predominantly White, English-speaking students versus the multilingualism of predominantly racially minoritized English-learning students). Where necessary and/or possible, develop a plan of action to improve language policies. Be sure to equitably and justly include multilingual students and their families in all language policy development work.

## You Make It Work!

Purpose: To make the ideas from Explore work in your own practice.

Design your own activity (or tweak one of ours) to ensure that you are spending your time doing work that is most useful and relevant to you and your students. We recommend starting with the critical reflection and complexity thinking questions. Then clarify for yourself which level you are working at (intrapersonal, interpersonal, or systemic) and build your effort to make this module's learning work for you from there!

 ## Share

Share is your opportunity to engage with your peers and receive feedback about the work you have done and what you have learned in this module. Begin by revisiting the reflection you wrote at the beginning of the module and revise it to include your thinking now, noting any changes and what they might mean for your practice. Be sure to attend to opportunities to strive for justice and equity and to potential barriers to achieving it. Don't shy away from the complexities that come up—embrace them. Think about different ways of being and doing in your classroom that could address those complexities. Once you have completed your reflection, be prepared to share it with your colleagues along with a description of the work you did in the Make it Work section. By sharing what you have learned, you have the chance to both solidify your own learning and thinking and expand your opportunities for growth by learning from your colleagues.

# 2

# Dominant Cultural Narratives

This module continues to delve into context by discussing some of the dominant cultural narratives that surround multilingual learners as well as ways we can disrupt them in our classrooms. Begin by considering these questions for critical reflection and complexity thinking: *What impacts do perceptions of difference held by me, and my students and their families and communities have on our classroom community? What do I need to do for differences to be positive and productive rather than a source of harm and marginalization for multilingual students and their families?* Be sure to preserve your initial reflection, notes, and ideas so you can revisit them during the Make It Work and Share sections of this module, paying attention to how your schema are changing and keeping track of your learning.

 **Explore**

Every society has stories that are told to pass on cultural values, define expected behavior, and explain various issues and/or phenomenon. While told from different perspectives, some versions are more often repeated and even institutionalized. These stories thus become the dominant cultural narratives, whether they reflect reality or not. They play an important role in shaping our perspectives and our cultural practices as well as distributing social power and privilege, even when we are not conscious of them. Dominant cultural narratives especially affect how we view practices, ideas, and ways of being in the world that are different from our own, like when our lives are dissimilar to those of our students and their families. These narratives are both explicit and implicit about everything and anything from historical events to gender roles in society, definitions of beauty, who can play which sports, or even parental roles and responsibilities. Something as simple as the idea that pink is a girl's color is transmitted through dominant cultural narratives. Dominant narratives play impactful, but often unattended to, roles in our curriculum and instruction.

Some narratives are more subtle and less overtly structured into stories but are easy to recognize once we pay attention. For example, without knowing anything about someone, we often make judgments about their educational background, their status in society, and even their intelligence based solely on their accent or the variety of English they speak. In the US, some accents or varieties of English such as British or Australian are often viewed as attractive, educated, and desirable, whereas others, perhaps from India or Nigeria, are positioned as difficult to understand or heard as an indicator of low socioeconomic status and/or education. Depending on where we live and what narratives we have consumed, other varieties of English, such as those from parts of Boston, New York, or the south, are dismissed as representing lower classes and the less educated. While the stories that inform our judgments of different accents are not necessarily overt, we are familiar with them and often laugh at jokes based on them, perhaps unaware of the linguistic, racial, economic, ableist, and gender biases these narratives have instilled in us.

Sometimes, dominant cultural narratives can appear to position a group positively but still have negative impacts for the oversimplified and stereotypical view of that group that is transmitted. One such dominant narrative is that of the "model minority," a myth that suggests that, among other things, all Asian students are well behaved and good at mathematics (for more on the model minority myth, see Lee, 2009). We've heard from many students with Asian heritage how their teachers made them feel inferior because they weren't actually good at math and their teachers openly wondered why. We've heard from others about how they were good at math but sought to hide it from their teachers and peers so as not to be viewed as an Asian stereotype.

## Difference as Deficit

An overarching dominant cultural narrative we have identified in our research and work with teachers is the view that difference means deficit. This narrative applies to many aspects of identity, including religion, language, gender, and sexual preferences. The difference-as-deficit narrative is common across our whole society, not just in schools, but plays an especially damaging role in classrooms and schools when anything that isn't the "norm" or "normal" is considered a problem, creating the context for some students to be embraced and others marginalized.

Despite rhetoric about public schooling being the great equalizer, the education system in the US very clearly sorts students into predictable categories based largely on race and social class and consistently relies on a deficit narrative especially regarding ability and language. We label students who aren't "normal" as having disabilities/deficiencies or as "English language learners" and then we work to treat the cause of those labels as intensively as possible until the child can be considered "normal" again. Another way this gets expressed is that students who don't speak English are broken and our job is to fix them. However, they are by no means broken because they don't yet speak English.

It is common for multilingual students' home languages to be positioned as problems to overcome, ignoring students' ability to move and work in multiple languages. Because of this, most programs for multilingual students are created and implemented just for the purpose of fixing the perceived problem of not yet being proficient enough in English to do schooling without linguistic supports. In these situations, success is defined only in terms of English proficiency, not in terms of multilingual proficiencies. Yet the research is very consistent and clear: programs that are developed to support bilingualism and biliteracy have the best outcomes, in terms of both English proficiencies and bilingual abilities (e.g., Genesee et al. 2005; Umansky and Reardon 2014). Despite this evidence, high-quality bilingual programs are not the norm in schools serving multilingual students.

According to a great deal of research (as cited in Miller et al., 2013), when we consider a student as normal and thus able, we are more likely to offer them help and praise, give better grades, and provide more chances and also fewer punishments. When we view students as different or abnormal, we are more likely to punish children, ignore them, give them lower grades, and label them as resistant or learning disabled. We give them less choice and validation for their work and worth.

### The Problem with Assimilationism

Undergirding the narrative that difference is deficit is a commitment to assimilationism. This common ideology works with our dominant cultural narratives to create perceptions of what is normal or correct. Anyone who doesn't meet those expectations or criteria should change and assimilate to them. Assimilationism is closely tied to white supremacy. It positions certain people, ideas, cultural practices, and ways of being as superior and the people who can't or don't subscribe to those ways of being and thinking as inferior. Race scholar and historian Ibram Kendi (2017) has documented the role of assimilationism in our history and how it continues to impact issues around racial equity and justice in the US and beyond. His work illustrates how problematic assimilationism is and how it perpetuates racist practices and inequities. He also shows how commonplace assimilationist thinking is, even when we think we are striving for equity.

Equity in schools today is typically operationalized around the notion of giving everyone what they need to succeed and not just doing the same thing for everyone. There is an image that is often used to describe the difference between equity and equality. Three people of different heights are standing behind a fence where a baseball game is occurring on the other side. One can see over the fence, two cannot. Equality is illustrated as giving everyone the same size stool. One person doesn't need the stool but gets it anyway, and one person still isn't boosted high enough to see over the fence. Equity is then illustrated as giving a different-sized stool (or even no stool to the tallest person) so that everyone can watch the baseball game over the fence. Some images of this scenario claim that justice or liberation would be to take down the fence entirely.

However, we'd like to look at this image from another angle to shed light on how assimilationism can be operating even as we attempt to make things more equitable. In this image, assimilation is operating as the assumption that there is one notion of success-seeing the game over the fence. In the case of the people behind the fence, if we define their needs as being able to watch the game and success as having a clear view of the game, then providing the people of different height with different-sized stepping stools is a great solution. But who defined the people's needs and the desirable outcome? Did anyone ask these three people why they were standing on that side of the fence and what they were seeking to accomplish? What are the implications

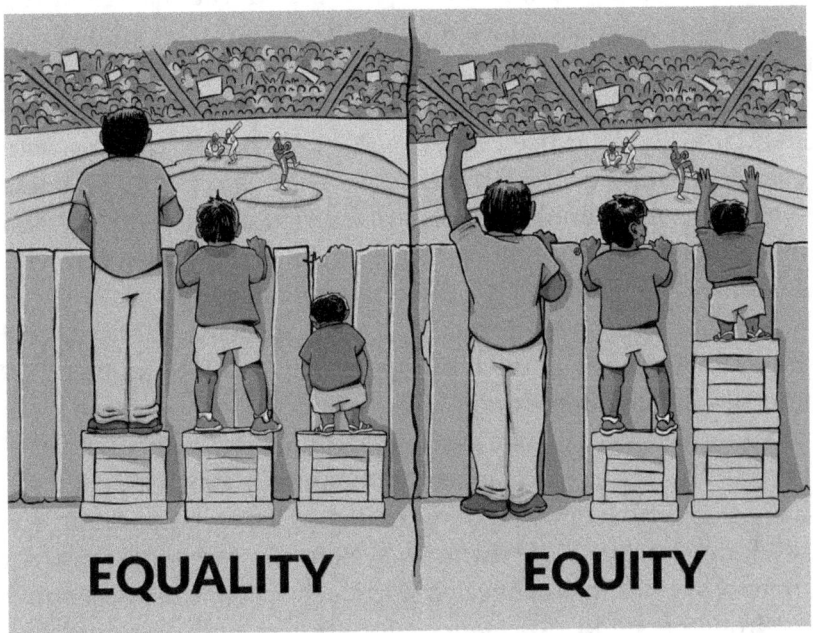

**FIGURE 2.1** Equality vs Equity.

of defining someone's needs without their input? Who benefits? Who is disadvantaged?

In this case, what if the game tickets are too expensive for a minimum wage worker to afford? A stool can help them see the game, but it doesn't get them close to the action in a comfortable seat. What if one of them wants to play in the game, not just watch it? Are their needs met with a stepping stool? What if another person would like to sit and have a picnic while they watch the game and perhaps throw some balls around themselves? Tearing down the fence would help the latter person meet their needs and version of success, but it wouldn't help the others who want to either sit in the stands or play in the game. So, is that justice? Liberation? When we view these three people and their needs and successes from a monolithic predetermined lens based on either dominant cultural narratives or our own perception of what their needs and successes are, our interventions only serve the purpose of helping them assimilate to our idea of success versus actually helping them achieve what matters *to them*.

It can be a bit mind-bending to wrap our head around this because virtually all of schooling and the educational enterprise have been designed and operationalized through assimilationism. Students, parents, or communities are seldom allowed to determine for themselves what success looks like. We have state standards, standardized tests, neoliberal policy reforms, and even legislation constantly being passed that control and name what can and should happen in curriculum and instruction inside classrooms. Success is largely defined externally and typically focused on narrowly prescribed outcomes.

What happens if, instead, we give students, families, and communities a say in what success looks like? We can then further discuss and agree upon what we can do to meet those ideas of success. As educators committed to justice, equity, and creating humanizing pedagogies with multilingual students, we have a variety of opportunities to disrupt assimilationism in our thinking, practice, and education system. We can move toward a more open and interconnected approach where we co-construct environments and expectations for success with our students, families, and communities.

## Alternatives to Assimilationism

We can begin to disrupt the difference-as-deficit narrative in our classrooms by putting aside dominant ways of thinking and creating spaces for multiple learning pathways, ideas, languages, and cultural practices. One way to reject assimilationism is promoting acculturation, a process where students are supported to successfully participate in a new culture and language while being encouraged to hold on to the things that matter to them from their home culture and language. Research has shown that students who engage in acculturation processes, versus assimilation ones, do better in school and in their personal lives (e.g., in their relationships with family members) (Birman & Addae, 2015).

Alim et al. (2020) go beyond acculturation, which focuses on the individual, and advocate for creating spaces where adaptations to new ways of thinking and being happen in all directions or for the collective. A core part of what they call culturally sustaining pedagogies is decentering whiteness as the norm. Whiteness is not just the state of being someone in a White body. Rather, whiteness can be understood as the dominant cultural narratives and practices that view the cultural practices and perspectives of those in White bodies as superior to those who are not in White bodies. Whiteness plays a major feature in the difference-as-deficit narrative as it positions the culture, language, religion, and social class of the majority of White people as the norm. Anything and everything outside of that norm are positioned as less than. Whiteness, assimilationism, and dominant cultural narratives are tightly woven together. They affect each of us at the intrapersonal, interpersonal, and systemic levels. In order to be equitable and just in our classroom practices, we have to decenter any narrative that suggests there is just one acceptable way to be. Through that disruption, we create space for other ways of being in the world to be valued, embraced, and elevated.

Assimilation is all about individuals changing to fit the expected norm of the collective. To counter this, we recommend that instead we change as a collective to embrace the assets and needs of each individual. This can be done through approaches that elevate students' cultural practices and decenter whiteness/dominant cultural narratives to make space for new cultural practices to be co-constructed with everyone. For example, a newly arrived student from Afghanistan was appalled to see students and the teacher using the thumbs up gesture in class as that is a very vulgar and inappropriate symbol to use in her community. The teacher learned that she was upset and decided not to just force the student to start using a symbol that was vulgar to her. Instead, the teacher wanted the new student to feel valued and welcome in class. So, she brought the issue to the classroom community.

In their morning circle, the class talked about how different symbols and gestures can have different meanings in different cultures around the world. She shared with the class how their new community member had a different interpretation of the thumbs up gesture than theirs. And while they want their new classmate to learn about the cultural practices and customs in the US, they also considered how they wanted her to feel safe, valued, and supported in their classroom community. The class then discussed what other hand gestures they could use instead of thumbs up. Through this conversation, they learned together that the "OK" symbol (when we form a circle with our thumb and index finger) is also offensive in Afghanistan, so that would not be a suitable replacement. The students enjoyed the opportunity to be creative and design their own hand gesture for their class community. Together they decided to use the "raise the roof" gesture instead of the typical OK or thumbs-up signal. Students had a lot of fun with this and felt energized by the collaborative problem-solving.

It can feel scary to let go of the predetermined norms that dominant cultural narratives of assimilationism offer us as teachers. We can, however, recenter our learning communities by creating our own norms and values as a learning community (for more on this, see Module 4). In this way, our ideas, values, perceptions, and wishes along with those of our students and their families and communities can play a role in creating a new collective that works for all involved. By treating the concerns, ideas, needs, and wishes of each community member as valid and important, we can create different kinds of communities not only within our classroom but also in our learning.

We have visited an impressive school where educators have made concerted efforts to open up the learning process to embrace the inherent differences in their students. At this school, the faculty agreed on key learning outcomes for the different grade levels and content areas grounded in the requirements set by the state. But then for each unit and lesson, they developed additional inquiry questions to guide the students' learning. In the process, they created space for varying cognitive, cultural, and linguistic practices to be utilized as part of instruction.

As an example, we observed a sixth-grade mathematics class where the lesson was focused on this question: How can you annotate the number line to prove you are correct? As we watched this lesson, we saw something very interesting. The purpose of the lesson was for students to learn a new method for solving the problem (annotating the number line). However, one student insisted on solving the problem his own way (without annotating the number line). The teacher encouraged him to try out the new way they were learning just to expand his problem-solving repertoire. However, he didn't and kept using his own approach to successfully solve the problem.

The teacher allowed the student to use his method because his different way of thinking and doing math was not viewed as a problem. The teacher knew the student was meeting the overarching learning target beyond this specific lesson as he was able to solve the problem correctly. So, his different approach to solving the problem was not treated as an issue in the classroom. This teacher did not perpetuate the difference-as-deficit narrative and in doing so potentially avoided a frustrating experience for both the teacher and student.

External factors, however, sometimes push us to do what we know isn't in line with our goals. Some might argue that the teacher should have insisted that the student learn the new method knowing, for example, that the tests used for accountability accept only one right way and it would reflect badly on the school's scores if the students didn't know it. The tensions we need to resolve are around what we envision as the learning we hope will take place and the constraints that we are working under that make it harder to enact that vision, especially for the diversity of learners we are working with. We find that such tensions are often most productively resolved when they are openly discussed and shared with students. In this way, they can help create solutions and maintain their agency as they continue on their learning journeys.

### Language-Specific Narratives

An aspect of the difference-as-deficit narrative that particularly impacts multilingual learners is that home languages are a problem to overcome rather than assets for learning and life, something touched on above. We often hear educators say something along the lines of, "My students don't know English or their home language," suggesting that students don't have any language. This common yet harmful view of multilingual learners focuses on what students can't do rather than on what students can do with language. Noting that students' range of vocabulary might be smaller than expected should not be equated with thinking that these same students don't have the capacity to expand their vocabulary, which they certainly do. The reality is that, all students come to classrooms with complex and extensive communication skills, even those with various cognitive or physical differences. They may not be the skills that we know or recognize or that are typically valued in our schools, but these skills have helped them to successfully navigate their world to that point in their life. Additionally, what it means to "know" a language is quite complex and deeply entrenched with power and privilege issues.

It is beneficial to learn about the language skills of students and help them make use of those skills to further learning. In the process, we need to examine our own views of students' language practices and whether we are seeing them through racial lenses. If we are, we are likely privileging the language practices of White students over the racially minoritized. We might even be policing the language practices of students we don't view as using standard language practices, a view that is often informed by our perceptions of race. If we do these things, we are creating inequities in our classrooms.

Additionally, it is important for us always to remember that multilingual students' language practices won't and shouldn't look exactly like the language practices of monolingual children or youth. Assuming that all students' language practices should be identical is highly problematic and perpetuates the difference-as-deficit narrative. For example, the way multilingual students use or don't use English can lead to inappropriate special education labels and perpetually relegating them to basic skills/low-level classes. Instead, we can embrace differences in language practices as expected, valued, and important.

To accomplish this, we must expand our perceptions to include varied language practices as part of what learning and school success look like. For example, we can allow students to demonstrate their knowledge and ability on various grade-level content standards through languages other than English or other communicative mediums like art, video, collage, or performance (see Module 5 for more on Humanizing Assessments).

Along the same lines, the knowledge that students have from their lives outside of school or even outside of the US is often ignored or considered irrelevant. Instead of seeing home language(s) and transnational lives as problems, we can position languages other than English in the classroom as strong assets for learning. Instead of seeing limited experience with certain ideas or practices as limited ability, we can position students with diverse backgrounds as teachers themselves who bring that diversity to the learning community to benefit the learning of all.

## Perceptions of Parents/Families

Parents, or other family members, behaving differently than the expected norm often results in their being characterized as unloving, uncaring, and overall less-than in their role as caregivers. This most typically happens to parents from racially minoritized backgrounds whose varying cultural and linguistic practices may not match the stereotypical norm of White middle-class English speakers. We've seen teachers use this difference-as-deficit narrative about parents extensively.

Assimilationism, white supremacy, and dominant cultural narratives are working together here to perpetuate a status quo where parents and students (most frequently, racially minoritized students and parents) are likely being misunderstood as well as mislabeled. Often parental behaviors regarding school involvement—seen by many educators as an expression of parental love—do not match the cultural expectations of teachers and schools. The response is to suggest that parents need to assimilate to the school's perspectives to be good parents. A parent who doesn't regularly attend parent–teacher conferences or family nights at schools is often seen as not caring. This also happens with a parent who doesn't participate regularly in pickup and drop-offs, thus missing regular interactions with their teacher and other school officials, or a parent who doesn't do homework with their children the way the school and/or teacher expects them to.

The flip side of this narrative, and equally as destructive, is that while parents may love their children, they can't really help them with schoolwork because they don't speak English or have advanced literacy skills. To the contrary, families always have a role to play in deepening their children's understandings of the world based on their own experiences and wisdom. It is up to us to be transparent in our belief that this is so, communicate it to families, and provide opportunities to connect families to the topics being studied in school so they can add in the knowledge and wisdom that exist in every home.

An example of this is from a fourth-grade team that was studying earthquakes. When we proposed that the teachers involve families in the work, they sent home a description of the movement of tectonic plates and told the families to teach the content to their children. This is absolutely not what we were suggesting! Even as teachers with extensive formal education, most of us would have to study earthquakes in depth before teaching it to our students. But we all have schema around earthquakes and that is what families can help to deepen through any language, just through conversation or sharing family stories. The questions we then brainstormed together for the teachers to share with families included the following: What do you know about earthquakes? Have you ever been in one or felt the ground tremble? Where have you gotten information about earthquakes—from the news, movies, or stories from family members? Do you think it's likely there will be an earthquake where we live? What would we do if there was an earthquake or any other type of natural disaster? The teachers then chose a couple of visual images to send home along with the discussion prompts translated into the families' languages and an encouragement to dig into the topic together. The students were thrilled when they shared in class what they had learned from their families.

There are also many reasons why some multilingual families may not feel comfortable in the school environment. Depending on the cultural and schooling practices in their countries of origin, some may not see it as their role to be involved in their children's formal schooling. They don't want to be seen as interfering with the work of teachers. They may also be remembering their own negative experiences in US schools or lack confidence in the educational processes that are culturally foreign. Families may feel left out when meetings at school are conducted only in English. Instead, they may prefer face-to-face conversations with interpreters or want to bring the whole family with them for meetings and events. We have often seen these requests spark negative reactions from school personnel who see the presence of multiple family members (often times young children) as additional burdens. In other cases, family members' perceived failure to show up at school is simply because meetings are held when they are working or there is no childcare provided.

Families' seeming unwillingness to engage with the school may also be because of the treatment they received the first time they entered the building. For many immigrant families, the school office is their first contact with the US education system and its abundant bureaucracy. The reception they receive sets the tone for the rest of their experiences with the schooling of their children. The way that school personnel engage with families through their words, body language, and facial expression can make families feel welcome or not. When families arrive to enroll their children, many are nervous about communicating in English and most don't know what will be expected of them. Some may even fear for their safety. Families have recounted to us how frustrating it is when everything is only in English, office personnel roll their eyes, and then talk loudly and very slowly.

Sometimes, they have been directed someplace else not accessible by public transportation. As professionals, we can do better.

One way to do better is to shift our orientation from expecting families to come to us and be willing to go to them. Rather than waiting for or expecting families to come to them, many schools and educators proactively go to families, building relationships, creating successful communication strategies, and collaboratively partnering for the benefit of the students they all love and care about. In order to prevent burnout, we need to work together as faculties so that these efforts don't fall on the shoulders of just a few teachers. The labor needs to be shared across the school. A similar shift in orientation is useful in our classrooms. As humanizing pedagogues, we shouldn't be waiting for students to come to us with issues and questions. We should be proactively going to students, creating the context for them to communicate their issues and questions with us, and not putting the burden on them to "ask if they have any questions."

## Reimagining Family Engagement

An important way we can disrupt the difference-as-deficit narrative is to reimagine how we position and interact with the families and communities of our students. Building community inside the classroom is strengthened by connecting to the community outside the classroom. At the center is shifting from a unidirectional approach to family engagement and moving toward collaboration and reciprocity. Such relationships with families are possible only by giving careful thought to how they are welcomed into our community.

We can begin by taking a tour of our building to get a feel for what it might be like for multilingual families to visit our schools. First, imagine you don't speak English. As you walk around, ask yourself: What makes me feel welcome? What might discourage me from trying to participate in school activities? Would I be able to navigate around the building on my own? What kinds of resources are visible in languages other than English? You can also follow the in-take process when a new family arrives at the school and ask if any of the practices might create obstacles for multilingual families. Is there evidence that they and their students matter in the school? Is there a message that all students belong here and have a voice? You can also review the information that is provided to families both online and in hard copy, taking notice of what is available in which languages and how easy the information is to navigate.

An important part of building an inclusive school community is to make visible the languages of all our families. Obvious actions are to post signs such as "Welcome!," "This Way to the Main Office," and then to have materials available in multiple languages. This lets new families know that their arrival has been anticipated and their language is honored. "Point to Your Language" posters are easily downloaded from the internet and can help school personnel connect families with documents and resources in their home languages right away. These may all seem like small gestures, but they send a strong signal that multilingualism is valued and that differences are viewed as assets.

Other ideas include the following: display pictures of staff and faculty with their names and room numbers in a central area, arranged by grade level or subject area; label hallways with words and pictures to indicate which grade levels or subject matter are taught where; have welcome packets designed by current classes, families, and community members that send a message of joy and care that the family has joined the school community; follow up with families after their first visit and beyond to ensure that they have what they need to join the school community successfully.

The families and students already attending our schools are likely to have helpful insights into how to make the school a welcoming space for themselves and other members of the community. Some schools we know have made welcome videos with information about school procedures and opportunities. These are dubbed and closed-captioned in multiple languages so that families can learn about the building itself, typical routines, requirements, and expectations (e.g., school timetables and calendars) as well as meet various members of the school staff. The videos often end with an invitation for the family to join the school community and share their ideas and suggestions to help improve the school from their perspective and experiences with schooling.

Other schools we know have developed groups of peer mentors who work together to welcome new students and their families. They meet and greet families and students from their same language group and take them on a short tour of the building. They create student welcome packets and/or guides for newcomers to give them the best possible start at their new school. Such guides utilize multimedia resources and student popular culture relevant to the incoming students' interests. These are just some of the steps we can take to disrupt dominant narratives about multilingual students and their families and in turn help to build trust and strong collaborative partnerships.

 **Make It Work**

In the Explore section, we discussed important ideas regarding dominant cultural narratives (especially the difference-as-deficit narrative) and assimilationism. They illustrate possibilities for creating collective learning communities where differences are assets for learning rather than a problem. Now is your chance to play further with these ideas and make them work in your practice! Below, we have provided some options of how you can do that, thinking about the intrapersonal, interpersonal, and systemic levels of engagement. Any of these could (and potentially should) be done just by yourself but also could be accomplished through learning activities with your students. As you choose an option, keep in mind the module's critical reflection and complexity thinking questions: *What impacts do perceptions of difference held by me, my students, and their families, and communities have on our classroom community? What do I need to do for differences to be positive and productive rather than a source of harm and marginalization for multilingual students and their families?* We encourage you to revisit the components of humanizing pedagogies from the introduction and think about the implications of what you learned from engaging in this module in relation to context, orientations, and pedagogy. When you have completed your Make It Work activity, reflect on your findings to share them with your colleagues.

## Make It Work Options

### Intrapersonal: Dominant Narratives Autobiography
Purpose: Dig into how dominant narratives have operated/operate in your own life in relation to one or more aspects of your identity (race, gender, class, language, nationality, religion, ability, sexuality, or family roles).

Reflect on the following questions:

- What various identities do I have? (Consider race, gender, class, language, nationality, religion, ability, sexuality, family roles, etc.)
- How have those identities been associated with expectations by my family, community, or society in general?
- Where did those expectations come from? Whom do they benefit? Whom do they harm?
- How were they communicated to me?
- How did those expectations fit me? Or not fit me?
- Did the dominant narratives that were told to me about who I should be and how I mattered in the world match my own sense of myself and who I wanted to be in the world? If they did, how? If they didn't, how?
- How have I responded to one or more dominant narratives told to me in my life?
- How have the dominant narratives surrounding me affected how I engage with the world?

Then draft a narrative regarding your own personal relationship with dominant narratives in your life. Be sure to include the ways you may have disrupted dominant narratives imposed on you. Also consider how dominant narratives impact you now in your work as an educator.

### Interpersonal: Dominant Narratives in the Classroom
Purpose: Identify the overt and covert messages that students might be receiving from your curriculum and instruction.

Record what is happening in your classroom (or a classroom you are observing) over at least a one-week period. It would be useful to video-tape yourself (be sure to follow all student privacy rules/guidelines from your school or district) or work in partners to observe one another and consider the following:

- Which students get attention (positive or negative) from the teacher in front of the whole class. What was the attention for?
- Which students get one-on-one attention (positive or negative) from the teacher. What was the attention for?
- In the curriculum that was engaged with, which authors, characters, populations, geographic locations, etc. were attended to? Can students see themselves, their families, and their communities in the curriculum? Take note of the connections: are they positive, stereotypical, absent, etc.?
- In the visual space around the classroom, which students can see personal connections to the people, ideas, geographies, languages, and images presented?
- What kinds of interactions occur among students? Take note of who appears to receive a lot of attention from peers and who might not and whether it seems positive or negative.

You can look at more than one aspect of identity as your lens (gender, race, language, etc.) simultaneously, or you can spread your observations out over a longer time to go more deeply on each. Use the data you collect to uncover any dominant narratives that may be operating in your classroom. Reflect on what you discover and what steps you might take to disrupt harmful or inequitable practices communicating negative narratives to students about various aspects of themselves, their families, or their communities.

**Systemic: Welcoming Families**
Purpose: For new multilingual families joining the school community, proactively create welcoming policies and practices that will communicate care, belonging, and opportunities for engagement.

Start a grade- or department-level or whole-school conversation on growing/creating a welcoming school for multilingual families. Depending on where your building is currently, you could examine in-take policies, procedures, and online information provided to new families. Explore and utilize mechanisms in place to get input from families. You could also review resources about multilingual family engagement, identify potential peer mentors, or collaborate with students and families to create welcome packets or a multilingual welcome video and tour of the school. Draw from the ideas in Explore as well as your experiences in your school community and create and implement a plan that proactively creates a welcoming experience for all new families in the school community.

**You Make It Work!**
Purpose: To make the ideas from Explore work in your own practice.

Design your own activity (or tweak one of ours) to ensure that you are spending your time doing work that is most useful and relevant to you and your students. We recommend starting with the critical reflection and complexity thinking questions. Then clarify for yourself which level you are working at (intrapersonal, interpersonal, or systemic) and build your effort to make this module's learning work for you from there!

**Share**

Share is your opportunity to engage with your peers and receive feedback about the work you have done and what you have learned in this module. Begin by revisiting the reflection you wrote at the beginning of the module and revise it to include your thinking now, noting any changes and what they might mean for your practice. Be sure to attend to opportunities to strive for justice and equity and to potential barriers to achieving it. Don't shy away from the complexities that come up—embrace them. Think about different ways of being and doing in your classroom that could address those complexities. Once you have completed your reflection, be prepared to share it with your colleagues along with a description of the work you did in the Make it Work section. By sharing what you have learned, you have the chance to both solidify your own learning and thinking and expand it by learning from your colleagues.

# 3

# Toward a Multilingual Classroom Ecology

This final module in the Context section brings the topics explored in Modules 1 and 2 regarding immigration, migration, language policy, and dominant cultural narratives to our own classroom contexts. We explore how to work toward a multilingual classroom ecology as we attend to the complex relationships among language, identity, and education.

To begin, consider the following questions for complexity thinking and critical reflection: *How do policies and current practices impact our (me, my students, their families, their communities) perceptions of varied language practices and our willingness to engage in communication across differences? How can I open my classroom as a space where varied language practices (languages, dialects, registers) are utilized for the purposes of teaching, learning, and effective communication?* Be sure to preserve your initial reflection, notes, and ideas so you can revisit them during the Make It Work and Share sections of this module, paying attention to your growth and keeping track of your learning.

 **Explore**

We recently visited a class where second-grade students who were fairly new to English were reading a text together. Every so often, one of them lifted one hand and said a word in English and then they lifted the other and said a similar word in Spanish. They then clapped their hands together saying twice (in both English and Spanish), "That's a cognate!" As students were reading, they were spontaneously identifying words that have similar spelling, pronunciations, or meanings across two languages. The teacher was thrilled as she had asked students to always be looking for cognates as a way to connect languages. This was unmistakenly a classroom that valued multilingualism, not just from this practice but from the broad ecology of the class.

The word ecology evokes for us a complex ecosystem with multiple components that interact and support one another in order to thrive. Classrooms as ecosystems are composed of teachers and learners (and their families) as well as the ideas, materials, language(s), policies, and orientations we share with our students. A multilingual classroom ecology can appear in big and small ways. In many classrooms, we see some evidence of attention to multilingualism—a poster with a motivational quote in a language other than English, greetings in multiple languages, or even a poster with vocabulary words translated into several languages. We applaud such approaches knowing they are the seeds of a multilingual classroom ecology. However, they are just seeds, a place to start and efforts that require further growth and attention.

## Creating a Multilingual Classroom Ecology

A multilingual classroom ecology opens possibilities for multilingualism to thrive with an openness to and acknowledgment of the assets that multilingual learners bring with them.

## Language

Understanding language development is key to creating a thriving multilingual classroom ecology. At its most basic, language is a vehicle for humans to represent their understandings and experiences of the world using a set of commonly recognized symbols. Humans are biologically predisposed to acquire symbolic communication, either through spoken language using sounds or through sign language using gestures. The acquisition of language begins at birth (or before) and happens though exposure to people who speak or sign the language. This can happen through one language or several languages simultaneously, meaning that when babies or young children are consistently exposed to more than one language system, they become multilingual from the beginning (Menyuk & Brisk, 2005).

There is both commonality and variety in the ways that the world's many languages express human experience. For example, all languages and dialects can locate things in space and place events in time. They can all describe what things look like and how people are feeling. Speakers of any language can express what has happened in the past, what is going on right now, and what will happen in the future, though they may use different grammatical structures to do so. For example, in some languages, verbs are conjugated to indicate tense, like in English—*walk, walked,* and *will walk.* Other languages use the equivalent of *today walk, yesterday walk,* and *tomorrow walk,* and still others depend on context to indicate to the listener or reader when something has happened.

In addition to varying grammatical practices, languages convey different cultural perspectives and ideas about the location of things in space, the placement of events in time, and descriptions of what things look like and how people are feeling. There is not always a direct word-for-word translation or one-to-one correspondence of ideas, even though all languages and dialects can communicate these important aspects of the human experience.

Some students may not yet know the language of instruction when they arrive at school. They have, however, acquired language itself and all the capabilities that come with it through their varying life experiences and efforts at communication.

This understanding, that students come to school with language skills, is *essential* to creating a multilingual classroom ecology.

We've heard so many educators, from classroom teachers to a state commissioner of education, talk about students as not having any language, which is simply not true. Seeing what students *can do* with language, focusing on the communicative skills students *have* versus perceived deficiencies in their English abilities, is a core asset orientation that is necessary for a multilingual classroom ecology to thrive. This idea is so important that we are going to repeat it: *Students who do not yet know English still have language, and they can use their existing linguistic resources for a wide variety of purposes.* All human beings develop mechanisms for communication; it's just that those mechanisms may not be the ones we are already familiar with or value in school.

Becoming proficient in an additional language (like English at school) means, in part, figuring out how each language is organized to express human experience. Negotiating the differences among languages is a key aspect of multilingualism. In order to learn about languages, sometimes people examine the structure of language looking at the discrete aspects of the ways that sounds, words, and sentences are put together. Instruction from this perspective focuses on learning the rules of the language to produce grammatically accurate utterances or text.

This approach has been critiqued at times for how it treats language as separate from the human beings who use it (Flores & Schissel, 2014). A solely structural view of language lends itself to prescriptivist approaches in classrooms where we act like language police, rewarding students for the "right" ways they use language and punishing students for the "wrong" ways. Certainly, there are more and less effective ways to communicate ideas to a variety of audiences in a variety of contexts. However, the notion of "right" and "wrong" when it comes to language practices is grounded in power relationships that cannot be separated from the people using language or the contexts and purposes for which they are communicating.

Spoken languages are all composed of the same basic building blocks—sounds (phonemes) organized into units of meaning and words—that can be formed into phrases and sentences which can be put together into larger units of discourse. For example, every spoken language or dialect has a set of sounds, which is referred to as its phonology. Sounds are important because a difference in a sound can make a difference in meaning. The words *tin, ten, ton, tan,* and *tune* all have distinct meanings but only slightly different sounds. In some dialects of English, all the words are pronounced differently, while in others, two or more of the words may be pronounced in the same way. A person learning English may not even hear the difference in the vowel sounds across those words, depending on the language sounds their ear is accustomed to hearing.

Languages such as Chinese and Vietnamese use additional sounds called tones to carry meaning. In these languages, how the speaker's voice rises, falls, or remains flat for the same set of sounds will differentiate the meaning of one word from another. For example, in certain dialects of Vietnamese, the phoneme /ma/ can mean ghost, mommy, however, tombstone, an old Chinese word for horse, or young rice plant, depending on the tone used.

The way people sound to us plays an invisible role in how we perceive and treat them, too often resulting in language-based discrimination and prejudice. Prescribing the "accurate" ways to use a language often places an overemphasis on accent. Our accents are simply an assembly of the sounds we use to communicate. We often don't hear an accent when the people we interact with use the same sounds we do.

How we hear people's language is intricately intertwined with race. A study (Kang & Rubin, 2009) conducted with college students had them listen to an audio recording of a lecture and then respond to questions about the intelligibility of the speaker. One group heard the recording while looking at a picture of the purported speaker, a White person. Another group did the same, but the picture they were presented with was a Chinese person. The students all listened to the same audio recording, yet the students who thought they were listening to a racially minoritized speaker rated that speaker as harder to understand than the students who thought they were listening to a White speaker.

Our perceptions of speakers, their ideas, and the language practices they use are impacted by white supremacy and the racial hierarchies that exist in society today. As teachers, we are not immune from the biases generated from living in a world where power and privilege are linked to various racialized language practices. We all have work to do to examine our attitudes and move toward an orientation of openness. To embrace different, legitimate language practices, even if they are unfamiliar to us, we can and must move away from prescriptivist language-policing approaches that dismiss or marginalize them.

Within any language, certain dialects or accents will typically be considered "standard." Accents and dialects that deviate from that standard are often perceived as uneducated or less than. We may even tell students that when they speak or write with those non-standard dialects their use of the language is "wrong" and needs to be fixed. This is especially complicated and problematic in some approaches used today to teach reading. Approaches that suggest the cornerstone of reading is mastering sound symbol relationships typically focus only on "standard" language practices and dialects. This creates difficulty for students whose language practices differ from that "standard." We've seen teachers teaching phonics lessons struggle with "standard" pronunciation of various sounds, realizing that students pronounce those same sounds differently because of the dialect they speak. There doesn't always appear to be plans for what teachers should do in that context and how students should understand the different ways that language is used. Rather, what we have seen is an insistence on the "standard" pronunciation as right and no further discussion.

There is another issue that we have often seen with how language sounds in the classroom. If a student speaks English without what the teacher perceives as an accent, they may not even realize that student speaks another language. We've visited classrooms and asked who speaks languages other than English and been told that there aren't any multilingual students in the class. But, by the time we leave, we've had conversations in Spanish with several students. Because students speak English without what appears to be an accent and likely do not have the "English learner" label, teachers often completely overlook an important aspect of who the student is and what they bring to the learning space-their multilingualism.

## Multilingual Language Development

Research from the field of linguistics frames many people's understandings of how we expand our linguistic repertoires. In education, multilingual language development is most often discussed in terms of "second language acquisition." Some students do enter US schools with virtually no formal exposure to English. It may be, however, that it is the third or fourth language they are acquiring. Students born in the US may have limited or extensive exposure to English depending on their family's circumstances.

There are some typical stages of language development that appear both in initial language acquisition and for languages that are learned later in life. Becoming familiar with them is helpful, but they should not be seen as rigid or deterministic. Language skills are built based on the opportunity to use them, and individual trajectories will differ depending on context, access to input, opportunities to express oneself, and motivation.

More than 40 states in the US use standards and assessments developed by the WIDA Consortium. They label the stages of language development as entering, beginning, developing, expanding, bridging, and reaching. For each stage, WIDA provides descriptors of what students are typically able to do across the domains of reading, writing, speaking, and listening. These descriptors are helpful because they provide general guidelines of what students new to English can do and where they are heading. The downside is that often multilingual learners are referred to according to the numerical rating they receive on the language assessments—*He's a 3, she's a 1*—dehumanizing the students and making it harder to see their assets. In addition, a single number masks that students are often at different places across domains and that their movement forward may be uneven from one year to the next. Their assessed level of proficiency will vary depending on familiarity with the content and importantly on literacy skills already developed in English and other languages as well as how well they perform on tests.

The ways we use language are grounded in meaning-making, communication, and contextualized within societal power hierarchies. Part of creating a multilingual classroom ecology is stepping away from seeing languages through a monolingual lens. A typical monolingual lens that is put on multilingualism is in terms of judging the abilities of multilingual learners in the language they are learning.

Stop for a minute and consider what you think it means to know a language. For instance, once we were speaking in English with a colleague from Germany with whom we had presented at conferences in English and published academic papers in English. This colleague, who was raised and educated in German, said they did not think they were bilingual. We were stunned. What would it take to be considered bilingual if presenting and publishing papers in another language weren't enough? What would it take for you to consider yourself bilingual or multilingual?

Does it mean you can say a couple of words and use simple phrases to meet everyday needs? Or does it mean that you can handle most situations and successfully communicate your ideas and needs? Or does it mean you have to be able to easily understand everything you hear or read and also be able to express all of your thoughts and needs with nuance and detail? Or can you only be bilingual if your proficiency in another language mirrors that of monolingual speakers of that language?

A monolingual view of multilingualism suggests that to "know" a language is to sound and operate like a monolingual speaker of that language. We disagree with this perspective heartily. In fact, we argue that multilingualism is much more widespread than many believe because it starts with being able to say words and use simple phrases to meet everyday needs. For some multilingual people, this means simple language uses like calling taxis, bargaining at the market, or being able to give directions to get home. For other multilingual people, this means extensive reading, writing, speaking, and listening in various languages.

Along with understanding that multilingual language development is a varied trajectory for each individual, it is important to recognize that success on that trajectory is highly individualized. Schools typically position students learning English as deficient versions of monolingual English speakers (e.g., through data comparisons of multilingual students versus monolingual students). Rather, we suggest focusing on the multilingual abilities of students and thinking about their success on the terms that make sense for the trajectory they are on and related to the learning goals they have. For a student in high school who has newly arrived and is eager to join the workforce, their multilingual language development is going to look different than for a student born in the US entering kindergarten speaking Chinese and starting to learn English. In our efforts to create multilingual classroom ecologies, we need to embrace and elevate these varied language development trajectories and open our perspectives around what it means to be multilingual.

## Languaging and Translanguaging

Ofelia García (2009) refers to the ways we use language as "languaging" and describes how these practices are codified into named languages like Italian, Hindi, Farsi, or Hmong. "Translanguaging" then encompasses the varied and multiple communicative strategies that are used by those who can access more than one named language or dialect to communicate.

Early research on learning and teaching languages treated the languages inside a multilingual's brain and their use of more than one language as distinct and separate. However, multilingual individuals are not just the sum of two monolinguals. A translanguaging perspective minimizes the borders and boundaries between named languages and embraces a more complex view. It positions multilinguals as having one comprehensive linguistic repertoire that they draw from as they decide, consciously and unconsciously, how to effectively communicate. Their choices are grounded in the expectations and power hierarchies that are embedded in the communicative context.

There is a fair amount of debate, discussion, and disagreement about how translanguaging can or should be used in the classroom. We do know that multilingual learners benefit when their teachers embrace creative possibilities around languaging and legitimize the full linguistic repertoire of an individual or community. We can use these understandings to disrupt inequitable hierarchies in school and society, beginning with rejecting that there is a right or wrong way to use language. This is at the core of building a multilingual classroom ecology.

Any individual's personal repertoire develops from their life experiences (languaging) and the varying language practices they are exposed to. This includes the multiple dialects that exist for every language as well as different registers. Language registers are the different ways we use language in different contexts for different purposes. A common distinction made in schools is around social language registers and academic language registers.

This distinction gained heavy traction when the terms Basic Interpersonal Communicative Skills (BICS, for social language) and Cognitive Academic Language Proficiency (CALP, for academic language) were introduced in the early '80s. These terms were put forward to explain why it takes several years for multilingual learners new to a language to demonstrate proficiency on par with their monolingual peers in classrooms. Amid critique, the original conception was modified to include the variability of cognitive demand and contextualization as a feature of any interaction. This reframing did consider some of the multiple factors that affect how language is used in different contexts but still perpetuated an unhelpful hierarchy.

Unfortunately, the simplistic BICS/CALP dichotomy has never gone away and is still widely used by educators. It perpetuates the false assumption that interpersonal communication by definition lacks cognitive demand. It also suggests that "academic language" is the only acceptable way to communicate in school. The result is a discriminatory narrative that "social language" used outside of school, at home and in the community, is inferior to the "academic language" used inside of school. The result diminishes the language practices of students in their homes and communities. It also simply isn't true. Very complex ideas can be shared through language that is considered more informal or social. Also, informal/social registers of language are often used in school to support various academic efforts, including demonstrations of learning.

Indeed, we communicate differently in different settings (at school, at home, on the bus, in religious institutions, with friends, with strangers) and for different purposes (to learn, explain, convince) both orally and in writing. Our choices vary according to the level of formality, the power relationships between the participants, and the types and purposes of the interaction.

As noted above, linguists describe this as register. We shift language registers frequently as we interact throughout the day. We converse with a neighbor in one way and differently in a parent–teacher conference. Our grocery lists look different from postings on social media. We prepare a job application in one way and an essay for a class in another. Importantly, all registers and dialects can express complex thoughts and represent critical and abstract thinking.

Our comfort with or fluidity in a particular register reflects in part how frequently we have opportunities to use it. The communicative practices we are best at or view as easiest are typically those that we have used the most. Interactions in schools may be perceived as more challenging than interpersonal ones in part because we have had fewer opportunities to use specific academic vocabulary and genre conventions. Some students' oral dialects are closer to the way ideas are represented in print in school. They may adopt academic register more quickly, but it is not because they are smarter.

One consequence of viewing some ways of speaking as problematic is that many people feel the need to adopt practices in majority spaces that do not necessarily represent their authentic or most-desired identities. For example, some transgender people who are transitioning may not feel safe to use their actual name and pronouns in all spaces. Or People of Color hold back from using their home dialects in majority White spaces in job interviews or even after many years at a workplace. These examples are indicative of how the hierarchies in our society related to race, class, gender, and sexual orientation can negatively affect people's lives. It is important to pay attention to the relationship between language and power, something we can proactively map and pay attention to, especially in order to disrupt inequity and injustice (see Make It Work Options below).

To create a strong multilingual classroom ecology, we need to shift away from binary thinking that assigns more social value and privilege to some language practices and denigrates others. One way to do this is to explore with our students which language practices receive more validation and power in which contexts and to the benefit (and detriment) of whom. This rejection of either/or is central to developing perspectives that move us beyond naming "correct" and "incorrect" language uses. As teachers, we can work with students to explore the different choices we make in order to communicate effectively in different contexts. In the process, we can identify and develop tools to communicate well in a wide variety of circumstances.

## Multilingual Language Detectives and Architects

The topics discussed above provide the backdrop for ways we can deconstruct and reconstruct language to develop multilingual classroom ecologies that center inclusivity, equity, and justice. Together with our students, we all can become both language detectives and language architects. As we move between the two roles, we can uncover the ways that languages work and creatively use our entire linguistic repertoires to represent and effectively communicate our thinking and understandings.

### Multilingual Language Detectives

Language detectives in a multilingual space explore the varying ways that people use language across different communicative contexts (e.g., a ballgame, a science class, or a party) and their relationships to power and privilege. Through detective work, we can see how a variety of language practices are legitimate and successful mechanisms for communication and others may be less so across the language domains of reading, writing, speaking, and listening. Our role is to notice and uncover, not to judge what is the right or wrong way to say or write something. We can examine languages we know as well as those we are unfamiliar with. Through these investigations, we can uncover how power operates through language and see how social hierarchies, especially those related to race, class, and gender, influence how we perceive and treat different people.

A place to start is becoming familiar with the linguistic landscapes that surround us both inside and outside of school. In our buildings and out in the wider community, students can document through pictures, recordings, or written descriptions how the different environments they spend time in incorporate the languages of their families and communities. These investigations can be done broadly or fine-tuned to relate to a specific topic we are studying. Students can review the images and descriptions in small groups or as a whole class to analyze which languages appear in which spaces, related to what topics or activities. This can lead to discussions about what messages they receive and how those messages affect them. We can then use what we learn about how languages can be valued or diminished to craft a linguistic landscape in our classrooms that affirms students' multilingual realities.

Language arts teachers we know do language detective work when they examine mentor texts to support students' writing development. They help students notice how language is used in different genres, how the text is organized, or what kind of imagery the author uses. They also use mentor texts to find examples of language usage they would like their students to try out. Bilingual teachers can examine texts in more than one language so students can compare similarities and differences in styles and conventions across genres. For more on this approach, we recommend the work of María Estella Brisk (2022).

As language detectives, students can uncover how different languages describe events or processes and how they indicate the past tense or conjugate verbs. For example, students might note that in Spanish adjectives typically follow nouns but that in English they go before. This can lead to a discussion and exploration of how adjectives and nouns work together in different languages to provide more detail and interest. By reviewing mentor texts, students might explore how effectively an author uses adjectives and nouns. For instance, when we did this with students, they noted that adding precise adjectives in front of nouns in English is a useful way to integrate more detail into students' writing. This is something teachers often ask students to do (add more detail to their writing), and students often struggle with how to do it. Therefore, using mentor texts to see how successful authors accomplish the skills students are developing is a strong application of language detective work.

Another example of language detective work is a homework assignment where students explore how words/concepts introduced at school are represented and used in the language(s)/dialect(s) used at home and in their communities. Students can ask questions and note when they hear the words and ideas in English or in other languages/dialects. Some teachers we've observed used information that came from students' detective work to create multilingual word walls. Others displayed how different mathematical terms are represented in different languages and how certain algorithms like division are visualized in different cultures and languages. Some teachers have students demonstrate the different ways to talk about ideas across dialects and languages.

Language detective work is most successful when we provide examples to model and encourage students to continue their investigations inside and outside of school. At times, we have turned students' findings into class datasets and charts to use in math activities and social science lessons. Language detective work always produces interesting content for language-focused lessons.

Detective work can extend beyond language itself to some of the cultural practices of people who speak that language on a regular basis. Community leaders and families can also play a role in these investigations, especially when we invite them into our classrooms to share how they navigate different language practices in their own lives. They can explore with us where across the world their languages are spoken and perhaps how many people speak the languages. They can help us identify people from different linguistic and cultural backgrounds who have contributed to the knowledge around the topics we teach.

We encourage our students to come up with their own questions and ideas for further exploration and to help us learn about their language practices. We invite them to pose questions about what they find perplexing or confusing. In this way, students can exercise leadership, agency, and curiosity in their learning as they become experts on aspects of language in their world and community. From pop cultural references to youth innovations with language (think slang), to ideas and practices around how racism, ableism, and sexism are conveyed through how we use language, these conversations can be provocative, insightful, and empowering.

Developing curiosity about language practices can extend to explorations into complex and challenging topics such as race, gender, or sexuality. In a classroom community that has established the trust needed to discuss difficult topics, students can investigate the overt and covert ways that people are marginalized and oppressed by how people talk about them or how they are represented in course materials. Together we can analyze these examples to help students understand that the ways we use language are related to our own and other people's positionality in the larger society. Most importantly perhaps is that we and our students consider how the ways we use language can perpetuate or disrupt harmful dominant narratives. Students can talk about how different language practices affect them personally as well as the people around them. Our hope is that we, and our students, will be more intentional about the ways that we, and they, use language going forward.

When we ground our conversations around language in curiosity to understand the variety of language practices at play in our students' lives, we can help them develop tools to use language creatively. The knowledge they gain as language detectives then becomes the basis for their work as language architects, capable of building creative language practices that meet their various communicative wishes and needs.

## Multilingual Language Architects

As multilingual language detectives, we open ourselves to learning about language, how it is used across contexts for different purposes, and how our language practices affect others. The next step is to apply the understandings and become multilingual language architects, constructing and reconstructing the ways that we use language to express our ideas. This doesn't mean anything goes. As suggested by Nelson Flores (2020):

> Like a building architect, language architects are not free to simply do whatever they want. If this were the case,

> buildings would be unsafe and communication efforts would fail. Yet, beyond some broad general parameters, both must adhere to in order to successfully complete their tasks, there is a great deal of decision-making that both make that reflect their own unique vision and voice.
>
> (p. 4)

Language detective work builds students' awareness of the "broad general parameters" around language and provides them some tools to creatively communicate their ideas. As multilingual language architects, students are in a constant process of building and remodeling their linguistic repertoire as they learn to communicate effectively across different contexts and languages. They can use different registers and conventions to express the same ideas and compare their potential for getting their meaning and intent across to a particular audience.

Further, creative multilingual language architects can make careful decisions about their communication practices, perhaps choosing to intentionally defy conventional linguistic norms. The process is multidirectional. As language architects, multilingual learners can work back and forth among different language resources to hone their understandings of the ideas as well as how to best communicate what they know.

Recognizing and affirming students' multilingualism open up possibilities for more authentic and meaningful communication in terms of their identity and understandings of the world. Just like building architects, the true test of students' language architecture work is the soundness of the structures they create—meaning how well their ideas are communicated. If a student can communicate ideas well without using conventional linguistic norms, that is great.

When we provide tools in the classroom for students to learn and communicate their learning in languages other than English, we create the opportunity for more expansive language architecture work while we send a message that school learning is not just an English activity. We can create a space where every language in the classroom community, including local Indigenous language(s), has a legitimate place in academic products and processes.

One way is to design culminating projects that include opportunities for students to use multiple languages to display their knowledge. Students can also create language autobiographies or passports to integrate multilingualism into academic work across multiple language domains. There are varying technology tools available today that can support the work of multilingual language architects. When available in the language(s) of our students, online translators, while not perfect, can help us check their grasp of key concepts and try to answer students' questions.

Further, as multilingual language architects, students can use their home languages to deepen their understandings and share with their families what they are learning. Students can also create short videos where they talk about their work in school that we can text to families or share via school websites. Obviously, we will not be able to provide feedback and assistance for students who are developing products in languages we do not yet know. However, we can still connect with families to share the multilingual work their students are doing in our classroom. This allows them direct access to what students are learning. In some cases, parents have provided feedback to our students and let us know their sense of the quality of students work. This sharing can be done through multiple modalities and technologies to involve all families, including those who don't yet have literacy skills in their home languages.

By building relationships with language and cultural brokers/leaders from students' communities, we can further support multilingual language architecture. We can invite community members for in-class visits to give students quality feedback on their work. Or visitors can help students either one-on-one or in small groups plan what's next. We can also ask community members to share their expertise with the whole class. Connecting with multilingual families and communities is no small task and no one person should need or have to do it alone. The benefits of building such relationships are tremendous, especially when they are part of a school-wide effort where each staff member can contribute.

When we focus on multilingual language architecture, we are focusing on what students will be able to design and build with language across their whole linguistic repertoire. Our role is to design activities where students can be creative with language. It is not important that students "speak like a book" when they are actively engaging in their learning. We want them to have the space to generate new ideas and grow their thinking while they experiment with expressing their ideas in varying contexts. In the end, we want students to be able to have the choice about whom they communicate with, in which ways, and to what ends. This is much more important than just mastering the conventions of standardized English.

 **Make It Work**

In the Explore section, we discussed key ideas regarding language, multilingual language development, and languaging and translanguaging. We also looked at some of the ways we can collaborate with our students to create an interconnected multilingual classroom ecology. Building on those understandings, we can engage with each other as multilingual language detectives and architects. Now is your chance to play further with these ideas and make them work in your practice! Below we have provided some options of how you can do that, thinking about the intrapersonal, interpersonal, and systemic levels of engagement. Any of these could (and potentially should) be done just by yourself but also could be accomplished through learning activities with your students. As you choose an option, keep in mind the module's questions for critical reflection and complexity thinking: *How do policies and current practices impact our (me, my students, their families, their communities) perceptions of varied language practices and our willingness to engage in communication across differences? How can I open my classroom as a space where varied language practices (languages, dialects, registers) are utilized for the purposes of teaching, learning, and effective communication?* We encourage you to revisit the components of humanizing pedagogies from the introduction and think about the implications of what you learned from engaging in this module in relation to context, orientations, and pedagogy.

When you have completed your Make It Work activity, reflect on your findings to share them with your colleagues.

## Make It Work Options

### Intrapersonal: Reflect on your Stance Toward Language Differences

Purpose: Examine your perceptions of how people use language in a variety of ways, noting what you may need to do to be more open to language differences, especially multilingualism.

Reflect on the following questions and connect your responses to specific life experiences you have had. Think about how these experiences might impact your current or future work in the classroom, especially how your perspectives might be impacting students and families.

- How do I feel when I'm in the presence of languages that I don't understand? Where do those feelings come from?
- What is my response to language uses that don't meet my expectations of correctness? Where does that response come from?
- What perspectives, life experiences, or expectations might support or prevent me from creating a multilingual classroom ecology?
- What would it mean for me to expand my own linguistic repertoire?

As you reflect think forward to the work you would like to do to successfully co-construct a multilingual classroom ecology with your students and their families. In deciding where to go next, we suggest you plan some specific experiences and ideas to explore as you set goals for yourself.

### Interpersonal: Plan and (if Possible) Conduct Multilingual Language Detective or Architecture Lesson

Purpose: Create the opportunity for your students to do multilingual language detective or architecture work.

For multilingual language detective work, identify an aspect of language that students might investigate. It could be mentor text(s), how language is used in different contexts, or anything else that interests you and them. Think about the most feasible ways for students to record what they find. Consider what you will do with the results of students' investigations and why. If you are able to teach the lesson, reflect on how it went and possible next steps for students engaging in multilingual language detective work.

For multilingual language architect work, identify opportunities for students to engage in creative uses of language in your class and support students in doing that work multilingually. This can be grounded in the creative uses of language that students already engage with. Or it could be a new project entirely (like perhaps doing language biographies, something that is common in European classrooms; see https://www.coe.int/en/web/portfolio/the-language-biography). The focus should be that students are generating language and have the freedom to use their entire linguistic repertoire. Additional resources for this kind of work can be found online with the CUNY NYSEIB (City University of New York – New York State Initiative on Emergent Bilinguals) project: https://www.cuny-nysieb.org/.

**Systemic: Map Language and Power in Context**
Purpose: Understand how power operates through differing language practices in varying contexts and use the information to transform inequitable power distributions.

First, list several different communicative contexts like math class, grocery store, playground, and living room. Be sure to choose contexts that are relevant and part of either your daily life or that of your students. Then take one context at a time and list out the people who communicate in that context, the kinds of communication that happens, and the kinds of language practices that are expected. Paint a comprehensive picture of how communication typically occurs in that specific context and then deconstruct that picture by considering whose language practices are privileged in the context. How does power operate in relationship to the language practices used? Who gets to decide which language practices are expected or "appropriate" for the context? What happens when people use language practices that do not meet the expectations for that context? Pay attention to how silences get created and enforced, how communication can break down, and what would create the possibility for more openness and agency in communication practices in that specific context. Move through each context mapping out power related to language practices in context and consider what you (and perhaps your students) can do to change the communication patterns in various contexts to create more equitable power-sharing. Be sure to include communicative contexts in schools!

**You Make It Work!**
Purpose: To make the ideas from Explore work in your own practice.

Design your own activity (or tweak one of ours) to ensure that you are spending your time doing work that is most useful and relevant to you and your students. We recommend starting with the critical reflection and complexity thinking questions. Then clarify for yourself which level you are working at (intrapersonal, interpersonal, or systemic) and build your effort to make this module's learning work for you from there!

 **Share**

Share is your opportunity to engage with your peers and receive feedback about the work you have done and what you have learned in this module. Begin by revisiting the reflection you wrote at the beginning of the module and revise it to include your thinking now, noting any changes and what they might mean for your practice. Be sure to attend to opportunities to strive for justice and equity and to potential barriers to achieving it. Don't shy away from the complexities that come up—embrace them. Think about different ways of being and doing in your classroom that could address those complexities. Once you have completed your reflection, be prepared to share it with your colleagues along with a description of the work you did in the Make It Work section. By sharing what you have learned, you have the chance to both solidify your own learning and thinking and expand it by learning from your colleagues.

# Section II

## Orientations

# 4

# Co-Constructing Learning Communities

After three modules focusing on context, we now shift the focus to orientations. Our orientations determine the direction of our decision-making and practice. They are derived from the ideologies, beliefs, and attitudes that we adopt. While there are many ways that we can orient ourselves as educators, we have identified six orientations that are especially important to humanizing our pedagogy: *openness*, *interconnectedness*, *agency*, *shared responsibility*, *creativity*, and *curiosity* (see Viesca et al., 2024). Each is intertwined with the others.

In this module, we foreground *interconnectedness* and *openness* as particularly useful for co-constructing multilingual learning communities. We emphasize the importance of building authentic relationships as part of humanizing our work. One way we can do this is to move away from seeing classrooms as places we alone manage and control, toward co-constructing strong and vibrant learning communities.

To begin, we ask you to consider these questions for critical reflection and complexity thinking: *How can I orient myself and my students toward interconnectedness and openness to build a strong community where we can collaboratively solve problems, disrupt inequitable issues, and create a sense of belonging? What systems, policies, and practices impact my ability to establish these kinds of relationships with students and families?* Be sure to keep your initial reflection, notes, and ideas so you can revisit them during the Make it Work and Share sections of the module.

## Explore

We once conducted research in a middle school where we followed a multilingual student across the whole instructional day. Another student not part of the research was in all the classes. She was clearly very bright, often raised her hand, and was actively engaged in every class we observed. As we entered the last period classroom, we were surprised to see the teacher immediately chastise the girl (before she had even entered the classroom) and then send her away with no discussion. To that point in the day, we had seen this girl as the brightest, most capable, and engaged student in each class. But this teacher instantly saw a problem and dismissed her. The student did not return, and we didn't see her again.

There is no way for us to know exactly what happened, since it would have been unethical under our research protocols to ask. But we were shocked to see such a contrast to what we had observed for the rest of that day. Certainly, there was a history there, and we assume the student had done something that the teacher had told her was unacceptable. The teacher acted authoritatively, decisively, and with stern consequence. The student was silenced, judged, and sent away. We were disheartened as it brought to mind so many other classrooms where we have seen similar treatment of students. Such practices do not create strong relationships or humanizing pedagogies. Our hope is that we can replace them.

## On Community

People learning together in a class, a program, or an institute do not inevitably form a community. Within the walls of too many classrooms, some students thrive while others feel left out or at the margins because of their identities or to what extent they conform to imposed rules. A true community is more than the presence of people in the same space. It is a place where people find connection, care, and belonging and can develop authentic relationships.

Dr. Martin Luther King Jr. articulated a powerful vision of community centered on love and compassion, built on understanding, forgiveness, and mutual respect. He called this the "beloved community," the key elements of which are justice and equality, a place where everyone has equal rights and opportunities. In a beloved community, we recognize and act as if we are all part of one human family. This was central to Dr. King's commitment to nonviolence and finding peaceful ways to achieve social change.

Given the world we live in, it can be difficult to imagine the beloved community on a global or even national scale. But perhaps we can envision it on a smaller scale. Our classrooms and schools could be spaces where we can counteract the inequities that surround us so that beloved learning communities can thrive. We think so because we've both seen and been part of them. Such learning communities do not just happen, they take work and commitment.

One roadblock to building a true community is the dominant cultural narrative around *difference as deficit* (See Module 2). Indigenous scholar Donald Dwayne (2021) writes about how colonialism created what he terms "relationship denial"—that is, the myriad ways we live separated from one another—in denial of the respectful and reciprocal relationships we should foster across the human and non-human world. We gravitated toward his idea as it illuminates why it's often challenging to build authentic relationships within the systems, practices, and policies that are common in modern Western society.

There are many examples of how we discount and deny relationships in our decision-making. They include prioritizing district curriculum pacing guides and state standards over the learning interests and timelines of our students. It happens when we dismiss or police the way students use language to express their ideas or when we tell a student "There's nothing I can do" as we enforce a policy that they are frustrated with. Relationship denial is in play when we punish students strictly according to imposed classroom management plans without talking to them to find out more about the context surrounding disruptive behaviors.

Dwayne teaches us that we counteract relationship denial by focusing on "relational renewal" and "ethical relationality." He describes this as acknowledging and honoring the significance of the relationships we have with others, how our histories and experiences position us in relation to one another, and how our futures as people in the world are similarly tied together. This can happen in many ways.

Take the example above of strict adherence to pacing guides regardless of students' understanding of the material. To focus on relational renewal, we might slow down our work across the curriculum or even just focus on larger ideas. Rather than just pushing through, we could have conversations with students and be open with them about the demands and where we think there might be opportunities to slow down. They can work as collaborative problem-solvers when we face tensions between district demands and the actual pace of the learning occurring in our classroom.

Relationship renewal requires being open to and curious about students' cultural and linguistic practices and encouraging their creativity and experimentation. It thrives when we express empathy, explore alternate possibilities, and even advocate for change. Relational renewal is a key part of conflict resolution. Instead of jumping to punishment with students and instantly assuming that they have done something wrong, we ask, "What happened here? Are you OK?" to all involved. We search for solutions and next steps that preserve everyone's autonomy and dignity while seeking to repair any harm caused. Orienting ourselves toward interconnectedness and openness with our students and their families and communities moves us toward humanizing our instruction.

## Orienting Toward Interconnectedness

When we orient toward interconnectedness, we acknowledge how we all are part of a complex whole where our own well-being is bound to that of those around us. When we ground our teaching and learning practices in love, belonging, and care, we can better attend to everyone's needs, wishes, and interests. Striving for each person to be and become the best, most desired version of themselves as part of a supportive whole requires us to accept that what we do and say impacts those around us, regardless of our intentions.

Orienting toward interconnectedness disrupts the dominant narrative that an individual's achievements result solely from their own efforts, an embodiment of relationship denial. Great classroom learning communities are constructed through individual and collective effort and support, particularly when the strengths and abilities of each member are elevated. When each member sees themselves as interconnected and part of an authentic, caring, and loving community, negative practices like domination, exploitation, manipulation, and control can be diminished or even extinguished.

Our positionality in the larger society also affects how much our true essence is seen or overlooked in classrooms. When difference is viewed as a deficit, students from marginalized groups may never feel their value seen or reflected back to them at school. Their validation may come only from their family or their peers.

Building opportunities for each person to see their own great qualities and abilities as well as those of the people around them is a way to build community through moments of affirmation. Such moments of affirmation may happen at home, at school, or out in the larger community. We remember how deeply we were affected when, for example, an elementary teacher noticed our talent for drawing and encouraged us to use that skill in our classwork instead of scolding us for doodling, a college professor took time to discuss our writing outside of class because she found the ideas compelling despite many technical errors, a debate coach fostered our leadership, and a former student yelled out in the grocery store: "She changed my life when she taught me to read!"

Creating and ensuring that moments of affirmation occur regularly for each of our students take planning and intention, especially to ensure that these affirmations are authentic and honest and don't come only from us as the teacher. We need to teach students how to affirm one another, notice each other's strengths, and express gratitude and provide compliments for the good work we see each other do. Providing students with specific sentences or sentence starters as well as practice opportunities is useful. There might even be time set aside in class for students to praise one another verbally or through written notes. We've done an activity where each student writes their name at the top of a paper and all the papers circulate around the class and each member of the class writes a positive statement about the student. They can choose to sign their name or leave the compliment anonymous. Some of our students have mentioned this sheet of compliments from their peers as one of their treasured possessions.

Relationship-building grounded in interconnectedness is an ongoing practice, not just a one-time activity. For example, some middle school teachers we know were concerned about reports from their multilingual learners that they were getting bullied and made fun of for the food they ate at lunch, the way they pronounced English words, and not knowing aspects of popular cultural, like music, movies, social media fads, or slang. The teachers thought they could address the concerns by celebrating these students' diversity. They hosted a culture night where the whole school was invited to bring food from their cultures and wear typical clothes or perform traditional dances. The turnout was high among the multilingual families, but few White monolingual English speakers attended. Everyone there had a great time celebrating diversity, but the event had little impact on the relationships back in the classroom. Different efforts were needed if multilingual students were to be fully seen or feel a sense of belonging at school.

In contrast, we've worked with an elementary school that annually hosts a Global Gala during a school day where the multilingual students in the school create learning stations around their language and cultural backgrounds and the whole school cycles through the stations learning language, playing games, learning songs, and so forth. It's had a powerful impact on how multilingual students are seen and valued in the school, including teachers viewing students as capable experts rather than simply students with English deficiencies. It's been so popular and well received that many other students have asked to be able to teach about various aspects of their lives and background as well.

The Global Gala was designed to foster interconnectedness. The community cultural night was designed with the idea of celebrating diversity and perhaps did accomplish that, but it did not foster interconnectedness. It is important that we orient ourselves and our decision-making toward interconnectedness to create authentic belonging for multilingual learners in our classrooms and schools.

Many teachers do community-building activities during the first day, week, or even month of school and then stop. To sustain a sense of interconnectedness, community-building activities need to be ongoing throughout the year. We regularly hold morning meetings or beginning of class community circles to connect, share, and problem-solve. Sometimes, we post open-ended prompts that students see when they enter the class. Other times, we have postcards or pictures spread out and they pick one and then talk about what they like or see. In these activities, we encourage students to share with others what is important about themselves and their likes, interests, and wishes. It is always their choice what to share or reveal. One prompt that we use over and over is "What is something that is making you happy today?" Even if a student answers "nothing," it tells us something.

There are a variety of ways to organize students to engage in community-building. Students can find a partner with the same birthday month, favorite color, or type of shoes they are wearing that day. Or students can line up alphabetically by the first letter of the word or phrase they will share (like what is making them happy in the moment). You probably have many other ways that take just a short time for members of the learning community to get to know more about each other in a relaxed setting. This does not take time away from academic work; rather, it solidifies the relationships needed to learn together. The goal is for every student to be able to work well with every other student in the classroom, something that will not happen without building in efforts for students to find points of connection across differences.

Sharing activities work best when they are centered on typical human feelings or experiences that are less culturally bound. For instance, instead of asking about a particular holiday in the US, we might ask, "What is something you like about winter?" Over time, we can deepen the conversations to acknowledge and address how students experience the larger society and how it affects what happens in the classroom. To foster the participation of multilingual learners, especially students newer to English, we may need to provide supports in advance or during the activity, like sentence starters, vocabulary visuals, or the opportunity to do the activity in a language other than English.

## Classroom Communities Versus Classroom Management

Teachers are often taught to think of the way we run our classrooms as classroom management. This can often be operationalized as the teacher as the sole person in charge, holding all the power and authority to police, judge, and sentence. In such contexts, students have little agency or voice in any of the processes. Because of these approaches, we've seen teachers "manage" classrooms in ways that are biased, discriminatory, culturally insensitive, and problematic. And let's be honest, at times we've done this ourselves. However, we have found that different approaches are possible and successful.

Now we seek to construct open and equitable classroom communities by orienting our work toward interconnectedness. Instead of us managing our classrooms, we want to be part of a strong collaborative, interconnected community that works together to learn and transforms the typical schooling narrative. We strive to co-construct spaces where we are all teaching, learning, and belonging.

## Shared Agreements

At the beginning of every course and even in workshops, we take time to set shared agreements. In building a beloved community, we try to center these agreements about how each of us can contribute toward it. Sometimes, the parameters are set for us by school-wide expectations that everyone must adhere to, such as "Be responsible, be kind, and be prepared." The conversation then is about how we want these mandates to appear in our classroom. What does it mean and what does it look like to be responsible? To be kind? To be prepared? What will we do to help each other do and be these things? What will we do when we fall short?

We usually begin by asking students about their expectations for themselves, for each other, and for us as the instructor. We share our own perspectives as well. Out of this discussion, we draft an initial set of agreements or even a statement of our shared values. We go over them together to ensure that they reflect everyone's input and come up with examples of what it means to enact them. These are always open to revision for additional topics like grading policies or what our class absence policy should be. We've seen teachers and students act out the agreements demonstrating what they both do and don't look like (often in super funny ways). Sometimes this takes 15 or 20 minutes, in other classes it takes longer, but we always take the time needed to ensure that everyone agrees. Refining our shared agreements and community values is ongoing throughout the class. We regularly revisit them to see what adjustments might be needed.

## Accountability

Accountability is most often enacted in schools through punishment. Students who break the classroom rules are sent to the office or their parents are called in by the principal. People who use the school parking lot without a permit get a ticket, even if it was an emergency. Students get suspended for disrupting an assembly, even though the speaker was offensive and demeaning. If our test scores do not meet externally imposed expectations for either proficiency or growth, we are threatened that the state will take us over, or we'll lose our jobs, or the principal will be fired.

Punishment often creates harm, suffering, and disconnection. Indeed, sometimes when we punish students, they change their behavior. There is abundant evidence, however, that especially harsh or "zero tolerance" punishments do not transform or even deter unwanted behaviors. Sometimes it isn't clear to students why they are being punished, in particular multilingual learners new to US schools. Their takeaway may be that we don't or won't see their perspectives or that they aren't valued or cared for. These disconnecting feelings can be exacerbated when student identity markers are different from our own.

Insights offered from the modern-day abolitionist social movements help us reconceptualize accountability (see Cullors, 2022 or Kaba, 2021) and orient it toward interconnectedness. Their vision of community is built on strong relationships grounded in self-actualization in reciprocity. Being our own best selves is tied to others being able to do the same. These activists argue that punishment as accountability is rarely effective and never humanizing. They advocate for creating accountability through transformational consequences in our problem-solving and conflict resolution efforts. When we do so, we can more easily center students' learning and our community interconnectedness. It does take work to create an accountability system that is aimed at repairing harm and building community. When we engage in accountability grounded in transformational consequences, our agreements help everyone be productive, engaged, and valued members of the community.

Collaboration is essential as we create our shared agreements as well as establish the consequences for not meeting them. These agreements then become tools for problem-solving when there are troubles, missteps, or conflict in the community. For example, instead of getting suspended for spraying graffiti on the bathroom walls, students could have to provide labor and/or materials to clean it off. They may also need to talk with the custodians to learn about the extra work their actions created. In turn, students might suggest designating or constructing a wall where graffiti is allowed where they can express their creativity as long as it doesn't violate agreements around respecting others. We need to find multiple ways to be accountable for our actions and explore what that could look like.

For example, as we were co-creating agreements with a group of eighth graders, they suggested that a positive consequence for meeting the agreements would be accumulating points toward a reward. Each day the whole class met expectations they would earn a point. After accumulating a certain number the points, they would take one class period to do something fun together of their choice, like walking to a nearby coffee shop. When some said they couldn't afford it, others offered to create a "coffee fund" so everyone could participate. We were skeptical of this kind of extrinsic reward system and also surprised at how well it turned out. We would have never chosen a point system, nor would we have thought the class would want to have a collective reward. But it became a powerful tool to work and grow in this learning community. It was so popular that students in other classes asked their teachers if they could do the same thing.

It does take work to create an accountability system aimed at repairing harm. An orientation toward interconnectedness helps us move away from focusing on punishment and toward transformational consequences that either grow or keep strong community connections intact. It this way, we can better build authentic relationships, co-create shared agreements, and hold one another jointly accountable for the well-being of the whole learning community.

## Orienting Toward Openness

Closely related to interconnectedness is an orientation toward openness. Through openness, we can counteract the dominant difference-as-deficit narrative by embracing multiple ways of being and knowing. It's also how we can have grace for problems and mistakes knowing that humans are always flawed and that missteps will occur even when doing our best.

Openness requires humility and accepting that our own experiences and ways of viewing the world are not the only truth. In our society, a pervasive message is that there is one right way to be or see the world and we should all assimilate toward it. What is seen as the "right way" to look, talk, and behave is grounded in racial, gender, and many other social hierarchies. "Normal" then is equated with straight, White, male, Christian, and so forth. These power dynamics impact our perceptions of students, families, and their communities as well as students' perceptions of each other. Negative views of one another result in students making fun of or policing each other's behaviors. Openness means accepting that there are multiple ways of knowing and being different from our own that are valid and true.

We use a simple a game (Barnga) to illustrate how differences in ways of knowing and being are often subtle yet destructive if not understood. Students initially learn to play the game in groups of four. Once they can play comfortably in their groups, we hold a class tournament. In the tournament, communication is through gestures and images on paper. No one is allowed to speak or use words in writing during play. Though they don't know it yet, each group of four has learned to play the game given slightly different rules about which cards are high, which are low, and which suit trumps the others. When the tournament begins, each group is playing by their own rules. At the end of the first round, the two lowest-scoring players from each group must rotate to a new table for the second round (a rotation that continues with each subsequent round).

In the second round, confusion always ensues and external power dynamics immediately surface. Very often, the rules of the people who stayed at their tables remain in place and the new players just have to adapt (a typical assimilationist approach). At other times, we have seen those with more social power and capital (most often White men) impose their game rules on everyone else, even when they are new to the table. As the rounds progress, sometimes players get upset with each other and frustrated at not being able to communicate well. Sometimes players give up, stop trying to communicate or figure out the rules, and just do as they are told. Others openly resist and rebel against or sabotage a game that is clearly rigged. At times, when players realize that they have all learned different rules, some try to agree about how they will play the game before the next round starts. They see co-constructing the rules as necessary for anything reasonable to occur as they play the game.

Co-Constructing Learning Communities ◆ 101

Barnga is a simple analogy for how different cultural practices play out in human interactions. We have all learned sets of rules to follow as we navigate through various social and educational situations. While on the surface it may look that we are similar and following the same rule book, there are diversities and corresponding oppressive factors like racism, linguicism, or homophobia that impact how we interact with those around us. Barnga highlights the need for openness toward differences as we co-construct shared agreements in our classroom communities.

We also use a popular meme to discuss that different perspectives on the same situation are legitimate (Figure 4.1).

This picture illustrates how two people can be looking at the same thing and have two different yet accurate interpretations. Unless we are open to understanding the other person's perspective, we may dismiss them as wrong, uneducated, or brainwashed. Importantly, our place in the larger society which affects our life experiences, engagement with social structures, values, and interests also influences whether we are positioned to see the 6 or the 9 or perhaps even something else.

Our positionality in society affects our perspectives and interpretations. Openness allows us to move from a place of seeking only right answers to embracing that there can be multiple truths and multiple positionalities. The question becomes how we can do this work in a way that attends to differential power

**FIGURE 4.1** 6 or 9?

and privilege based on our positionality. These are the kinds of issues that an orientation to openness forces us to grapple with.

It's important to create rich contexts for learning rather than shut down dialogue or the opportunity to learn from one another. We have conversations with our students to explore problematic, oppressive, or harmful ideas. While these conversations are challenging, all of us, by orienting ourselves toward openness, can better understand where different ideas and perspectives might come from and how to disrupt inequities and hopefully move toward learning and growth. Rather than dehumanize, call names, and shut people down, we can—with openness—explore different points of view and try to understand them.

By being open, we can also help multilingual learners explore and make sense of their experiences in and outside of school. Newcomers to the US are not just learning English, they are also being racialized in ways that can be difficult to understand. The way racism is enacted in the US is often very confusing. Imagine that a multilingual student who is a Person of Color, but not Black, uses the n-word in class and they get punished. They are confused because it's a word they have often heard other students using and it's in the music they listen to. They know it's a powerful word but they don't know the full context of its oppressive history. While the word has been reclaimed by part of the Black community, they may not understand that it's not appropriate for others to use it or why. If we take an open, interconnected approach to this situation, we can find out that the student used the word unaware of its full weight. A transformational consequence in this situation might be the student researching the word and its history. They could then teach what they learned to the class accompanied by an apology for the harm done and a commitment to changed future behavior.

This is a contrast to what we usually see in classrooms when a student says something harmful, like attacking a classmate with racist, homophobic, or anti-Islamic name-calling. More attention is paid to punishing the offender than trying to address the harm caused. What we need to do is tease out what happened and why it happened. Then we can work to repair the harm and try to prevent it from happening again. When we remain open and refrain from jumping to punishment, we can facilitate learning as well as relational renewal.

Another example of the complexity of racial stereotypes came up when we were talking with a group of teenage girls who were wearing hijabs. They told us that they were really jealous of their brothers. They had all been in the US for many years and spoke English without any noticeable accents. Their brothers were seen and treated inside and outside of school as simply "cool Black boys." The girls said their experience was quite different. As visibly Muslim, they were often called "terrorists" and told to go back to where they came from. This never happened to their brothers. We should make space in our classrooms to discuss with students how to find their way through confusing and hurtful racist cultural experiences.

This can include articulating in our shared agreements and accountability plans how we will say and hear "ouch." It is inevitable that, even with the best efforts and intentions, members of the learning community will step on one another's toes. How we prepare for and handle it can either foster connection and openness or shut it all down. Learning ways to hear about the impact of our missteps and repair the harm caused by them is an important aspect of developing a beloved learning community.

## Getting to Know Students and Their Families

An orientation toward interconnectedness and openness spurs us to learn as much as we can about our students and their families. Schools do collect some information we can access—mostly assessment scores—but the pictures they paint can be misleading. For example, in a fifth-grade classroom with many multilingual learners, nearly all the students were assessed to be reading below grade level in English. The monolingual English-speaking literacy teacher assigned to work with the class assumed that only three or four of the students spoke or read Spanish, since they used only English with him. In his view, they were "struggling readers."

As part of a research study, we conducted reading assessments in the class in both languages. Right away, we discovered that only three students *didn't* speak Spanish and that most read at higher levels in Spanish than English, several at the middle school level. The students' excitement at being able to demonstrate their capabilities and have them recognized was palpable. The teacher's perception of the learners and how he approached literacy instruction in English both changed when he realized many were strong readers in Spanish. He told us that in the future he would definitely talk with multilingual students to learn about them and their experiences.

Teachers' views of their multilingual learners' facility with English too often are based solely on grammar-based language assessments. Low test scores position some students as stagnant or extend their label as "English learner" when they have actually made substantial growth in English. Many teachers are surprised when they learn of the sophisticated ways that students use English outside of school. We've seen students act as interpreters and translators for their families at doctor's offices, community service agencies, and the grocery store. Others we know are responsible for setting up service calls with the utility company or negotiating with landlords. But these skills and abilities are not assessed in school.

With curiosity and creativity, we can develop a more open and complete picture of students. On the first day of school, an elementary teacher we know takes a photo of each student under a sign that says, "Welcome to our 3rd Grade Classroom!" in English and the languages of the students in the school, including local Indigenous language(s). She asks the students what names they want to be called, languages they know or want to learn, what they are good at, and a little about their families. She points out where different languages are spoken, noting local Indigenous languages as well as different alphabets. She makes it clear she values what students know in any language, as it contributes to their success in school. For homework, students are given a copy of their photo on a small poster that contains similar questions to complete with their families using words, drawings or decorations. In the following days, they use the posters for activities like a gallery walk to learn about each other and find similarities and differences among themselves. Each time a new student arrives, they are added to the photo gallery, and the class spends time getting to know them. These activities form a basis for their community-building and relational renewal.

Another example is from a science teacher we know. Early in the semester, they ask students to create a Science Autobiography in comic book form. Students use drawings and words to reveal their great and horrible science moments up until now and are encouraged to ask their families about their views on science as well. Another strategy we use is to survey students about their language backgrounds and schooling experiences. Sometimes they create language autobiographies in which they document the languages they hear and use in their families, neighborhoods, and larger communities. The students tell us who they are as multilinguals and what they do with the different languages they know.

To get at literacy skills in languages other than English, we often give students an interesting picture and encourage them to write a description in their home language(s). We do not need to be able to read or understand what they write to get a sense of their comfort engaging with the task—whether the student seems at ease, how quickly or belabored their production of text is, and if they insert words in English or leave blanks.

Too often, a classroom community is seen as being made up of only teachers and their students. By opening it up to include families and communities, we can expand our understandings of who our learners are. We have found that when we ask family members, they respond by sharing their hopes for their children and visions for their future. Their participation contributes to building a beloved, multilingual learning community where both students and their families feel welcome, embraced, and valued for who they are and what they uniquely bring. In this way, students and families can share who they are on their own terms. They also generate data for us to use that supports learning, engagement, and belonging for both students and families in the learning community.

Some students and families may be reluctant to share information about themselves due to their experiences with authorities before coming here or the kinds of documentation they hold. Or they simply don't want their children labeled as "English learners" for fear that they will experience discrimination or suffer from low expectations. Letting them know we view them as partners in their children's education and that we are open to their input can help ease some fears.

Teachers sometimes hold negative ideas about students' families, judging and blaming them or holding them in contempt. We may not agree with their families about everything, but they also should be part of the efforts we make toward interconnectedness and relational renewal. Some teachers shy away from engaging with multilingual families because of a language barrier. It may take a little extra effort, but we need to be open to a variety of opportunities to build strong relationships with families, even when there is a language barrier. These can be overcome much more easily today as there a variety of ways to communicate through technology. We can also access translations services that districts are under legal mandate to provide. Further, we can communicate with teachers at other grade levels or content areas who serve students from the same languages to share resources and information.

Finally, we can create our own portrait of our students by combining test scores, our observations, anecdotal notes, information gathered from homework and classwork, and conversations with families and students. In this way, we can more accurately and authentically acknowledge the unique values and strengths of our students and mirror those back to them. Being oriented toward openness helps us generate the best possibilities of learning about students to be able to see and support their most true, authentic, valued selves in our learning communities. Seeking the unique value in our students and their families can become a life practice. When we orient ourselves toward interconnectedness and openness, we never know for sure where our dialogues or inquiries will go. This opens the way for us to build on multiple ideas and perspectives to co-construct our classroom learning communities.

 **Make It Work**

In the Explore section, we discussed many ideas for co-constructing a strong multilingual learning community. We considered what a great community is, the role that relationships play, and how to foster authentic relationships to build beloved communities. We also explored two key orientations central to teaching multilingual learners: interconnectedness and openness. Now is your chance to play with these ideas and make them work in your practice! Below we have provided some options of how you can do that, thinking about the intrapersonal, interpersonal, and systemic levels of engagement. Any of these could (and potentially should) be done just by yourself but also could be accomplished through learning activities with your students. As you choose an option, keep in mind the module's critical reflection and complexity thinking questions: *How can I orient myself and my students toward interconnectedness and openness to build a strong community where we can collaboratively solve problems, disrupt inequitable issues, and create a sense of belonging? What systems, policies, and practices impact my ability to establish these kinds of relationships with students and families?* We encourage you to revisit the components of humanizing pedagogies from the introduction and think about the implications of what you learned from engaging in this module in relation to context, orientations, and pedagogy. When you have completed your Make It Work activity, reflect on your findings to share them with your colleagues.

## Make it Work Options

### Intrapersonal: Self-Analysis/Self-Study
Purpose: Deepen your understanding about relational renewal in a beloved community revolving around the orientations of interconnectedness and openness in order to contextualize them into your own life and practice. This includes exploring ways that you can grow in co-constructing strong learning communities

through attention to community, relational renewal, openness, and interconnectedness.

This option encourages you to use self-study or self-analysis, strategies teachers often use to explore their teaching practice and the impact of various instructional approaches. We encourage you to dig into how the features of co-constructing a learning community—relational renewal in a beloved community, interconnectedness, and openness—play out in your personal and professional life. We recommend picking one or more of those ideas and scrutinize how they appear (or don't) in your personal or professional life over time. You may choose to do this for a week, a month, or longer. You may choose to focus on one concept at a time and see what you notice and learn and then move on to the next concept. From your self-study, form ideas about what you can do to grow the beloved community in your classroom through relational renewal and orienting toward interconnectedness and openness.

### Interpersonal: Co-Construct Shared Agreements

Purpose: Co-construct shared agreements with students to guide classroom engagements and accountability plans based on orientations toward interconnectedness and openness.

Create (and, if possible, implement) a plan for co-constructing shared agreements with your learning community. If there are already schoolwide expectations for conduct or behavior, focus on making them authentic to your classroom. In the process, consider how you can move away from a one-size-fits-all approach. You might begin by thinking back on conflicts that have arisen in the past. Consider what you did and come up with some alternative transformational consequences you could have used to address them. More importantly, co-construct a plan with students regarding how to engage in accountability grounded in transformational consequences (e.g., the people involved co-construct the consequences that will repair harm as well as prevent future harm). Include in your plan how you will ensure accountability to the shared agreements and maintain everyone's human dignity and value. If you can implement the plan, reflect on what you might do differently going forward.

## Systemic: Explore and Improve Systems, Policies, and Practices Impacting your Classroom Community

Purpose: Understand and advocate for change in systems, policies, and practices that impact your classroom community.

A variety of systems, policies, and practices both inside and outside of our classrooms and schools impact our classroom learning communities. Some areas that may be worth investigating outside of school include opportunities related to local housing, transportation, employment, food, and childcare. Consider how external factors impact opportunities to co-construct an open and interconnected classroom learning community. Also consider changes that might be needed and how you could advocate for them.

Another possibility is to focus on specific policies in your school or district. How are students labeled "English learner" in your district? What academic opportunities are provided to them? When do they qualify for reclassification, and what does their education look like after losing the "English learner" label? Other policies to investigate include disciplinary practices and school sports and clubs' inclusion (or exclusion) policies and practices. How do these policies impact your classroom learning community? How might you advocate with your students to change discriminatory policies? The opportunities are endless, and the investigation and advocacy can be replicated across many different issues. Be sure to work with multilingual learners and their families and communities in these efforts as well as with an orientation toward interconnectedness and openness.

## You Make it Work

Purpose: To make the ideas from Explore work in your own practice.

Design your own activity (or tweak one of ours) to ensure that you are spending your time doing work that is most useful and relevant to you and your students. We recommend starting with the critical reflection and complexity thinking questions. Then clarify for yourself which level you are working at (intrapersonal, interpersonal, or systemic) and build your effort to make this module's learning work for you from there!

## Share

Share is your opportunity to engage with your peers and receive feedback about the work you have done and what you have learned in this module. Begin by revisiting the reflection you wrote at the beginning of the module and revise it to include your thinking now, noting any changes and what they might mean for your practice. Be sure to attend to opportunities to strive for justice and equity and to potential barriers to achieving it. Don't shy away from the complexities that come up—embrace them. Think about different ways of being and doing in your classroom that could address those complexities. Once you have completed your reflection, be prepared to share it with your colleagues along with a description of the work you did in the Make it Work section. By sharing what you have learned, you have the chance to both solidify your own learning and thinking and expand it by learning from your colleagues.

# 5

# Humanizing Assessments

In this module, we explore ways to humanize our assessments—those we are mandated to give and others we get to create in our classrooms. While *interconnectedness* and *openness*, the orientations considered in Module 4, are certainly applicable, in this Module we focus on *curiosity* and *creativity* as particularly important. When we orient toward *curiosity* and *creativity*, new ideas emerge for crafting robust assessment practices, procedures, and outcomes. It is not possible in a single module to fully explore this topic. We want to draw attention to the mindset and orientations toward assessment that can help our multilingual students flourish and accurately narrate their successes on their learning journeys. To take a deep dive into assessment with multilingual students, we recommend the work of Margo Gottlieb (2023) and her many useful books on assessments with multilingual students.

Before getting into the module, take time to engage with and reflect on these questions for critical reflection and complexity thinking: *How can I use assessment to create a complete and complex picture of my students? How is assessment data used to sort, label, and promote deficit narratives of multilingual students? What roles do or should families play in the assessment of my students? How do curiosity and creativity contribute to humanizing my assessment practices?*

DOI: 10.4324/9781032672199-8

Be sure to keep your initial reflection, notes, and ideas so you can revisit them during the Make it Work and Share sections of the module.

## Explore

Mari arrived in the US after a long journey with her family. Before she left home, she was an eager student and did well in all her subjects. She was especially interested in science and anything to do with growing things. When she got to the US, she was enrolled in seventh grade at a middle school with few other multilingual learners. Her teachers responded in various ways when told she scored Level 1 on the English language proficiency assessment, meaning that she was new to English. Her math teacher was doubtful about having a "non-English speaker" in his class. When Mari failed the course pre-test as well as the first two quizzes, he concluded that she knew only basic math concepts and was too far behind to catch up. To keep her busy, he gave her simple addition and multiplication worksheets, which she silently completed in the back of the class without asking any questions. She was miserable.

In contrast, her science teacher got to know Mari before deciding how to best support her. She consulted the school counselor and found out from intake records that Mari had strong literacy skills in Spanish and also spoke Portuguese, the language of her grandparents. The teacher used an app to translate a short interest survey that she uses with all her students to determine which life science topics they are familiar with and most interested in. Mari smiled and wrote two paragraphs in Spanish about her love for nature as well as growing and caring for plants. Her teacher searched for resources in Spanish online and gave Mari a journal to document her learning in words, pictures, and images, using all her languages. Mari also used the journal to pose questions, which the teacher then translated to English, so she and other students could help her. After just a few weeks, Mari was actively participating in small-group work and using many words and phrases to express herself in English.

These teachers' perceptions of Mari differed dramatically. In one class, she was seen as incapable and a burden due to her lack of English. Neither curious nor creative, the math teacher saw Mari as a problem, put her in a box, and made decisions that limited her opportunities for growth. In the other class, the teacher was curious, took time to get to know Mari, and found creative ways to encourage her learning. She positioned Mari as a literate multilingual student who could build on what she knew to learn the content. In one class, Mari was cut off from learning and connection; in the other, she was humanized, her assets were embraced, and she was given opportunities to be curious and creative herself. We can all be more like the science teacher and disrupt deficit narratives about multilingual learners.

## Learning Journeys and the Role of Assessment

Learning for us is a lifelong journey with countless destinations, detours, and an infinite number of stops along the way. To understand where we have been and where we are now, we use information from multiple sources to judge how successful a leg of the journey was or is and where we might need or want to go next.

At school, learning journeys are surrounded by expectations held by individuals, their families, and the society at large. Many current assessments craft inaccurate narratives about or limit students' possible learning journeys, especially multilingual learners. Assessments designed with and for monolingual English speakers often suggest that multilingual students' journeys are too slow, need to be repeated, or perhaps are headed toward the wrong destination. They overlook where students' journeys take them when they aren't in school and what they know and have learned in languages other than English.

Inaccurate assessment data make it difficult to fully know our multilingual students, especially when such data are used to represent complex human beings in very simplistic ways. There is much we can do to counter this. Our work is to ensure that no matter where our students have been on their journeys before we meet them, they can move forward to new destinations with a sense of agency and authenticity. We can use our curiosity to better know our learners and our creativity to overcome obstacles as we accompany them on their learning journeys.

## Difference as Deficit in Assessment

Assessment is used for many purposes: to guide instruction, evaluate performance, compare students, rate schools, and more. Many harmful assessment practices are grounded in the *difference-as-deficit* dominant cultural narrative (see Module 2). Too often, assessments are used to label, compare, and sort students while providing little guidance for day-to-day instruction. Before we ever see our students, assessments have helped determine who is in our classes, how they are categorized, and what their abilities are perceived to be. This affects how we view them and the learning opportunities we offer.

### Standardized Assessments and the Normal Curve

Different assessments are constructed for different purposes. They are either summative (to assess the ultimate arrival at a destination) or formative (as check-ins along the way to help us change or correct course as necessary). Whether it is one or the other depends partly on how the data are used. But both summative and formative assessments can be standardized and have some limitations when considering multilingual student learning journeys.

Criterion-referenced assessments focus on mastery of a predetermined learning trajectory against a defined set of standards. For example, per federal law, students labeled "English learners" are assessed annually to measure their language development against English Language Proficiency standards. Results provide a snapshot in time and aren't intended to be used to compare one student with another. Theoretically, every test taker can be at the same level—all test takers could be at Level 1 or 2 or 6. The data produced from these tests can be analyzed to determine how many kindergarteners are at Level 1 versus the number of first or fourth graders at Level 1, but these data cannot suggest that one grade level is doing better than another. One benefit of criterion-referenced tests is that they can capture student growth from one year to the next as the standards remain constant and tests are developed to measure performance against them. Therefore, these data seek to illustrate where students are on their English learning journeys. While no one assessment can fully and completely accurately illustrate everything about students' capabilities on their learning journeys, criterion-referenced tests can provide some useful insight, especially over time.

Norm-referenced standardized assessments typically measure content knowledge. The difference is that they are designed to compare an individual's performance in relation to all the others who take the test. Think percentile rankings. The point of the norm-referenced assessment—in contrast to criterion-referenced tests, where performance is judged against specific predetermined benchmarks—is to determine the low, high, and medium performers in the tested population. Test items are carefully piloted and selected to ensure that scores will be distributed in order to make claims about differences among the test takers.

Most of us recognize the image below of what is called a "normal" or bell curve. Many phenomena when graphed—from human behaviors to various happenings in nature—are purported to fall along this curve. In norm-referenced testing, it creates a convenient but simplistic story about low, medium/average, and high performers, which is used to sort and label students (Figure 5.1).

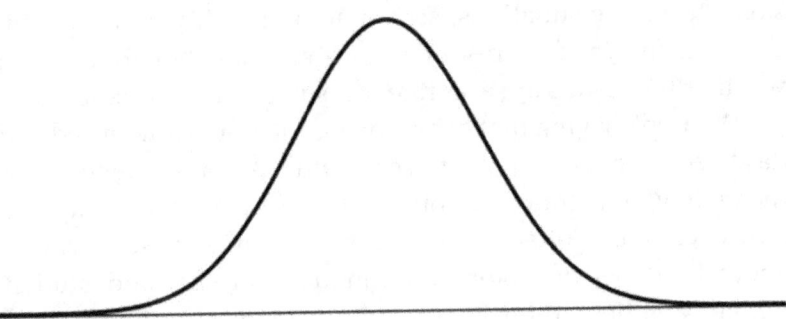

**FIGURE 5.1** Normal curve.

The normal curve has been widely critiqued for misrepresenting human differences (Dudley-Marling and Gurn, 2010; Gould, 1981). A common interpretation is that the people who constitute the middle of the curve are viewed as "normal" (rather than typical). This is where *difference as deficit* most often plays out. The people who are "different" from the majority in the middle are seen as outliers and thus "abnormal." They are often positioned as either less or better than those in the middle.

The problem with applying the normal curve to school assessments is interpreting the results as accurately reflecting intellectual capacity and personal effort, ignoring many other factors that affect how students perform. The content, format, and questions are benchmarked against a norming population that is often unrepresentative of all those who will take the test. Critiques of these tests include that the content is skewed toward the experiences of White, middle-class, monolingual English speakers. Results thus reflect oppressive hierarchies related to race, class, gender, language, and immigration status. Each line of identity may contribute to whether students have access to the knowledge and ways of expressing it needed to score well.

To use data wisely, we must understand the assumptions that underlie the assessments and the nature of the norming population. We can then critically reflect on whether the data provide an accurate picture of either our students or our teaching. Many who do well on norm-referenced standardized assessments are simply more familiar with or adept at a certain version of academic register. Discrimination is compounded when data are used to decide course placements, program and college admissions, teacher evaluations, school accountability and accreditations schemes, and/or resource distribution without questioning whether the results are accurate measures of performance.

We aren't saying that comparisons via norm-referenced standardized assessments are never useful. At times, such assessments have illustrated serious issues of inequity and injustice. However, more often, these data perpetuate false narratives about Students of Color, multilingual learners, and students with disabilities. To further complicate matters, testing is a multibillion-dollar industry with ties to politicians in high places.

Powerful lobbyists push national, state, and local legislative bodies to adopt their assessments. Test scores are used to make dubious claims about how public education is failing, often by those who would privatize schools and profit from a pay-to-go system. While generating huge corporate profits, the current over-testing regime is not responsive to the learning journeys of multilingual students, perpetuating inequity and discrimination.

## Issues Specific to Multilingual Learners

Humanizing assessment for multilingual learners requires taking into account the role that language plays in the assessment process. The language of the assessment matters. Results of tests given only in English often conflate content knowledge with English language proficiency. We once distributed a third-grade mathematics exam in Chinese to our mostly monolingual English-speaking college students. While their mathematics knowledge was far more advanced than what was needed to do well on the test, none passed or even got very far trying. The language of the assessment made it impossible for them to show their competence, which was quite frustrating and also enlightening for the students. We are not alarmed when students in the process of learning English don't do well on content tests designed for monolingual English speakers. The results simply confirm that students aren't yet fully proficient in English and tell little about their content knowledge. Our task is to create ways to get at their actual understandings.

One proposed solution is to test students in their home language. This can be useful but often is not feasible, even though there are some standardized assessments in languages other than English (mostly in Spanish in the US). Another option is to allow students to use all their linguistic resources in classroom-based assessments. While we do advocate using assessments in languages other than English, we urge caution if students haven't received any instruction in that language. Say a student learns about the solar system in school only in English. If they don't have the opportunity to learn the terminology or discuss the concepts in their home language, an assessment in that language may not capture what the student learned. In that case, using their home language for assessment becomes just another way to misjudge students.

Students' language development trajectories are much more complex than simple numerical labels derived from English language proficiency assessments (e.g., *she's a 1, they are a 4,* or *he's a 6*). Multilingual students often demonstrate different proficiencies across language domains (reading, writing, listening, and speaking) or move back and forth among them. We shouldn't be surprised when students don't progress in a linear fashion. Many students score higher one year and lower the next, even while exhibiting strong growth in our classrooms and personal interactions. With curiosity we can seek to understand students' trajectories over time to determine how to best support language growth in our classrooms.

A related issue is how data from assessments are (mis)used to judge a school's academic progress for accountability purposes. Among the complexities here are the wide differences among multilingual learners not as prevalent among monolingual English speakers. Every year, the tested population is different due to changing migration patterns, when in the school year students arrive, how old they are on arrival, and their prior schooling experiences. Even so, students labeled as "English Learners" are reported as a group and then compared with other subgroups of students not labeled as "English Learners." What do we really learn when the scores of students at the earliest stages of learning English are grouped with those who will soon be reclassified as fully English proficient? To us, it doesn't make sense to combine test results of students who've been in US schools for just a short time with those who've been learning English for several years. To understand multilingual student data from content assessments, scores need to be disaggregated by language proficiency, prior schooling, and literacy levels, something that in our experience seldom happens.

For example, whenever we disaggregate the test scores by language proficiency on literacy or mathematic assessments, we always find that students at the earlier stages of learning English (e.g., Levels 1 and 2) congregate on the lower end around unsatisfactory or not proficient on the content assessment. This is expected as language proficiency plays a role in how well they can show their content knowledge on the test. Students who have attained greater fluency (e.g., at Level 3) generally cluster around the proficient level; some are at or above and others are still below. Students at the highest levels of English proficiency (Levels 4 and 5) for the most part score at or above proficiency. This simple disaggregation gives us information that is more meaningful. Should we be concerned that students at the earliest stages of learning English are not performing well on a test of content knowledge given in English? Not really. In fact, the federal definition of "English Learner" is that they can't yet perform at grade level in English. We are much more concerned if students who are further advanced in their English learning (e.g., scoring at Levels 4 and 5 and in some cases Level 3), score poorly on these tests. In that situation, we need to ask whether the results are an accurate representation of students' knowledge and skills and what we can do to improve their learning journeys. If students can demonstrate their content knowledge in another way, we need to seek better ways to demonstrate to other teachers, students, families, and the community what students are capable of that these tests don't capture.

There are many reasons students further along in their English proficiency might not perform as expected. They may have a reading difficulty or an unidentified learning disability which makes it harder to answer the questions, especially if the test is timed. We have also known many students who because of negative experiences in the past are not invested in the test and don't even try. A related issue of concern is that many students get labeled "Long term English Learners"—or, worse, "ESL lifers"—when they don't test out of English as a Second Language (ESL) instruction even after several years of participation. Among the many problems with this label is that students are often treated as less than by their teachers and schools and even at times blamed for their perceived underachievement.

That multilingual students remain for an unexpectedly long time in English language development programs is a complicated systemic failure. Language development classes alone are not the solution. We need to be curious about the nature of the instruction students have received in all classes and how that is intertwined with the deficit narratives that surround them. When students remain labeled "English Learners" for many years, they miss taking challenging content classes and/or electives available to students perceived as more fluent English speakers, even though the former can also benefit from and succeed in such classes.

These issues related to multilingual students and assessment merit further attention. Data conversations regarding the performance of multilingual learners can't be based on standardized test scores alone. We recommend beginning with the work of Maneka Deanna Brooks, especially her book from 2020, and then exploring the work of scholars like Karen Thompson and Ilana Umansky. Their research illustrates the importance of having robust conversations regarding assessment data generated for multilingual students (see Thompson et al., 2023). We need to dig deeper into students' profiles and explore how their life and educational experiences affect the data. When we go beyond the numbers, we can uncover the complexities.

## Key Aspects of Humanizing Classroom Assessment

Humanizing assessment is a central feature of a just and equitable classroom. As a verb, it means trying to change the current state of assessment practices. As an adjective, it describes the strategies and approaches that can support students on their individual and collective learning journeys as full, complex, multilingual human beings. It includes being curious and gathering a body of evidence to explore where students' journeys began, how far they have come, and the possibilities for where they can go next.

Because of the diversity of multilingual students and the different assets they bring, there are many potential pathways to assess their learning journeys. Different journeys benefit from different approaches to assessment ranging from informal in-class observations to formal multimodal assessment practices. In our view, any assessment captures only the minimum and not the cap of what students can do. Any gaps in skills or knowledge uncovered by assessments do not represent failures but instead point us to the next place in the learning journey. With assistance, practice, and appropriate scaffolds, students can usually successfully arrive at any learning journey destination.

The kinds of assessments we recommend uncover who the learners are, their experiences, languages, and strengths they can continue to build on. They capture students' successes as well as their opportunities for growth. The assessments and tools we use should provide meaningful information so we can offer students useful feedback on their performance and fine-tune our assistance to support students in arriving at the learning destination. When we invite multiple perspectives and embrace different ways of being and knowing, including those of students' families, we can tell more accurate, positive stories about students' accomplishments and guide their learning to the next level.

Rubrics, portfolios, and journals all play a role in our assessments as they center curiosity for both us and our students. *Rubrics* offer stepping stones or routes to take and support student agency as they offer ever-deepening ways to display their knowledge. They are most useful when they are co-constructed, so that everyone understands the indicators and what is required to achieve them. *Portfolios* are like scrapbooks of our journeys. Students contribute by choosing artifacts that document where they began and how far they have traveled. Multilingual, multimodal portfolios allow students to utilize all their languages to craft strong narratives about their learning journeys, thus providing insight into what they learned, how, and for what purposes. *Journals* provide a space where students can reflect on their own learning, ask questions, and communicate with us directly. They are analogous to travelogues, capturing stories of what they are learning, how it makes them feel, and any questions that arise along the way. Journals can be done in writing, through voice memos or even on video, all using multiple languages.

Quick informal assessments also grow our understandings of our students. Strategies like thumbs up/thumbs down, exit tickets, anecdotal notes, and even checklists provide valuable information about students. They let all of us—including students and their families—know how students are progressing on their journey, when they get to the next stop, and where they can go after that.

## Learning Targets

Many aspects of students' learning journeys are out of their control—and ours. Factors like state standards, policy mandates, and district-determined curriculum externally impose what they are supposed to learn and on what timeline. This can be frustrating for teachers of multilingual students, especially when those students at the earliest stages of learning English are held to the same timelines as monolingual speakers. Such practices ignore the complex and challenging process of learning a new language.

However, there is much we can do to support students even with externally imposed learning targets. The first thing is to ensure that students have a strong understanding of what the learning targets are and where their learning is heading. This is perhaps the most important and most overlooked part of humanizing assessment practices with multilingual students—ensuring that students have a clear understanding of the learning journey destination they are working toward.

Learning targets can be presented in words and pictures as well as with actions and examples so students can internalize them to set the course for their own learning. We have often seen an emphasis on language and content objectives; however, we've rarely seen evidence that they are more than words on a board or an item on a checklist for an administrator doing an observation. There is a fair amount of work that needs to be done to ensure that students truly have a sense of the destination of their learning journey. We recommend spending time discussing the learning target, engaging in activities to ensure that it is well understood, and even backwards-planning together with students for how they will both meet that learning target and know themselves that they have arrived. We also suggest helping students work together toward larger learning targets and seeing how the day-to-day learning is moving them toward that larger topic.

For instance, students who are learning to read may very successfully engage with the phonics exercises and games in class but have no idea that the purpose of those games and exercises is to be able to connect sounds to the written word on the page and construct meaning through reading. Helping students build a conceptual understanding regarding the work they are doing and how it works together to move them toward an important learning target can be very motivating as well as supportive of stronger learning outcomes. For this reason, contextualizing those activities and connecting them to actual reading practices and the written word are critically important.

It is possible that students will be working toward different learning targets or even the same learning target but on different pathways. For instance, in a class of multilingual students learning to read in English, there may be some students who have already mastered blending sounds and feel confident doing it with several different sounds, while others are just starting to build that skill and are focusing on only a couple. However, they are all still working on the ultimate learning target: becoming proficient readers.

Some students may be able to say the learning target but still not be totally clear about their destination or the tools they will need to get them there. These students may need to participate in a few activities before having a clearer sense of where they are headed. For others, repeated opportunities to conceptualize and discuss their learning destination will be necessary. This highlights the importance of ongoing conversations and interactions with our students across the entirety of a learning journey. The goal is not only that all learners arrive at their destination but that they know when they have arrived.

Therefore, students should have ways not only to know where they are heading but also to monitor their own progress. We should offer feedback to students and support their journey, but the more students can take leadership over their own learning and use their own curiosity and creativity to guide it, the farther that learning will reach and more effective it will be.

## Using Multiple Modalities for Assessment

No one single assessment can reveal everything that our students know, understand, or can do. Humanizing our assessments is resisting the temptation to value certain kinds of data—such as standardized assessments, or written tests in English—over all others. Unfortunately, as a society, we tend to place our trust in the assessments most likely to tell false narratives about multilingual learners.

An orientation toward creativity is key to crafting an assessment system that incorporates multiple avenues for students to demonstrate their learning. Research suggests that the most accurate and robust information about multilingual students' understandings comes from combining different modalities—visual, written, oral, and performance (Grapin, 2022). Providing opportunities to use languages other than English is also vital. Each modality and each language provide a different perspective on the learner and broaden our understandings.

Students can show their thinking in traditional ways as well as via videos and podcasts. We encourage our students to use images, posters, 3D models, collages, skits, or digital shorts as well as illustrate what they are learning via multiple languages or even mediums that are not language-centric. We also use language-free assessments where students can show their thinking without having to use much English. For example, they can choose between two visuals and point to one to demonstrate their understanding of terminology or they can create a visual image of a concept. When we invite students to help decide how they will show what they know and can do, the possibilities expand even further.

When we do use assessments that are language-dependent, we also offer scaffolds like sentence stems to support students in showing their knowledge and thinking rather than getting tripped up on English conventions. Providing sentence stems to students newer to English is quite beneficial in formal and informal assessments. Examples of useful sentence stems in mathematics are, "To solve the problem, first I _____ and then I _____" and "I used _____ (table, graph, drawing, equation, and so forth) to solve the problem, because_____." We have worked with mathematics teachers who were amazed at how using sentence stems changed what they were able to see and understand about their students' learning.

We frequently use oral assessments (especially with our multilingual students) because they allow us to probe and ask questions. We find that dynamic interviews (Grapin, 2022) are quite useful. These are open-ended oral discussions designed to uncover students' understandings, misconceptions, and opportunities for growth. As we plan for the interviews, we set a goal for what we want to learn from students and prepare questions, visuals, and prompts to facilitate the conversation as students demonstrate their knowledge and/or skills. Our role is to listen carefully for the students' ideas, build on them, and dig deeper. We focus on *what* students say and not as much on *how* they say it for content assessments. We constantly remind ourselves that our focus is on content, not on English grammatical accuracy.

## Involving Students

Students of all ages benefit when they can participate in decisions about their learning and how to document their progress. As we seek to design a fully responsive assessment system, we share our ideas and perceptions with our learning communities and invite them to contribute theirs. We co-construct shared understandings to clarify the destination that students are moving toward and what success looks like.

We worked with a fifth-grade teacher who was especially skilled at helping all students, many of them multilingual learners, grow as writers (see Viesca & Hutchison, 2014 for more on this teachers' work). Ms. Hutchison had consistent, frequent, and ever-expanding conversations with her students. They learned what good writing looked like by deconstructing and analyzing mentor texts and writing texts together. Students then used these examples as tools to evaluate their own writing as well as each other's. These ongoing conversations helped students gain a strong sense of their strengths as writers and also where they could continue to grow. Over the course of the school year, discussions became more nuanced and complex as the class refined their shared vision of writing proficiency. Over time, as Ms. Hutchison continued to support students, each student also took on a leadership role in their own learning journey and supported their peers. Not only were students learning and improving their writing to a very high standard, the burden on the teacher as the only reliable source of feedback and assistance in the classroom was reduced.

Some assessments are a combination of teacher suggestions and student input and choice. With input from both teachers and students, no one has to come up with everything. The Make It Work section at the end of each module is an example of co-creating an assessment. We always offer a "You Make It Work" option so you can decide what is most applicable and meaningful in your own context and with your students. In our many years of using the Explore, Make It Work, and Share learning model, most teachers take what we have designed and then tweak our suggestions. Neither our ideas alone nor those of the participants end up guiding most of the Make It Works; rather, they are guided by a combination of the two.

Assessments are usually designed for individual students to show their independent learning. Virtually all high-stakes tests in the US as well as most assessments in classrooms ask what students can do without assistance. We can move away from focusing only on what students can do on their own and become curious about what they can do in collaboration with others. It is not wrong to assess what students can do on their own, but this does not create a full picture of their capabilities.

We have found it useful to have students work together to demonstrate their learning. The process of engaging collaboratively around the learning often furthers and solidifies conceptual understandings in more complex or in-depth ways than what one student could do on their own. By working together, they also learn important skills like compromise, communication, and leadership. This kind of small-group work also generates authentic languaging opportunities for students to grow their multilingual linguistic repertoire.

An approach to collaborative assessment we often use in our classes is having students teach their learning to each other. One group might read part of a book or research a topic and then teach the rest of the class what they learned on their own. Students are usually quite creative as they share their learning, answer questions, and solicit peer feedback about both the content and the format. This becomes part of the body of evidence we have about their learning. Inevitably, the presentations improve over time as each group learns from those who preceded them. Students often tell us that being able to teach the content to others is how they know they have actually learned something. Further, students consistently report that they learn more from their peers' teaching than from ours. This is actually great news and not surprising as well as something that can be utilized in classrooms of all grade levels. Even Kindergarteners can be co-teachers with the right supports and opportunities. Because of its effectiveness, this kind of activity has become a regular part of our instruction.

**Involving Families**
Curiosity about our students extends to their life outside of school. In K-12 settings, we always try to bring families into assessment conversations to help us learn about students' interests, knowledge, and strengths. We ask families for ideas of how to support students' learning journeys and even help shape their direction. Families open our eyes to ways we can be more culturally and linguistically responsive to students inside and outside the classroom.

In K-12 multilingual settings, families play an important role in the assessment process by helping us get a clearer sense of what students do know and understand. We have found that opening regular lines of communication focused on learning targets helps everyone better understand the learning journeys students are on and the learning targets we are working toward. We are aware that, as hard as we try, students newer to English are not going to fully capture content delivered only in English. This is why we let families know the broad topics that are being explored and encourage families to talk about them with their students in whatever language they would like. We also strategize with students about ways to participate in these conversations at home. Students who can effectively communicate to their families what they are learning and why likely have a strong understanding of the learning target. We are not asking parents to teach the content—just create a space for students to talk about what they are learning. This helps students consolidate information and articulate questions they have.

To the extent possible, we communicate with families in their home languages in writing, via text, or over email. We have used blog posts, letters home, or videos. We share discussion prompts and visual images as well as students' work products as sources of information. We also ask students to bring back the questions their families pose to share with the classroom community. We often compile those questions on a class poster and use them to expand the learning of the class collectively. They help us refine our inquiry questions and determine whether students have learned what they need to answer them.

We also welcome families to share with us any insights they gain and/or questions that arise from the conversations they have with their students. We use online translation tools as well as district resources so these conversations can be productive and meaningful. Of course, there are flaws in the process, especially when translation tools don't support the languages represented in our school populations. We still try to use our creativity to overcome communication obstacles.

Teachers often express a fear that when students explore content in their home languages, they will develop or solidify misunderstandings or misconceptions. This is a legitimate concern. We grapple with issues of misconceptions and quality of information all the time. In our classroom communities, we establish ways to collaboratively determine if information is valid and useful for our learning or if it is misinformation (or disinformation) that might lead to misconceptions.

At times, however, something we might think is a misconception or a misunderstanding is simply another way of seeing, knowing, or being in relationship to the topic. We need to be open to the ideas/perspectives our students and their families have. For example, there are different algorithms for doing long division in different countries. Across different cultures, narratives are structured in varying ways: some are linear, some circular, and some go off on tangents and return to the main idea. We try to explore where misunderstandings might come from and appreciate how they expand our own understandings of a topic. They may be just different understandings that can lead to expanded perspectives of the world and our content. Or there may be misconceptions and inaccuracies that need to be corrected.

It is a community process and shared effort where we use our collective curiosity and creativity to sort through these tensions. We do not have to single someone out with a "wrong" idea or make someone feel as if their thinking isn't valid. We can, however, interrogate all of the ideas that are shared and hold them to a standard in terms of what evidence supports the idea, where the evidence comes from, whom the idea impacts, and so forth. For us, this is an ongoing part of the community conversations we have in our classes.

## Make It Work

The essence of humanizing assessments is to paint comprehensive and accurate pictures of students' strengths and opportunities for next steps. In this Module, we addressed how we can provide a more accurate and dynamic picture of students' learning journeys in multilingual classrooms. We explored some of the issues surrounding assessment especially related to externally mandated, large-scale assessments. We also discussed ways to improve classroom-based assessments, by orienting ourselves and our students toward curiosity and creativity. We advocated including students and families in the process and using multilingual, multimodal, and multifaceted assessments. Now is your chance to play with these ideas and make them work in your practice! Below we have provided some options of how you can do that, thinking about the intrapersonal, interpersonal, and systemic levels of engagement. Any of these could (and potentially should) be done just by yourself but also could be accomplished through learning activities with your students. As you choose an option, keep in mind the module's critical reflection and complexity thinking questions: *How can I use assessment to create a complete and complex picture of my students? How is assessment data used to sort, label, and promote deficit narratives of multilingual students? What roles do or should families play in the assessment of my students? How do curiosity and creativity contribute to humanizing my assessment practices?* We encourage you to revisit the components of humanizing pedagogies from the introduction and think about the implications of what you learned from engaging in this module in relation to context, orientations, and pedagogy. When you have completed your Make It Work activity, reflect on your findings to share them with your colleagues.

## Make it Work Options

### Intrapersonal: Self-Study of Judgments

Purpose: Note the many ways you assess/judge students throughout the day and ensure that those judgments are just and equitable.

If possible, video-tape yourself and review it noting all the different assessments/judgments you made through the entire lesson. We are constantly assessing as educators and without critical reflection; we may be assessing in biased ways that limit our ability to see the full potential of our multilingual students. If you can't video-tape yourself, you may ask a partner to come observe you (and offer to do the same for them). Another option is to spend a day seeking to record in real time or through ongoing reflection during the small breaks you have to capture all the assessments you are making of students. After you have captured the data around your ongoing assessments/judgments, spend some time analyzing it and considering the impact of those judgments. Were you open to different uses of language? Were you curious about behaviors and actions? Was there anything you might have overlooked in the moment? After you conduct your analysis, consider areas to work on. For instance, perhaps you discovered that because of the busy demands of a large classroom with many students, you made quick judgments about a student you thought was misbehaving. But seeing the video and watching what happened from a different angle, you realize your judgment was inaccurate. They were actually trying to get help with work they were struggling with. Based on this discovery, what will you do next? With this example, it would be good to consider how to repair any harm with that student but also how to create a context where students can get the help they need without your having to be stretched so thin. How might students help each other and rely on other resources rather than only you for assistance? Further, what internal work would you need to do to respond in that situation differently, orienting toward interconnectedness, openness, curiosity, and creativity? If you aren't yet the teacher of record in a classroom, you could observe a teacher noting their ongoing assessments and engage in critical reflection for yourself as if you were in their shoes.

## Interpersonal: Plan and (if Possible) Implement a Multilingual and/or Multimodal Assessment

Purpose: Explore the affordances of using multilingual and/or multimodal assessments in your classes.

Design a multilingual and/or multimodal assessment for either immediate or future use. Consider a current monolingual, single-modality assessment you use and plan how you could make it multilingual and/or multimodal. Aim for a multifaceted assessment that gathers different kinds of data around student understandings to better capture their strengths and opportunities for growth (e.g., an assessment that includes both written and oral components) (see Grapin, 2022). Keep track of what you learn as you engage in the process, including any aha moments, challenges, or roadblocks. If you administer the assessment, reflect on how it went, what could be improved, and implications for designing creative multilingual and multimodal assessments in the future.

## Systemic: Explore and Advocate for Improved Data Pictures of Students

Purpose: Explore current assessment practices with multilingual students and, where necessary, advocate for improved assessments and/or ways to analyze and use the data.

Learn as much as you can about the current assessment and data use practices with multilingual students in your school and district. Explore the data picture that is created for multilingual students at your school and in your district. What are the assessments that students are required to take? What is done with that data? Many schools and districts collect and analyze data for multilingual students simply to meet compliance requirements with state and federal law. But in doing so, they might miss opportunities to paint more accurate and useful pictures of students' and teachers' accomplishments. Dig into the assessments that are used: are they criterion- or norm-referenced? What work has been done to ensure that these assessments are valid and reliable for multilingual students? What decisions are made using these data? Do those decisions create strong learning possibilities for students? Where necessary, advocate for changes and improved uses of data. Thompson et al. (2023) offer a strong framework to improve data analysis and use practices with multilingual students that your school and/or district could adopt.

**You Make It Work!**

Purpose: To make the ideas from Explore work in your own practice.

Design your own activity (or tweak one of ours) to ensure that you are spending your time doing work that is most useful and relevant to you and your students. We recommend starting with the critical reflection and complexity thinking questions. Then clarify for yourself which level you are working at (intrapersonal, interpersonal, or systemic) and build your effort to make this module's learning work for you from there!

**Share**

Share is your opportunity to engage with your peers and receive feedback about the work you have done and what you have learned in this module. Begin by revisiting the reflection you wrote at the beginning of the module and revise it to include your thinking now, noting any changes and what they might mean for your practice. Be sure to attend to opportunities to strive for justice and equity and to potential barriers to achieving it. Don't shy away from the complexities that come up—embrace them. Think about different ways of being and doing in your classroom that could address those complexities. Once you have completed your reflection, be prepared to share it with your colleagues along with a description of the work you did in the Make it Work section. By sharing what you have learned, you have the chance to both solidify your own learning and thinking and expand it by learning from your colleagues.

# 6

# Pluralism in Practice

When we were preparing to become teachers, we were taught to design whole-group lessons, which we were then supposed to tweak to differentiate for students with various learning profiles, including multilingual learners or those with identified learning disabilities. Planning for differentiation was an afterthought, time-consuming, and often ineffective. In this module, we provide guidance for how instead we can embrace the diversity of our learners in our planning and practice from the outset.

Embracing pluralism is integral to humanizing teaching practices. We find we can more directly address the varied learning profiles of our students when we create learning spaces where multiple activities and varied assignments are happening simultaneously, where students have a say in their learning journey as they complete assignments, where they use a variety of materials and can express themselves using all their linguistic resources, and where we share power with them. To do so, we need to orient ourselves toward *agency* and *shared responsibility*, built on the firm belief that students can and will rise to the occasion.

Before you get into the module, take time to reflect on and engage with this complex topic and consider these questions for critical reflection: *What role does pluralism play in your practice? In terms of control in the classroom, what is important to you? Where might you be able to give up some of it? Where might you struggle to offer students agency and shared responsibility in the classroom? Why?* Be sure to keep your initial reflection, notes, and ideas so you can revisit them during the Make it Work and Share sections of the module.

## Explore

We once visited a fifth-grade classroom where students were busy at work all around the room. They were mostly in groups of three—some at desks, some on the floor, and some on bean bags. Every group was deep in conversation and clearly engaged. The teacher was working directly with one group seated around her. They were nodding, taking notes, and sharing their ideas as they responded to the teacher's questions. Looking around, we realized that each small group was talking about a different book, referring to a materials packet that outlined various ways that students could take leadership over aspects of the work. The teacher explained that each group had selected their own book to read and used the support materials as needed to frame their discussions. Students developed their own plans, which they called "lesson plans," for how to run their book clubs. Students were actively participating, interested, and excited about their work.

Given the kind of independent work that students were doing, many would think we were observing a class for the "gifted and talented." They were making choices about their learning and taking turns to lead it. However, the teacher told us that most of the students were on an Individualized Education Plan (IEP) for learning disabilities or were labeled "English Learner" or both. In this class, students who often are positioned in terms of what they can't do were thriving and showing just how much they could.

There was abundant evidence of humanizing pedagogies in this class as the teacher elevated and sustained students' strengths and embraced their differences. She rejected the prejudices that positioned them as "other" or "less than." She was clearly guided by two orientations central to sharing power: *agency* and *shared responsibility*. These orientations make it possible to move from classrooms where everyone is doing the same thing at the same time to those where groups of students engage in different activities simultaneously—a multitasking classroom.

## The Multitasking Classroom

Currently, most classrooms are organized around monotasking—where everyone is expected to do the same task (often with the same materials and the same procedures) at the same time. The typical setup is whole-group instruction where the teacher leads the entire class in a discussion or activity. Monotasking is also in place when students work in small groups that are all doing exactly the same task or assignment with the same resources. For example, a science lab where everyone conducts the same experiment with the same hypothesis and the same materials is monotasking. Multitasking would be each group testing different hypotheses with different materials around a similar or same topic, thus setting up authentic opportunities to share, compare, and discuss results.

Monotasking has its roots in transmission models of teaching where students are viewed as empty vessels, waiting to be filled with the knowledge that teachers choose or are told to transmit. Orienting toward transmission makes it easy to fall into the script of teaching as surveillance and learning as compliance. Educators can often perform these scripts without questioning which (or whose) knowledge is being transmitted and to what effect. Transmission models of teaching perpetuate oppressive relationships and limit who teachers and students are and should be. They treat teaching and learning like mechanized, factory-like procedures. Such conceptions of teaching and learning also play a substantial role in the so-called culture wars that are currently leading to book bans and legislation limiting classroom discussions on race, LGBTQ topics, or any "controversial" issue. When teaching is viewed as simply transmitting knowledge, it's also easy to suggest that teaching is indoctrination.

However, teaching is not just about transmitting knowledge, nor should it ever be for the purposes of indoctrination. A variety of factors impact what we learn and under which circumstances. Our various identities, interests, motivations, perspectives, and life experiences affect how we engage with new ideas. We are not empty vessels, and neither are our students. By the time they start school, children have had years of life experience that shape how they see the world. They have developed ways of thinking and being in the world and figured out how to use the information they have access to. When we reject the empty vessel metaphor, we can embrace each student as a complex and agentic human being whose learning potential is expansive.

The narrative that teaching is transmission of knowledge is also problematic for how it positions us as teachers. Our role becomes no more than telling students what they are supposed to learn as if we lived in a vacuum. More and more as teachers, we are mandated to use scripted curriculum which deprofessionalizes us and limits our own agency. Too often, the result is boring and ineffective classroom practices like endless lectures or whole-group activities where many students are left behind. Certainly, human beings can learn from being told things. But when asked, most learners will describe that they learn the most when they are in action with others—learning by doing.

It is harder to implement humanizing pedagogies and draw on the strengths, assets, and learning abilities of all students when everyone is expected to do exactly the same thing at exactly the same time. Usually, some students are left behind or lost while others are bored and disengaged. When there is only one learning path and pace, there will inevitably be students who struggle. Multitasking approaches, in contrast, make it easier to address who students are, their interests, and what they bring to the learning goals of the unit. Multitasking, or pluralism in practice, provides a variety of opportunities to sustain and expand the cultural and linguistic practices students bring to the classroom. This makes learning more personal, meaningful, and relevant as students proceed on their learning journeys.

Activity centers are a form of multitasking. So is an elementary literacy class where during guided reading a small group of students works with the teacher while the rest of the class is engaged in independent or small-group activities—vocabulary games, spelling activities, writing or reading tasks, and so forth. Multitasking is possible across all grade levels and content areas, and it especially enhances learning in multilingual classrooms as it opens space for students to use their whole linguistic repertoire.

Multitasking classrooms support differentiation in the learning process, products, and outcomes. By building lessons around multitasking, educators provide students with different entry points, resources, and opportunities to accomplish their learning goals. Students can therefore engage in learning activities individually, with their peers, or with their teacher (and, where possible, other adults). In multitasking classrooms, students may read different books or do assignments in different languages or engage in entirely different assignments from one another. The individual learning paths that students take can come together through authentic opportunities to share/teach what they've learned. The varied learning approaches and outcomes can then actually build the whole class's understandings. With such practices, students' varied cultural backgrounds and linguistic abilities become clear assets for their learning journey as well as the learning of their peers.

We visited a multitasking seventh-grade social studies class with many multilingual students new to English. Two adults—the teacher and a paraprofessional—were each working with a small group. The adults stayed with their group for the full 45-minute observation and worked with their group as a full-fledged collaborator. As collaborators, these adults enabled the groups of students to successfully engage in group work that would have been too complicated or challenging on their own. The rest of the students were working individually, with a partner, or in small groups where they led discussions and collaborated to complete their assigned tasks.

On the board was a large matrix showing a variety of activities related to the learning for the overall unit. Students' names appeared several times in different boxes, showing both activities they had been assigned and others they had chosen. There was also a chart indicating when students would rotate and have time to engage in the varying activities. Plans included working in home languages or reading or writing in English at different levels and for different purposes depending on the student.

Many students' learning activity plans overlapped, but others were unique, each tailored to using their strengths to help learn and grow.

In our own multitasking classrooms and in many we've visited, we've found that initially both students and teachers are uncomfortable stepping outside of a one-size-fits-all, monotasking instructional approach. Students aren't used to having choices (agency) or having to be accountable to their peers (shared responsibility). Teachers are reluctant or unsure how to share power and not be totally in charge of everything that happens in the classroom. Over time, however, multitasking often becomes their preferred approach as it produces the best learning outcomes for students, simplifies planning, and makes teaching and learning much more engaging and joyful.

## Orienting Toward Agency

In monotasking classrooms, students are expected to do what the teacher tells them to do and when and how the teacher tells them to do it. In multitasking classrooms, students are expected to work independently and in small groups, where they have to follow different sets of directions, make decisions, and change tasks on a regular basis. When teachers and students have spent most, if not all, of their classroom experiences monotasking, the shift to multitasking can take some time and effort. Orienting ourselves toward agency is a powerful lever to make the shift.

A multitasking classroom runs completely counter to the view of teaching as the transmission of knowledge. This kind of interactive learning is even more important for multilingual students. Constantly listening to teacher talk in a language they are still learning is exhausting and can quickly become overwhelming. The most effective teaching and learning opportunities are grounded in hands-on inquiry, curiosity, and creativity—all of which require learner agency. We want to create learning opportunities where students become independent and critical thinkers, capable of engaging with new information as they grow their linguistic repertoires.

A Finnish teacher shared with us her experience teaching English to ninth graders early in her career. Her students that year included some who used English at home with their families and others who could barely produce a full sentence. The range of English proficiency was so wide that the curriculum she had been given was completely inappropriate. She decided to move away from whole-class instruction and take a very different approach. Her focus was on creating meaningful learning for each student at the level of English proficiency they were at.

So, she shared with the students a topic they were expected to cover from the curriculum. She then asked students three questions that they each needed to answer on their own: How do you want to approach learning this topic? What materials will you use? Who are you going to work with? All 26 students in the class created a proposal for how they would learn. Some students wanted to work independently with the assigned textbook. Others wanted to work in small groups and engage with various digital media in English (e.g., movies, social media, and popular music). The teacher worked with each student to ensure that their plans were both sufficiently challenging and resourced. She also ensured that she knew how to best provide each student with assistance for their learning success. The teacher was amazed at how learning skyrocketed in her class, commenting that this approach "worked famously." So, she continued to use it across the whole school year with each new topic.

That same year, her class was randomly selected to be part of the national assessments (students in Finland are not assessed on large-scale standardized tests nearly as frequently as students in the US are). The data she received confirmed what she witnessed in her class. Her students' average scores on the English test were dramatically higher than those of other ninth graders across Finland. This teacher embraced a multitasking approach imbued with agency, and her students had phenomenal learning outcomes because of it. She is now a veteran teacher who utilizes this approach in all of her teaching. For her, the greatest value is that everyone is learning for themselves. With her assistance, they set their learning targets as well as the pathway to reach them. Her students are enthusiastic and more interested in the learning. She found, as we have, that learners of all ages are more motivated and engaged when they have agency in their learning.

Having agency in the classroom can take many shapes and forms. Students have some agency when they can freely move about the room to get the materials they need, when they need them, without having to get permission or be a disruption, or when they can select from among a menu of possible activities to complete a unit. They have even more agency when they can choose the language(s) and or materials they will use or how they will represent their learning. A colleague and friend who teaches at a university in Norway recently told us about a time when her college students were clearly very tired and disengaged from the lesson. They were stunned when she asked them what they wanted to do. They weren't used to having a choice. And they had great ideas about how to make the learning more meaningful and engaging. They suggested simple tweaks to the schedule and to the grouping practices they had used. These small changes made a big difference and were ideas our colleague admitted she wouldn't have come up with on her own. Orienting our teaching toward agency opens possibilities for each learner to choose the tools and resources they need to further their own learning.

## Orienting Toward Shared Responsibility

To create a functioning multitasking classroom where pluralism flourishes, we also need to be oriented toward shared responsibility. In an individualistic society like the US, we often think of agency only in terms of personal freedoms and rights. What is left out is the responsibility that comes with freedom—personal responsibility for our actions and their impact on those around us in our communities.

We can begin orienting toward shared responsibility by examining how power is exerted in our classroom. Power is reflected in how we structure our classes, the nature of the relationships we develop, and the kind of learning that can happen. As teachers, we create the context for how students are positioned and what amount of autonomy they will have and thus what roles they can play. The power levers that are typically in our hands include how time is spent, how the space is organized, how students will access the curriculum, the resources they are given, and the pedagogical approaches we utilize. For example, many teachers determine classroom rules ahead of time and the accountability mechanisms for not complying with them.

Seeing ourselves and our students as having agency and sharing responsibility alters the power structures. All members of the learning community can have a say in decision-making while taking into account how our attitudes are shaped by external societal hierarchies. When we open up decision-making and together agree on solutions, they can become more inclusive, equitable, humanizing, and effective.

Sharing power can also be uncomfortable for students. They aren't necessarily ready to take on responsibility for how things will run from day one. This shouldn't prevent us from orienting our classroom community toward shared responsibility. Instead, we can scaffold their learning for engaging in the process in the same way we would any other topic. By crafting learning opportunities for students to develop the skills and knowledge to take on leadership roles and share power with other members of the community, we engage in an ongoing effort to help students become strong collaborative problem-solvers and leaders. As described below, briefings and debriefings provide an ongoing structure for these conversations as students learn to make decisions over their own learning while sharing responsibility for everyone's success.

When students can choose different pathways for their learning journey, the issue of fairness always arises. We have had multiple conversations with students over the years about fairness where the difference-as-deficit narrative is always in play. So much of schooling has been operationalized around doing assignments on time rather than around demonstrating authentic learning. Because of this, some students feel uncomfortable when others are not doing school exactly as they are (e.g., working on a different timeline or doing different assignments) and also earning good grades. When pluralism is in practice, some students may be allowed to miss more classes or turn in work late or study independently.

Rather than ignore the feelings or frustrations that come up for students experiencing pluralism in practice, we openly discuss these issues with students and remind them that our focus is on authentic learning rather than on performing compliance. We ask students to think through what it means for different members of the learning community to embark on different learning paths.

We also discuss our belief that, on their learning journeys, different routes can lead to high-level learning. We encourage students to appreciate that they have their own unique learning path rather than worry about what others are doing. The exception is, of course, when the learning paths converge, like when doing a group project. In these instances, we work with students to embrace the different strengths they each bring to the learning process and operate with an orientation toward interconnectedness and openness to resolve any conflicts that arise. Students also have to develop a sense of how their behaviors affect one another. Attending to the impacts of our actions (and inactions) as members of a learning community is a core skill to learn as we build shared responsibility and agency.

Multitasking entails changing groups smoothly, cleaning up quickly, and taking care of shared materials and workspaces. It is built on people working in cooperation with others. Success itself is a shared responsibility that can occur only when there is trust among all members of the learning community. There are many resources out there about cooperative learning that can help you and your students build various skills for collaboration to thrive. Kagan Cooperative Learning Structures are popular, and the work from Stanford University on Complex Instruction is also useful.

However, teaching students how to work in groups without attending to issues of oppression linked to the difference-as-deficit dominant cultural narrative is insufficient. We need to address head on the inequities and injustice generated for people based on various aspects of their identities—race, gender, sexual orientation, disability, nationality, language, religion, and more. Otherwise, we will not be able to enact humanizing pedagogies. We highly recommend beginning with the Social Justice Standards available for free online at learningforjustice.org. These standards provide valuable tools to work with students across four domains: identity, diversity, justice, and action. We have found that planning instruction around these standards has been essential in helping students successfully work with each other across differences.

## Trajectory Toward a Multitasking Classroom

Much of what we know about multitasking classrooms comes from extensive research done at the Center for Research on Education, Diversity and Excellence (CREDE), which was at the University of California Berkley in the 1990s and early 2000s (see Tharp et al., 2000; Hilberg et al., 2003). They conducted research on effective teaching in classrooms with multilingual learners and other diverse student groups. This research clearly illustrated the beneficial impacts of developing multitasking classrooms. These researchers also documented the kinds of preparation necessary to help students and teachers work together to create strong multitasking classes.

Skills that are integral in making the shift from compliant monotasking classrooms to agentive multitasking ones takes time and effort to develop. We have seen many teachers attempt to implement multitasking, only to give up before it had a chance to succeed. Usually, multitasking failures are a result of moving too quickly and jumping to multiple activities before building the interaction skills needed across the learning community.

Questions that teachers usually ask us include the following: How long should we spend on multitasking (e.g., all day and each class period)? Should multitasking be the focus of only one content area? And for how many days? How long should the learning activities be? The answer to each of these questions, and many others that are posed about how to do multitasking right, is the same: it depends. There is no *one way* to effectively put pluralism into practice, but from the research and our years of experience, we have some insights to offer. Therefore, we provide ideas for creating a productive context for multitasking rather than strict linear steps or phases. The process will look different if we begin on the first day of school than if we start well into the instructional year. It will also look different with different groups of students at different grade levels in different content classrooms. Again, it does take time. The path to effective multitasking may require weeks or even months to fully implement. It is an iterative path where we move back and forth between the various aspects described below.

When we first work with a new learning community, we share with them our orientations toward agency and shared responsibility. We emphasize our desire to establish a classroom community that can work across differences and learn together. We encourage students' independent thinking and let them know we believe they are all capable of leading their own learning. Our process is shaped around who our students are and the experiences they bring with them for cooperation and collaboration. We develop our plans in response to the humans we are working with in a way that underscores and elevates their and our humanity. We always return to things we've already worked on if it seems they need more attention. With the tools and ideas shared below, we are confident you can do the same.

## Briefings and Debriefings

Successful multitasking classrooms include ongoing, daily discussions around shared agreements, classroom routines, how assignments are turned in, or how people are being treated as well as the learning agenda we have with our students. Even in monotasking classrooms, during the first day or week of school, teachers often discuss or create agreements and expectations with students. These initial conversations are important but insufficient. They need to continue across the entire school year. Developing a multitasking pluralistic classroom has a dual focus. One is on process (How we are working together to learn?) and the other is on content (What we are learning?) as students engage in learning activities. This is where briefings and debriefings come into play. Instructional activities begin with briefings, a co-construction of understandings around expectations for both learning and behavior. They end with debriefings, time to reflect on how things went in both areas.

We use briefings and debriefings from the very beginning of every class we teach to set the stage for a dynamic, long-term, solution-oriented process. Briefings let students know what we have planned and ensure that they understand as well as contribute to what is expected of them in different kinds of activities. There is always time for questions, modifications, and clarifications. Sometimes we conduct briefings through 30-second reviews of classroom agreements and assignments. Sometimes we need more time to co-construct solutions to anticipated issues. Early in the formation of a learning community, briefings are usually longer. We model what it looks like to meet the agreements/expectations and then discuss the specifics of what supports they might need. We often even act out funny scenarios of not meeting the expectations, as humor helps break the ice.

When we are at the early stages of co-constructing our agreements, briefings and debriefings focus primarily on behavior and collaboration expectations rather than the content students are learning. Over time, the complexity and cognitive demand of the learning tasks increase, and we place more emphasis on what will be or has been learned. Their exact format varies as different activities may have different agreements or expectations in place.

Debriefings play a key role in the learning process and success of multitasking classrooms. They allow us to reflect on what has happened and what it means for moving forward, in terms of both learning and behaviors. We have used community circles, lineups, exit tickets, online polls, and other tools to gather information to use for deeper analysis and discussion. Through these efforts, we always discover where we need to go next with the learning or various collaboration/behavior issues that we need to co-construct solutions around as a community.

We often see teachers start right away with debriefings focused exclusively on the topic or the learning. We don't recommend this. It is much more effective in the long run to spend the time necessary to discuss the processes and practices of working together in debriefings, privileging that work over reviews or synthesis of learning. Over time, debriefings become less demanding in terms of time and intensity and focus on process, but they never lose relevance. While it can be tempting to skip them when time is tight (always), we shouldn't. Debriefings are where we can support students in having agency and taking shared responsibility for their learning and that of their peers. Through briefings and debriefings, we can revisit (and refine) classroom agreements as we examine what went well and what needs to be improved in any learning activity.

### From Monotasking to Multitasking with Affinity Groups

We have visited many successful multitasking classrooms but seldom in August or September. Routines and norms take time to be established. We do often see students working in small monotasking groups right away as part of co-constructing the necessary foundational understandings and agreements with the whole class. However, this is monotasking where all the groups are doing the same thing, and their guidelines are well defined. The goal is building relationships as we put our agreements into practice and internalize community expectations so we can move toward more multitasking.

When we initially form groups, they are composed of students who feel comfortable together and already have some connection, what researchers call affinity groups. Groups might be organized by language background, friendship, or skill level. We want students to feel confident as they build and refine the skills needed to work independently from us and collaboratively with their peers. Of course, this process is easier when we have other adults to help us—teaching assistants or volunteers—but we have managed to do this on our own even with very large classes.

Once the routines are established and students are comfortable with some small-group work, we move slowly and deliberately from monotasking to multitasking. When we move from monotasking to multitasking, we do it slowly. Students continue to work in groups where they already feel comfortable. We usually start with two simple activities. For example, two or three small groups work on one task and two or three other groups work on a different task. They then switch half-way through the class or the following day. We circulate among them to check on process and encourage students to refer to our agreements as we solve problems. At other times, some students are reading independently or working on the computer while others are working with us. Or we might have a large group working with us, and a couple of small groups working on a different task. Over time, students engage in learning activities individually, in pairs or triads, and in small groups.

When we have had success with two different activities occurring simultaneously, we increase the number of tasks and/or the complexity of the content. Ideally, we get to a place where three, four, or more activities are happening at the same time and students are in charge of their learning. This allows us more and more time to regularly collaborate with small groups of students while others are working independently. The ultimate goal of a multitasking classroom is to create space for us as teachers to take on the role of collaborator rather than knowledge transmitter. We should be aiming to move from being classroom monitors—roaming the classroom as students work—to collaborators in student learning by joining students as a contributing member of a discussion or group project. We have witnessed and been part of successful multitasking at all grade levels, from the youngest learners to students in graduate school. Of course, this looks different in kindergarten than in middle school and different if we have assistants or community volunteers. We are confident, however, that it is always possible.

## Multitasking Outside Affinity Groups

With the goal of having all students able to work with all other students, we need to have a strong understanding of the social contexts that students exist in and their impact on students' abilities to work together. Many popular classic movies about teenagers (like *Mean Girls*, *Clueless*, and *10 Things I Hate About You*) discuss the affinity groups that exist in high school. Beverly Tatum (1997) wrote a book called "Why Are All the Black Kids Sitting Together in the Cafeteria," illustrating the way affinity groups form in schools, often within oppressive contexts like racism, classism, linguicism, and ableism. As educators, we need to understand these groups, where they come from, and how they influence the experiences of our students inside and out of school.

Research has frequently shown how much discrimination multilingual students experience in school. This includes low expectations from teachers, being segregated in a variety of ways, or being mocked for how they use English or the cultural artifacts they wear. While we cannot control everything that happens with our students outside of the classroom or school, we can work very deliberately to create caring spaces of belonging within them. Building students' ability to work in multitasking spaces opens the possibility for a whole new world of learning and engagement. It is not enough to just put students who do not belong to the same affinity groups together and expect things to run smoothly. We have to prepare students and plan good collaborative activities so that minoritized students, especially multilingual learners, will not experience discriminatory or harmful treatment in their group work.

Starting slowly and having students work first with students they are comfortable with are where we start but not where we end. This is something we make clear to students from the beginning. Once students are successful in groups where they share an affinity, and we have strong processes and clear expectations for how collaborations unfold and members of the learning community are treated, we can change how the groups are formed so students can learn to collaborate successfully with all of their peers.

When we move to multitasking outside of affinity groups, we want every student to feel supported and safe interacting with everyone else in the class. This doesn't happen just because we say we want it to. Dehumanization linked to oppressive systems centered on race, gender, class, ability, and language as well as other markers of identity is deeply ingrained in our society. Dehumanization operates in our classrooms in obvious ways like name-calling or anger-filled body language. It also exists in ways we may not easily perceive, like isolating/silencing some students. We must grapple with these challenges and inequities if we want to create a multitasking classroom where all students are able to work well with all other students. Depending on the composition of our learning community, this can be a harder or easier task. Some students may already share a lot of affinity with others in the learning community. Others may be skeptical of one another or even openly dislike each other, sometimes based on a negative history together.

At this point, we should have already done a lot of work to disrupt the difference-as-deficit dominant narrative (see Module 2) that plays out in classrooms, youth culture, and the larger society to help multitasking work go smoothly. We should have set agreements and co-constructed expectations for the whole learning community (see Module 4). We should be orchestrating ongoing community building efforts to counter negative perceptions that students may have of one another because of oppressive social hierarchies. Our explicit goal that each member of the learning community sees all other members of the community as fully human, capable, and worthy of getting to know and learn from should be very clear. This clarity comes in part from having engaged in ongoing collaborations that position each member of the learning community as capable and valuable. We will know that effective multitasking is in place when we feel confident about the ability of all students to engage in high-quality learning while enacting the established agreements and working collaboratively in many different configurations.

We are fairly certain that some readers are thinking something along the lines of, "This sounds great and idealistic but there is no way I can do this in my setting." We know it's a journey of many steps, big and small. We have tried to provide a vision of what it can look like, knowing it may take weeks, months, or even years to integrate all these practices, knowing that it may be possible at first in only one subject area or section/group of students. There is, however, always something we can do to recognize our students as active contributors to the learning process and value what they each can offer to the entire learning community. The possibilities of this approach are sizeable and have been proven via decades of research to be deeply beneficial for multilingual student learning.

 **Make It Work**

In the Explore section, we discussed the possibility of orienting our learning communities toward agency and shared responsibility as we develop multitasking classrooms and put pluralism into practice. Now is your chance to play with these ideas and make them work in your practice! Below we have provided some options of how you can do that, thinking about the intrapersonal, interpersonal, and systemic levels of engagement. Any of these could (and potentially should) be done just by yourself but also could be accomplished through learning activities with your students. As you choose an option, keep in mind the module's critical reflection and complexity thinking questions: *What role does pluralism play in your practice? In terms of control in the classroom, what is important to you? Where might you be able to give up some of it? Where might you struggle to offer students agency and shared responsibility in the classroom? Why?* We encourage you to revisit the components of humanizing pedagogies from the introduction and think about the implications of what you learned from engaging in this module in relation to context, orientations, and pedagogy. When you have completed your Make It Work activity, reflect on your findings to share them with your colleagues.

## Make It Work Options

### Intrapersonal: Take Inventory and Reflect on Roles of Teachers and Learners

Purpose: Critically reflect on the roles you and your students play in your classroom (or a classroom you are observing or have participated in as a student yourself) and where more agency and shared responsibility might be created.

Review a lesson you have recently taught or will soon teach (or observed, or experienced as a student yourself). If possible, create a video of yourself teaching it. Pay close attention to the roles you play and those of your students. Who is leading? Who is deciding? Who is talking? What does teaching look like? Is it transmission, exploration, dialogic, or monitoring? What does learning look like? Is it compliance, curiosity, creativity, collaborative, self-determined, or a combination? Is there any blurring of the boundaries/roles between teachers and learners? Are there moments when power is shared? Where you keep control? Then reflect. What role do you play in setting the context? What would sharing more power with students mean for you? How would you feel if students had increased responsibility for what happens in the learning community? Based on your reflection, what are the opportunities for change you see in your own practice, especially in relation to agency and shared responsibility? What are your next steps to work toward that change?

### Interpersonal: Plan and (if Possible) Implement Next Steps Toward a Multitasking Classroom

Purpose: Prepare for and get started with moving toward a multitasking classroom using briefings and debriefings and increasing the number of activities happening as well as who students will work with over time.

Plan for how you can integrate briefings and debriefings into your regular practice and, where possible, start to do them. Consider the dual goals of learning to work together (having more agency and shared responsibility) and deepening content learning. It's best to already have done the work in Module 4 regarding co-constructing expectations and agreements so you can use them as a foundation for the briefings and debriefings. Be open to making changes that students suggest to better support their learning. Note how having these kinds of conversations regularly affects what is happening in your learning community and implications for moving forward.

Also, plan for how you can integrate some multitasking into your classroom and, where possible, start doing it. Consider the process and examples discussed in Explore and use them to decide where you and your learning community are now and what you are ready to try out. Include in your plan how you will do that work and reflect on how it went afterwards. Capture what went well and what needs improvement. Think about ways to keep moving forward toward more and more multitasking in your classroom for the purpose of high levels of meaningfully differentiated learning to be possible.

## Systemic: Affinity Group Mapping with Attention to Oppressive Projects

Purpose: Develop strong understandings of affinity groups occurring in your school, why they exist, and how they connect to larger oppressive practices in society.

We recommend starting with different spaces and times of day in school, like lunchtime in the cafeteria, and observing, Who sits together? What affinities do they share? Who appears to not be included? Why? Replicate this during other times of day and in other spaces like hallways before and after classes/school, pick-up and drop-off, the playground/recess, and so forth. Take special notice of where multilingual students are and are not as well as which groups have the most social power in the school and which appear to have less. As you map out the affinity groups that operate in your school, consider how these groups impact the learning community(s) in your classroom. Do the ways that students interact in your classroom reflect what you have observed outside the classroom? What will you need to do to make sure students from each different affinity group will be able to work with students from each other affinity group? How will you help students find connections? How might they come to see each other as fully human, as people with abilities and skills and worthy of collaborating with? Seeking the answers to these questions may require building deeper understandings of various forms of oppression like white supremacy, heteropatriarchy, linguicism, classism, and ableism. We recommend exploring responses through books, classes, and discussions with colleagues or friends to learn from or with. Reflect on how you can address these hierarchies in order to help students in your class(es) develop the ability to work well together with all other students in your class.

## You Make It Work!

Purpose: To make the ideas from Explore work in your own practice.

Design your own activity (or tweak one of ours) to ensure that you are spending your time doing work that is most useful and relevant to you and your students. We recommend starting with the critical reflection and complexity thinking questions.

Then clarify for yourself which level you are working at (intrapersonal, interpersonal, or systemic) and build your effort to make this module's learning work for you from there!

 **Share**

Share is your opportunity to engage with your peers and receive feedback about the work you have done and what you have learned in this module. Begin by revisiting the reflection you wrote at the beginning of the module and revise it to include your thinking now, noting any changes and what they might mean for your practice. Be sure to attend to opportunities to strive for justice and equity and to potential barriers to achieving it. Don't shy away from the complexities that come up—embrace them. Think about different ways of being and doing in your classroom that could address those complexities. Once you have completed your reflection, be prepared to share it with your colleagues along with a description of the work you did in the Make it Work section. By sharing what you have learned, you have the chance to both solidify your own learning and thinking and expand it by learning from your colleagues.

# Section III
## Pedagogy

# 7

# Meaningful Collaboration

Now that we have explored some important aspects of context and orientations, we are shifting to focus on pedagogy, weaving together all the skills and knowledge necessary across each domain to build humanizing pedagogies. With an orientation toward pluralism in practice, we begin with how to meaningfully collaborate in a multitasking classroom.

Before you begin this module, critically reflect on and use complexity thinking to respond to these questions: *What tensions and complexities need to be addressed in my classroom for collaboration to be meaningful, equitable, and just? What opportunities exist and what barriers do I have to overcome for me to work as a collaborator in student learning?* Be sure to keep your initial reflection, notes, and ideas so you can revisit them during the Make It Work and Share sections of the module.

## Explore

When we were young, there was a popular soda commercial where people from all over the world are singing, holding hands, and declaring that they want to buy the world a soda. It was a feel-good commercial suggesting we can all just come together and achieve harmony. We understand the draw of these kinds of representations of unity. However, in diverse classrooms, the idea of simply bringing together people who speak different languages, live different cultural lives, and have different positions of power and privilege in society and expecting instant harmony is unrealistic and can actually limit collaboration. Too often, those with the most power and privilege do enjoy feelings of unity and acceptance while those with the least feel marginalized, left out, and/or silenced.

Additionally, we often hear about how much employers want to hire people who can work in teams and be great collaborators and how diversity is an asset for strong collaboration in teams. Unfortunately, this kind of open, creative embrace of collaboration is not always found in classrooms. Dominant narratives about some voices mattering more than others can inhibit the participation of some students, especially those who are the targets of racism, ableism, sexism, or other forms of oppressive behaviors.

The vision we have of meaningful collaboration is an approach that supports linguistic and conceptual development through authentic opportunities to interact as well as be curious and creative around ideas and texts. This approach helps students build connections and relationships with one another while linking learning at school to their lives, experiences, and understandings of the world. For us, meaningful collaboration is forward-looking and capable of generating creative new ideas, solutions, and ways of thinking while involving everyone in the learning.

## On Collaboration

Often what is called collaboration actually is contrived, forced, or grounded in assimilationist perspectives and therefore not meaningful. An example of this is what many teachers have described to us regarding required data discussions among colleagues where students' test scores are used to determine learning progress and teacher effectiveness. While these data discussions were painted as collaborative conversations, the teachers had little control over what data were being analyzed, how the data were disaggregated, or how the data were presented. The conversations had specific set agendas that were typically given to teachers rather than set by teachers themselves. Further, expectations around the use of predetermined rubrics and analysis protocols guided most of the "collaboration", tools that teachers had no say in developing and that did not reflect the developmental trajectories of many of their students, especially multilingual learners. These supposed collaborations were rarely deemed meaningful by the teachers we've talked to.

We have also experienced this as participants in classes and professional developments where we just do a task rather than connecting, engaging, and belonging. As we think about what collaboration means to us and what we want it to look like in our classes, we have to ask ourselves if we might be doing the same kind of thing with our own students. Do we tightly control the ways students work together, the kinds of efforts they are allowed to engage in, or the language(s)/dialects they use? Might collaboration efforts in our classroom feel like hoop-jumping exercises for our students rather than authentic opportunities for learning, connecting, belonging, and exploring? Do we believe the students can handle the responsibilities?

It can be challenging to teach our students to collaborate especially if we work in settings where teachers are in competition with each other and never have opportunities to participate in decision-making and planning regarding what teaching and learning look and feel like. Often, we are told that the students can't handle that kind of work, that some kids never do their share, or that they can't work without monitoring. We ourselves have felt exasperated when we have planned an activity that requires high-level collaboration, and it falls flat. While all of this can be frustrating, we are confident that all students can become effective collaborators across differences with the appropriate preparation and support.

We use backwards planning to achieve meaningful collaboration in the same ways we use it to plan content lessons. We determine where we want to arrive on our collaboration journey (e.g., what we want the collaboration to look like) and create a sequence of activities that can help us get there. In this way, we can provide students the chance to develop all the necessary skills and approaches for meaningful collaboration to take place. From the beginning of the year or semester, we can teach different ways to work together rather than just expecting students to be able to do high-level collaborative work from the outset.

We recently worked with a second-grade teacher of newcomer multilingual students who knew her students would do an inquiry project in the spring that aligned with the second-grade curriculum—a unit on insects. We began preparing for that work in the fall, thinking about the kinds of skills (as collaborators but also in terms of content and language) that students were going to need to do the collaborative inquiry work the teacher envisioned.

Over months, students learned to work more independently in a multitasking classroom, taking leadership over their own learning, and providing support to their peers as strong collaborators. They also improved on their English language skills, using their home languages as a support for their multilingual language development. In the spring, students collaborated to successfully complete the planned inquiry project. They researched different insects and demonstrated their learning about the life cycle of their chosen insects. Using some scaffolds, students also wrote entire paragraphs about their bugs. All of that backwards planning and skill development paid off in strong learning outcomes grounded in meaningful collaboration. A very important collaborator in this process was the teacher herself.

## Teachers as Collaborators

As we know, relationships between teachers and students play a crucial role in supporting high levels of learning. When we organize our classroom to be able to collaborate meaningfully with our students, we create the context for strong relationships to develop with and among each of our students. When we position ourselves not as transmitters of knowledge but as collaborators, we can guide students through modeling and questioning, gradually assisting them to higher levels of thinking and understanding. Such a teaching approach is more like an apprentice model for teaching and learning and provides students with access to important assistance and scaffolding to accomplish challenging things together that they aren't yet ready to do on their own (think Vygotsky's zone of proximal development here).

In our experience, during small-group work teachers typically walk through the room, responding to questions groups have, and help keep students on task. Obviously, there is benefit to this approach. But what we are aiming toward instead is preparing students to work together so well without us that the need to rove and monitor becomes unnecessary. Then we can work directly with a small group of students for an extended period.

Research consistently shows that various forms of collaboration in classrooms are important and that when teachers engage in small-group collaborative activities with students, learning soars. A space is created where we can facilitate the learning by being part of it, not just telling students what they are supposed to know or do. As we do the work *with* students, we can act as a guide, scaffolder, differentiator, assessor, and learner all at once.

Two specific examples discussed below—joint productive activity and instructional conversations (Tharp et al., 2000)—are pivotal to establishing meaningful collaboration between us and our students. We cannot recommend these practices enough. Both provide many opportunities for us to act as facilitators of student learning and supporters of independent thinking.

By positioning ourselves as collaborators, we can get to know our students better and more quickly. We can more easily see and learn about individual students' strengths and opportunities for growth and use this information to inform our instructional decisions as well as devise in the moment scaffolds and differentiation. What we do might vary with each different group to support the learning opportunities that exist within that specific group, even when we use a similar text or are exploring a similar topic across all the groups in the class.

An additional benefit of this kind of collaboration is the seamless way that assessment can be embedded. When we collaborate closely with students, we easily witness things that are relevant to understanding students' abilities, strengths, and opportunities for growth. These understandings inform both how we might need to differentiate and what other instructional practices seem to be most effective in deepening learning. As collaborators with small groups of students, we can also successfully foster a sense of belonging and agency among all members of the learning community.

## Joint Productive Activity

At its core, joint productive activity is very simple: it's when people work together to jointly produce a product. The products can be either tangible or intangible. Tangible products are easier to picture (text, graphic organizer, posters, reports, pottery, plays, games, debates, and so forth). What is harder to envision are the intangible products, which we may already be co-producing without realizing or naming as joint productive activity. They include more accurate or elaborated understandings of a concept, procedure, or an idea.

The guided reading group, which is an approach to developing literacy skills, is an example of a setting with the potential for joint productive activities. During guided reading, the teacher works with a small group of students while the rest of the class engages collectively or independently (or both) in a variety of literacy activities. At times, guided reading with the teacher in a small group may not actually be joint productive activity. So, we need to be clear about what we are suggesting here.

Joint productive activity is not just the physical arrangement of the teacher sitting with a small group of students while the rest of the class works collaboratively or independently. Rather, joint productive activity is about the actual interaction that occurs within that physical arrangement where students and teachers co-produce. In the case of guided reading, that joint productive activity could be about co-producing reading comprehension, concepts about print, authors intent, differences among genres, and so forth. It could also be a tangible product like collaboratively reconstructing a story with images, a co-constructed graphic organizer, and so forth.

While ideally enacted in small groups, joint productive activity can occur in whole-class settings. We observed this in a second-grade classroom in Finland, where the whole class was collaborating with the teacher on an intangible product—gaining a conceptual understanding of multiplication. In this lesson, the teacher used manipulatives, images, and students' bodies to create formulas on the board that illustrated how multiplication works. She started by asking a group of students to come to the front of the class. Then she gave each student three pieces of fake fruit. Each student was asked how many pieces of fruit they had while the teacher wrote their responses on the board: 3 + 3 + 3 + 3. She described how there were four students and each student had three pieces of fruit. This activity was replicated with images of dogs on the board (e.g., How many paws does each of the five dogs have? Tails?). The teacher also replicated this with student body parts, including legs, hands, fingers, and feet. The students and the teacher worked together to capture their counts on the board and talked about the connection between the numbers on the board and the real-life images or body parts that helped to create the math problem. In this lesson, they never got to actual multiplication. The purpose was creating a foundation to comprehend the larger concept. The whole lesson was a strong example of meaningful collaboration using joint productive activity in the whole-class setting.

One challenge we often face in developing effective joint productive activities is the need to hold all students accountable for their contributions to the joint product. Sometimes because of this, we fall back on activities where students sit together but do independent work. There are times and good reasons to do this, but such tasks are neither collaboration nor joint productive activity. There is no co-produced product and students can easily sit in silence and work independently without any interaction or co-production.

There are many successful ways to include accountability measures that track student learning, engagement, and participation. We can gather evidence of student participation in the group collaboration by using exit tickets before moving on to the next activity or class with targeted questions they must respond to about their learning and their role in the group or product. We have also found peer assessments to be strong tools for accountability in collaborative group work as long as the success criteria are co-constructed and clearly defined.

We can gather anecdotal notes based on informal observations and conversations with students regarding their own and others' participation in group work. We've observed teachers set the expectation that after students have worked together, anyone in the group should be ready to be called on to talk about the group's work to the class. Other teachers require that when a tangible product is developed, students indicate their individual contribution by using a specific color marker, pen, or even font when the work is done electronically. We do not need to let our interest in holding all students accountable for participating stand in the way of implementing joint productive activity widely in our instructional practices.

## Instructional Conversations

The second approach we recommend for engaging in meaningful collaboration is through instructional conversations whose purpose is to spur dialogue with and among our students. These are not just any oral exchanges. They are *intentionally planned conversations* around the learning topic. They occur when we are working with a *small group of students* and the *students are doing more of the talking* than we are. These are also not mini lectures. Instructional conversations are beneficial for all students and play an important role in multilingual classrooms. They are especially helpful for multilingual learners as it is much easier for students newer to the language of instruction to participate in content discussions with smaller groups of people.

We may be inclined to organize into small groups and then do direct instruction or basically mimic a whole-class lecture to a small group of students. However, doing so does not constitute an instructional conversation. An important characteristic of an authentic instructional conversation is that teacher talk is occurring at a lower rate than student talk. We want students' voices to be heard more than our own, so we can listen carefully, taking note of how students are understanding the content and using their linguistic repertoire. At times, this can be really challenging for some educators, especially those who have conceptualized teaching as telling.

Often teachers ask why it isn't an instructional conversation if it happens in a whole-class setting. The answer is simple: because there are just too many participants to meaningfully interact with each student. Whole-class discussions can quickly become overwhelming for some students, especially multilingual students at the earlier stages of learning English, and often lead to students checking out and not participating. In whole-group discussion, we typically end up interacting with just a small number of students while the rest of the learning community watches. Small-group instructional conversations offer the opportunities of deeper engagement and for each student to be actively involved. Students have a better chance of participating and we have a better chance of knowing when a student might need additional support or scaffolding to fully participate.

We observed a second-grade classroom in Germany where the teacher exhibited high levels of expertise in engaging with students through questions, a major feature of great instructional conversations. The group of students was working on ordering words according to alphabetic order. They "fished" a word from a "pond" of words and had to decide where it should go to be in alphabetic order in relationship to other words fished out. The teacher almost exclusively asked questions to assist students in the task. *Where does it go? Does that align with the alphabet we see on the wall (referencing a visual resource available to assist students)? Do we all agree?* The teacher never weighed in on student answers but rather turned the opportunity back to the group of students to decide if they agreed or not. When students were thinking in an incorrect direction, she continued asking questions until they sorted out the right answer.

At one point, a student "fished" out a word that started with the same first letter as a word that had already been fished out.

Students decided that they would order the word before or after the word they already had with the same first letter based on how many letters the word had. This led to a series of questions by the teacher like what will we do if we have two words with the same first letter and the same number of letters in the word? Students grappled with this and discussed various possibilities, finally deciding that they would look at the second letter of the word to determine alphabetic order (and then the third, fourth, and so forth). The teacher never once told the students an answer, but through her expert use of questions, the students discussed ideas, tried out possibilities, and eventually discovered an important understanding through their own efforts and engagements. This is what characterizes a powerful instructional conversation.

Now imagine if this same lesson occurred in a whole-class setting where there were some students who were new to English. Would they be leaving the lesson with strong understandings of alphabetic order? Likely not. However, if the teacher worked directly with students in a small group, she could modify the lesson and use communication practices (like gestures, images, the students home languages, and so forth) to make the learning possible and clear for the multilingual learners. The instructional conversation would look different than one with all monolingual speakers of English but would be successfully scaffolded and differentiated to support strong learning for the students involved. This is the power of instructional conversations with teachers working in small groups.

To plan for instructional conversations, we have to have a clear learning target in mind. For instance, in a ninth-grade biology class where homeostasis is being discussed, we can think forward to some of the questions that students might have as well as what we want to be sure they walk away from the conversation understanding. Perhaps it is early on in the unit and our instructional goal is simply that students start to understand basic aspects of the concept like that it is the tendency of our bodies to resist change in order to keep a consistent internal environment. If that is the understanding students should leave the conversation with, what questions do we need to prepare? Also, considering the word *homeostasis* and its prefix, which is similar to the prefix in *homosexual*, how will we ensure a conversation ensues that is inclusive of all student identities and doesn't turn into a bullying or exclusion situation? How can we use language detective skills to help navigate this situation effectively? (See Module 3 for more on language detective skills.)

In addition to our own planning for instructional conversations, we have to help students learn how to effectively participate in them. When we started implementing instructional conversations, even when we posed great questions, students' responses were often limited and typically directed only at us. Students were inclined to talk to us but not to each other. Students need to learn about the purpose of instructional conversations and how they work and to have the chance to build the skills necessary for effective participation.

It is also useful to build instructional conversations around authentic problem-solving. This creates the context for our questions to be more provocative and for students to have more motivation and inclination toward engaging as well as talking with each other. Collaborative problem-solving through instructional conversation is also a great way to create authentic languaging opportunities for multilingual learners as well as opportunities for students to connect and improve their relationships with one another through collaboration.

## Collaboration Challenges

Situating ourselves as collaborators in the classroom generates so many exciting possibilities for deeply impactful learning to occur. It also can create some challenges that have to be addressed. When we are part of a collaboration with students, we can mediate conflict and help students build their abilities to talk across difference. However, we cannot be in collaboration with all students at all times. Therefore, we have to teach students how to address the challenges that come up in collaboration.

## Conflict Resolution

In any situation involving more than one person, it is inevitable that conflict will arise, either from the inherent flaws that we all have as human beings or from the simple reality that people with different interests, backgrounds, and personalities working together will likely see and interpret things/actions differently. Additionally, in the current context of growing political, economic, and social divides, opportunities for oppressive behaviors in classrooms thrive. In multilingual classrooms, conflicts can arise among students of different races, languages, genders, abilities, or other identity markers. Harmful attitudes among students and teachers can result in hurt feelings, anger, or withdrawal. And too often, these harmful conflicts are left unaddressed.

Despite the ubiquitous nature of conflict, everywhere we have worked with teachers they express to us how poorly equipped they and their students are to deal with conflict in the classroom. One of the reasons so many of us feel this way is the mistaken perception that conflict is bad and should be avoided rather than an ongoing, and valuable, part of human interaction.

Conflict becomes negative when we do not have humanizing approaches to grapple with it. The inability to productively work through conflict has made our world more violent and dangerous. While difficult, working through conflict does not have to be negative. It can play an important role in helping us learn about different perspectives and ways of being in the world. It can also help us better understand ourselves, our needs, and our own opportunities for growth. Further, successfully navigating through conflict can grow better relationships and connections across learning communities. Classrooms can and should be places where this happens.

If we are not in a good place physically and mentally ourselves, we may not feel up to responding to our students in humanizing ways when challenges and conflict arise. Having strategies for self-regulation and ongoing work on our own healing and ability to stay present, calm, and loving in the face of classroom conflict is a good place to start.

It's also important for us to help our students learn to do the same. We need to help students understand how to be open to their feelings and emotions and develop positive pathways to channeling them. Some classrooms have created spaces where teachers and students can go to engage in self-regulating behaviors like listening to music, resting, reading, playing a game, and doing breathing exercises. Other classrooms have integrated meditation into their day, and some have regular conversations about emotions and how to feel them and learn from them.

There are myriad ways to model and teach good self-care and self-regulation. However, to be clear, these practices should not be viewed as solutions to harm and trauma caused within school to students. Working on self-care, self-regulation, and healing is not a substitute for changing systems of harm and oppression. As adults in the building, we need to be fixing the systems that are harming students rather than leaving those systems intact and trying to fix the students themselves (see Gorski & Swalwell, 2023). Taking care of ourselves and others is a life skill that we all need to develop in order to manage the inevitable conflicts we face in varying human interactions. It isn't an excuse to leave inequity and injustice intact.

In dealing with conflict, we want to create opportunities for students to be heard, valued, and co-creators of solutions. In a classroom community where students have co-constructed the norms and expectations, they can also co-construct solutions as problems and conflicts arise. We humanize our students when we treat everyone involved in the conflict with dignity, care, and respect. We can collaboratively determine norms and expectations in the face of classroom conflicts and also focus on learning and growth while we ensure that any harm caused is repaired. An important form of harm repair is the work to reduce the probability of that same harm being generated again in the future.

During a research focus group we conducted with teachers in Germany, a teacher shared an incident where students in her class from a minoritized religious background were shouting racist epithets and becoming physically aggressive. The teacher described what happened and how she shut it down, stating that she "couldn't tolerate intolerance." The students were punished. The class moved on.

Another teacher in the focus group addressed this situation, describing how they have been able to avoid, as well as overcome, such difficult classroom conflicts through drawing on shared community agreements and negotiating the situation with students (rather than just punishing them). The second teacher felt that the incident was an important teachable moment. We agree.

As meaningful collaborators in conflict resolution, students learn invaluable lessons—that they matter (their ideas, their perspectives, their feelings), that conflict is an opportunity for growth rather than just something negative that leads to punishment, and that actions have consequences. They can also lead to learning, improvement, healing, and better human connections in the learning community rather than sadness, anger, disconnection, and issues with self-worth.

To learn more about these kinds of approaches, we recommend engaging with perspectives on trauma-informed education and practices (e.g., Venet, 2024) as well as abolitionist perspectives on community, accountability, and transformative consequences (e.g., Hayes & Kaba, 2023; Kaba, 2021). At its core, meaningful collaboration thrives when we have in place practices that treat each person involved in a conflict as an important human being with dignity and deserving of care and respect while harm is repaired and future issues are prevented/minimized.

## Communicating Across Differences

Promoting divergent thinking and considering multiple points of view are essential in equipping our students to effectively interact with people who may have different views, positionalities, or experiences. An issue of great concern in our society today is the growing unwillingness or inability of people to talk across differences or to engage in conversations around topics that are contested and thus deemed difficult or controversial. Avoiding confrontation and the desire to remain comfortable (a typical feature of white culture or whiteness) often shuts down conversations before they can even begin. In classrooms, the result is that problematic issues go unaddressed and important learning opportunities for students to understand themselves, their positionality, and their relationships with others are lost.

We want to be the kind of educators who lean into the teachable moments that happen every day to help students build community and engage with one another as strong collaborators rather than shut them down (in other words, the "I can't tolerate intolerance" approach). The point isn't to tell students what to think but to help develop their independent thinking and ability to express their authentic ideas *while they account for how their words and ideas impact others.*

First, we recommend helping students see the purpose of communication as seeking understanding. This is in contrast to a debate-style conversation where one side (or both) is trying to convince the other side of their rightness. It is also in contrast to a sermon-type conversation where one side (or both) is trying to convert the other to their morally superior perspective. Communication across differences can and should be about seeking understanding, not about agreeing or having the same perspective.

Students will need help being able to do this. It's best to practice these skills with topics that are less controversial though still interesting to discuss. We often start with things like favorite pizza toppings and movies. Students who do not believe pineapple should be on pizza can practice having a discussion with students who love it on theirs. Then we work with students to help them prepare for how to have a discussion and build an understanding of why the other side thinks the way they do.

One tool that is useful here is something called the ARE method (Shuster, 2007). "A" stands for "assertion," "R" for "reasoning," and "E" for "evidence." We encourage students to use the ARE method and speak from their own positionality and use "I" statements rather than developing assertions that denigrate the opposing point of view. For instance, in the pizza topping discussion, a poor use of the ARE method would be *Pineapple on pizza is gross because the people who eat pineapple on pizza are gross.* This is both hurtful and unhelpful in efforts to seek understanding. A better approach would be *Pineapple on pizza is gross to me because I do not like the texture. Pineapple is stringy and gets caught in my teeth.* This example uses "I" statements and provides better reasoning and evidence that supports the assertion without denigrating those with a different perspective or experience.

Students can practice preparing for discussions using the ARE method and review each other's work, offering feedback and advice on how to present their ideas. They can work together to ensure they are communicating from their own positionality and bolstering their view rather than denigrating others.

After the conversations occur about pizza toppings, students should share out the understandings they gained. For instance, those on the pineapple-should-be-on-pizza side need to express their understandings of why people argue pineapple shouldn't be on pizza. Then vice versa. The class can co-construct a chart illustrating the different understandings that were garnered from the conversations. Then each side can weigh into the accuracies of the understandings gained. Having ongoing briefings and debriefings around the experiences of being in these conversations and how they can be improved to meet shared agreements is important (see Module 6 for information about briefings and debriefings). Then as students learn to discuss across difference for the purpose of seeking understanding and get better and better at it, the topics of discussion can become more challenging.

Another important part of this work is helping students build a sense of accountability both to themselves and to others in the context of communicating across differences. This is essentially a willingness and ability to say and hear "ouch" as well as repair harm. There are several reasons that someone might not be willing to say "ouch" when something hurtful has been said in a classroom conversation. They frequently converge with the person weighing out the cost of saying something versus the benefit. Too often, students have a great deal of evidence that the cost of speaking out will be too high and without benefit. When students feel this way, they stay silent in the face of poor treatment and problematic issues go unaddressed. This is not OK and is also not easily changed. However, one of the biggest things we can do to create the possibility for students to be willing to say "ouch" is to ensure we and all the members of the learning community are developing the skills to hear "ouch" and repair the harm that has been expressed.

On the surface, this may seem simple. If someone trips and falls and says "ouch," we are great at hearing it and helping that person get to safety and the medical care they need. But do we work with the same kind of care and urgency when the person says "ouch" because of an opinion we have expressed? Or an action we have taken?

Too often, the answer is no. We've both witnessed and been part of myriad situations where an expressed "ouch" is met with responses like "Don't be so sensitive," "I was just kidding," "It's not my fault," or even laughter and disdain. Rather than our hearing "ouch" and treating the person who said it with humanizing care, these kinds of responses are dismissive and hurtful. They will quickly make the person saying "ouch" regret it and decide not to do it again.

Communicating across difference in a world riddled with oppression and inequity requires that we all learn how to hear the "ouches" expressed to us, even when we don't understand or agree with them. We've worked with students around this complicated and challenging issue by focusing on how it is more important to be in right relationship than to be right. Meaning when we are willing to hear someone's pain, even if we don't understand it, we can treat them like their pain matters.

In this way, we can be accountable to one another, striving to be in caring, reciprocally beneficial, humanizing relationships. Care is especially well communicated when we work to repair harm. Once we have successfully heard an "ouch," we will also need to find out how to make things better and prevent the harm from occurring again. Sometimes all of this can be quite tricky and complicated. However, even when things are challenging, choosing to treat everyone involved like they are an important human being whose feelings and ideas matter is core to finding a humanizing way through the issues.

## Transforming Inequity Through Meaningful Collaboration

Meaningful collaboration in our classrooms can be a powerful lever to transform inequities and work toward justice. We've worked with many teachers who dedicate the time and energy to put both joint productive activity and instructional conversations into place on a regular basis in their practice. They use meaningful collaboration in their classroom to help students explore issues from a variety of perspectives and find their own solutions to tangible problems in their immediate world. Then as a classroom community, they continue to collaborate to actually put their solutions into practice and not just learn about inequity or injustice but to actually work together to change things.

Very often teachers tell us that this kind of work sounds nice, but they see it as an add-on that there isn't time for. However, all of the teachers who have shared their experiences with us were also focused on meeting grade-level standards and growing multilingual language proficiencies. Their collaborations with students were integrated throughout their content and language-learning efforts. A study on this kind of work from teachers illustrates exploring inequity, finding solutions, and then actually enacting the solutions together produces the strongest and most impressive levels of student learning, even on standardized content and English language assessments (Teemant & Hausman, 2013).

One sixth-grade teacher told us about how her students identified bullying in their school as an issue that they wanted to do something about. Through their work in English language arts as well as social studies, they explored the issues and came up with some potential solutions. The class together started what they called the SMART movement: "Student Movement Against Rude Treatment." They developed and enacted a variety of measures to combat bullying in their school. These included providing content for the daily announcements reminding students to be SMART and ways they could join their movement. The class created artwork around their movement and wrote and received small grants to be able to print t-shirts and purchase pencils exhibiting SMART artwork to give out to students across the school. They eventually were featured on the local news because their work was having a positive impact and impressing so many.

Another story is from an elementary school teacher who encouraged her students to always explore issues from a variety of perspectives to identify solutions and then collaborate to act toward a resolution. One of her students took the learning from their class and applied it in her life outside of class.

This student participated in an after-school program where they often watched movies. She went to the program organizers to ask if they could watch a princess movie one day. The organizers responded with something like "*No. Probably not—most of the kids here don't want to watch princess movies.*" The student pushed back with an argument, saying,

> *Yes. You are right. Most of the kids here don't want to watch princess movies, which is why we are always watching* Teenage Mutant Ninja Turtles *and* Transformers. *Those aren't my movies, but I watch them. I think it's my turn to have us watch a princess movie like I like to watch. If I have to always watch a movie that I don't want to watch, the other kids can watch just one that they don't want to watch either.*

The teacher was happy to report that her student got to watch her preferred movie and that the program organizers were really impressed with her ability to advocate for herself with a strong argument and a solution. We couldn't help but wonder what additional solutions might have arisen if the program staff took the problem to the whole group to solve together!

To us, this is really the point. We need a world of problem-solvers, people who can explore issues from a variety of perspectives, suggest solutions, and then actually put those solutions into practice. Students deserve to learn these skills, even in the earliest experiences in school. And through meaningful collaboration, we can support students to grow as effective and impactful independent thinkers and problem-solvers.

## Make It Work

In Explore, we discussed various aspects and possibilities for orchestrating meaningful collaboration in our classrooms. Now is your chance to play with these ideas and make them work in your practice! Below we have provided some options of how you can do that, thinking about the intrapersonal, interpersonal, and systemic levels of engagement. Any of these could (and potentially should) be done just by yourself but also could be accomplished through learning activities with your students. As you choose an option, keep in mind the module's critical reflection and complexity thinking questions: *What tensions and complexities need to be addressed in my classroom for collaboration to be meaningful, equitable, and just? What opportunities exist and what barriers do I have to overcome for me to work as a collaborator in student learning?* We encourage you to revisit your reflections from the beginning of the module and think about the implications of your work in relation to context, orientations, and pedagogy looking through intrapersonal, interpersonal, and systemic lenses.

## Make It Work Options

### Intrapersonal: Preparing for Conflict and Controversy

Purpose: Engage in the internal work necessary to be someone who can meaningfully collaborate with students and help turn conflict and challenging communications into important teachable moments.

Many factors impact how we respond to conflict and challenging communication in our classrooms. It is important that we look internally as we prepare for such work. We know many teachers who absolutely clam up when controversy arises, who have a strong resistance to any form of conflict, or who become very dysregulated in the face of controversy. We ourselves have been that teacher at times too. By doing the internal work ourselves, we continually seek to understand what our own challenges are in the context of conflict and/or controversy and how we can prepare to engage in caring, connected, and open collaborative work with our students. For each of us, this work will be different as we take time to reflect on our experiences with conflict and controversy. Questions to consider: What are your typical responses to conflict? Will those responses help students learn to engage in meaningful collaboration? Where do your responses come from? Is there trauma you need to address? When you freeze, get flustered or frustrated in moments of conflict and/

or controversy, what can you do to re-regulate yourself? Spend time thinking about and critically reflecting on the various complexities and tensions in your own engagement with conflict and controversy. Then make an initial plan for what you personally need to do to best prepare yourself to support meaningful collaboration and authentic learning even in the face of conflict and controversy in your classroom.

### Interpersonal: Plan and (If Possible) Implement a Lesson with Joint Productive Activity or Instructional Conversation

Purpose: Increase your repertoire of strategies to build meaningful collaboration in your classroom.

Think about an upcoming lesson where you could start working on joint productive activities and/or instructional conversations with your students. Focus on creating opportunities for you to be a collaborator with a small group jointly producing either a tangible or intangible product and/or engaging in an instructional conversation. If you are planning joint productive activity, have a clear sense of what the joint product is that you are collaboratively producing with a small group of students and how that collaborative production will unfold. If you are planning an instructional conversation, set a clear learning target for the dialogue and plan/write questions to help you spur more student talk than teacher talk and try to engage in a productive dialogue. Review your plans and consider what students' strengths are for the success of these activities as well as what supports they may need to be successful. After you teach the lesson, be sure to reflect and think forward about how to continue to grow in your implementation of joint productive activities and instructional conversations.

### Systemic: Teach to Transform Inequity

Purpose: Plan and, where possible, implement lessons/units where students explore varying perspectives and co-construct solutions to problems that address issues of inequity or injustice.

Grounded in the content learning expected for our classes are opportunities for students to examine the myriad complexities that exist in the world, identify issues to try to solve, create solutions, and then actually act to solve them. This does not happen in one short lesson and needs to be carefully planned. But it is a very powerful approach to collaboratively addressing systemic issues with students that has been illustrated to have a formidable effect on student learning. We recommend starting with students to identify an issue they would be interested in exploring (e.g., like the students described above who created the SMART movement to address bullying in their school). Then explore that issue from a variety of perspectives in order to develop a complex and complete understanding of the issue. From there, students should co-create a solution that they can also enact. Then students should enact the solution, utilizing meaningful collaboration all along the way. Be sure to document your planning and work along the way in order to share with your colleagues and to be able to use what you learned in future projects.

**You Make It Work!**

Purpose: To make the ideas from Explore work in your own practice.

Design your own activity (or tweak one of ours) to ensure you are spending your time doing work that is most useful and relevant to you and your students. We recommend starting with the critical reflection and complexity thinking questions. Then clarify for yourself which level you are working at (intrapersonal, interpersonal, or systemic) and build your effort to make this module's learning work for you from there!

 **Share**

Share is your opportunity to engage with your peers and receive feedback about the work you have done and what you have learned in this module. Begin by revisiting the reflection you wrote at the beginning of the module and revise it to include your thinking now, noting any changes and what they might mean for your practice. Be sure to attend to opportunities to strive for justice and equity and to potential barriers to achieving it. Don't shy away from the complexities that come up—embrace them. Think about different ways of being and doing in your classroom that could address those complexities. Once you have completed your reflection, be prepared to share it with your colleagues along with a description of the work you did in the Make It Work section. By sharing what you have learned, you have the chance to both solidify your own learning and thinking and expand it by learning from your colleagues.

# 8

# Grouping in a Multilingual Multitasking Classroom

In previous modules, we explored multitasking classrooms and meaningful collaboration, including how to position ourselves as collaborators as well as attend to conflict and differences. We've argued that all students should be able to work with all other students and provided ideas for how to make it possible. In this module, we continue to explore collaboration with a focus on how we can group and regroup students in both whole-class and small-group situations. We suggest that teachers and whole school communities need to attend to these configurations in varying circumstances and with different learning ends in mind, all through a multilingual lens. Thoughtfully grouping students allows us to attend to students' varying language profiles and importantly maximizes their use of their home languages.

To get started on this module, consider these questions for critical reflection and complexity thinking: *Whom do students typically get to work with in my classroom? Across their whole school day? What markers of identity get attended to in determining such grouping? How can I group and regroup with multilingualism in mind? What other factors need attention to ensure that inequities are not perpetuated as my students work together in different groups?* Be sure to preserve your initial reflection, notes, and ideas so you can revisit them during the Make It Work and Share sections of this module, paying attention to your growth and keeping track of your learning.

 **Explore**

We recently saw a video on social media gushing about certain celebrities who spoke more than one language. The video called their multilingualism "surprising" as they were stars who were raised speaking English but now are quite comfortable users of other languages. This perspective of multilingualism is pervasive. It is impressive or an asset when English speakers are multilingual but overlooked in speakers of other languages.

This perspective is reflected in a variety of programming and policy decisions in schools that limit learning possibilities for multilingual students learning English. For example, extensive research worldwide establishes that bilingual education programs where students both learn content and develop language skills in at least two languages are the clear gold standard. Yet they are seldom offered to multilingual learners learning English in schools (Morita-Mullaney et al., 2020, 2022). Further, where there has been growth in bilingual programs recently, it has more often been for English home language students rather than for students new to English (Delavan et al., 2024).

To be clear, we would love for all students to have a fully multilingual education regardless of home language. Unfortunately, for too long the bi/multilingualism of students whose home language is not English has been and is treated like a problem, while the bi/multilingualism of students whose home language is English has been and is treated as an asset for their learning and future possibilities.

No matter what school or program students attend, they should be able to build and expand their full linguistic repertoires. If we ignore students' multilingualism, we lose opportunities to promote students' home languages as vehicles for learning. In addition, we might not create spaces in the general education classroom to support students' English language development. We believe opportunities for both can happen in virtually all content classrooms.

We definitely can create schools and classrooms where the multilingualism of students learning English is treated as an asset and a resource that they can regularly utilize in their learning while they continue to grow it. One way to do this is to group and regroup students (inside our classrooms as well as across the school) in ways that take their multilingualism into account and support its development.

There is, however, an important caveat—when we advocate for students' language profiles to be used as part of our decision-making around forming groups, it is *not* for the purpose of policing their language use. Our role is to support student learning, languaging, and translanguaging, not to control which language choices students make on their learning journeys. While we may encourage the use of one language or another in a particular group, in all settings students should be free to use whatever language practices work best for them to communicate with others. In this way, students can have agency as they work as language architects and construct their communication efforts in their own voice and perspective (for more on language architects, see Module 3).

## The Complexities of Grouping Students

We seek to create spaces where students are actively learning with and from individuals with different backgrounds, identities, skill sets, and experiences. We want to see students critically engage with the content of the curriculum, strengthen their language capabilities, and interact with all their peers in non-oppressive ways. This can be challenging when students' positionalities in the larger society serve to benefit some and marginalize others.

We recommend regularly grouping and regrouping students according to their language profiles, which requires us to pay attention to the complexities of such grouping decisions. We need to be cautious that we don't overly segregate multilingual learners from their monolingual English-speaking peers as this often coincides with separating students by their racial identities.

Racial segregation has a long ugly history in the US, and while intentionally segregating students is illegal, de-facto segregation still occurs across the nation. This is tied to the disparity of economic opportunities for families on the basis of race, class, and language. It also reflects the widespread lack of affordable housing, especially in gentrifying neighborhoods. Further, many White and/or wealthy families have opted out of public schooling altogether, sending their children instead to tuition-based private schools.

In terms of the education of multilingual students, there are a variety of programs and approaches that are utilized to support students learning English and grade-level content. Schools may be implementing pull-out, push-in, co-teaching, tracking, newcomer programs, bilingual approaches, sheltered English instruction, and myriad other possibilities.

Depending on the context and the use of available resources, any number of approaches can be successful and humanizing. They can also become inequitable and unjust especially if we view the language specialist's job (meaning the English as a Second Language or bilingual teacher) as "fixing" the students until they are fluent in English. For instance, we recently visited a second-grade general education classroom where a newcomer multilingual student was seated alone with an iPad. During the entire time we were in the class, we did not see this student do anything meaningful on the iPad nor with his teachers or peers. Because this student was pulled out of his classroom for a short time each day for English language development, his school was technically in compliance with laws and regulations regarding the education of students learning English. However, his education was woefully inadequate given that he had no further supports for his learning for most of the day. This is not OK and sadly is not an anomaly. In our experience, these kinds of situations occur all over the country on a daily basis.

Because of all of these problems and complexities, rather than suggest a particular type of instructional program, we want to spend time thinking about the context of students' learning to create humanizing pedagogies. Specifically, we want to think about who students are learning with and what affordances grouping (and regrouping) students offer multilingual learners.

The way we group students is affected in part by who ends up in our classrooms. A school that serves many students from diverse cultural and linguistic backgrounds will provide different opportunities than those that are composed mainly of White monolingual English speakers. In schools that have high percentages of multilingual learners, we have greater opportunities to group students with their language profiles in mind. Where there are few multilingual learners, it can be harder to support students' multilingualism, but it is not impossible. No matter the context, *no single way* of forming groups will provide students everything they need, especially if our goal is the full realization of students' potential.

In schools where instruction is only in English, especially those with a low percentage of multilingual learners, teachers and administrators often ask us whether they should put all the students not yet fluent in English in certain classrooms or assign them across a variety of classes and teachers. Similarly, within our classrooms, we must decide whether we should randomly assign students to groups (all the time, some of the time, or never) or more intentionally use language profiles, interests, skills, or some other criterion in our decision-making.

Combining or separating students on the basis of language profiles is often referred to as clustering versus scattering. The appropriate decision depends on the specifics of a school's demographics and the preparation of the teachers to work with linguistic diversity. Unfortunately, placements are often made on the basis of the individual preferences of teachers or the scheduling algorithm rather than whether one decision or another would be beneficial or harmful to the students themselves.

We have heard teachers ask that students not be put into their general education classrooms until they "speak English." Other teachers allow multilingual students to join their classes but don't modify the way they teach (like the second-grade class we observed and described above). This lack of responsiveness can occur because teachers don't see it as their role as a grade-level or content teacher to teach multilingual students. Or perhaps they haven't yet received the preparation, education, or support needed to do so.

One problematic argument that is used for scattering and randomly assigning multilingual students to classes is that it is "fairer" because it treats all students equally. Another is that the students will learn English faster because they will be totally immersed. A more troublesome argument we've heard is that scattering the multilingual learners provides monolingual English speakers with more access to "diverse students."

We worked in one school where this was happening until a new principal changed the policy. A teacher who initially vocally resisted the change admitted in a faculty meeting that she realized, to her dismay, that now that there were several students new to English in her classroom, she could no longer overlook them or fail to notice when they needed additional support. Several other teachers agreed that with strategic clustering they could more easily provide support, as they had a small group they could work with.

The main argument against clustering is that every teacher is (or should be) a language teacher so we shouldn't unnecessarily segregate students. However, because not all teachers see themselves, or have been prepared, as language teachers, we often argue for clustering students in classrooms led by teachers with specific experience and preparation to teach multilingual learners.

As the teachers above pointed out, putting students newer to English in one classroom provides a critical mass for forming groups. In addition, we have found that students often feel less isolated knowing that they aren't the only one new to English. When we group students with the same language background in a classroom, there is a context for students to use their home language in school regardless of the language of instruction. It also provides an impetus for gathering home language resources as well as expanding who students work with, as participants in home language groupings can also be confident speakers of English.

Student grouping decisions are complex and multifaceted and can create strong learning opportunities for multilingual students as well as dramatically limit them. Further, grouping decisions made without attention to various oppressive issues will not counteract the privileging of certain multilingualisms or ways of speaking English. Neither can our grouping decisions automatically thwart racism, classism, ableism, or linguicism. Possibilities to create equitable spaces are more likely to emerge, however, when we are thoughtful about how students from diverse language backgrounds can be grouped and regrouped to work together in non-oppressive ways.

## A Day in the Life

The scenario below follows Raúl, a seventh grader from Central America, as he moves through a typical day of instruction. It highlights different ways that multilingual students can experience school. As you read, take note of anything that stands out to you and what you might want to emulate or do differently in your classroom or school.

*Raúl was an excellent student before leaving home with his family. They arrived in the US several months ago, and his parents have found work in the meat packing industry while they seek political asylum. He speaks the local Mayan dialect of his community with his family and friends and is proud of his Mayan heritage evident in his appearance. He's surprised that none of his teachers or classmates knows anything about the Maya. They call him Latino and think of him as a Spanish speaker. He does also speak Spanish but learned it at school and didn't use it much outside of class before coming to the US.*

*Today, Raúl's first class is science. Most of the 32 students are monolingual English speakers, but there are several who speak Spanish and a few who speak other languages. Students sit in rows of desks in assigned seats. He and the other Spanish speakers have been placed apart. The entire lesson consists of listening to a lecture in English and then filling out a worksheet related to a reading in the textbook. He doesn't really understand the reading, but he can decode the words. He finds some answers for the fill-in-the-blank worksheet by matching words and pictures in the text to the worksheet. Students are expected to work independently, but he notices English speakers helping each* other. None of them speaks to him directly, but one points at him and laughs. The teacher who is working at his desk doesn't notice.

Next is English Language Development (ELD), a class of 24 students new to English. While they have all been assessed as Level 2, their facility with English varies. In this class, students are encouraged to collaborate, especially in English. Raúl is working with five other students on an inquiry project about schools and schooling practices around the world. The culminating activity is an oral presentation of similarities and differences between what they find and their own experiences. The teacher begins by checking in with the whole class to review vocabulary, answer questions, and go over the template for the final presentation. They then move into their small groups, and the teacher circulates among them.

The other students in Raúl's group speak Arabic, French, Somali, and two Indigenous languages from Africa. This is intentional so they have to communicate in English. They are using a graphic organizer the teacher gave them to document their findings about schooling in Japan. Topics include the weekly schedule, the length of secondary education, required subjects, whether school is compulsory and for how long, what meals they have at school, the kinds of transportation they use to get to school, and a place for anything else they find interesting.

The teacher has identified websites and given students books in English they can use to access information. When Raúl's group reviews the timeline for the project, they see they are ready to organize information for their oral presentation. They start by practicing the phrases for the language of comparison that are on the template. The students laugh together when, at first, they stumble over the phrases. Then they help each other with pronunciation. Raúl enjoys the project, especially comparing each other's experiences. At the end of class, students submit exit tickets to communicate with the teacher whether they are on track, need help, or have any questions.

It's a block day, so it's already time for lunch. Raúl leaves class feeling like he accomplished something. In the cafeteria, he and two Spanish-speaking friends eat together and then go outside for some fresh air. Raúl then heads to his afternoon classes—social studies and music—his two favorite subjects. During first quarter, all four sections of world civilization received the same overview of the different civilizations, past and present, as well as the overarching themes of the course.

For the rest of the year, each section is focusing on a different part of the world. Raúl's class is studying India. For the culminating activity of each unit, students create posters and videos to share their learning. The students will use them to compare and synthesize the findings across the four sections. The social studies teacher worked with the administration to assign students with similar language backgrounds to the same section so they can collaborate using their home language and cultural resources.

Raúl's group has been assigned the origins of Hinduism, which they know little about. In the prior class, they looked at resources in English; today, they will search for and review videos and websites in Spanish. The other Spanish speakers are from different countries and class backgrounds, notable in the different dialects they speak. Raúl finds it very helpful to work in Spanish, except that one of the other students makes fun of him, calling him "Indio." He also mocks him, saying Raúl doesn't speak real Spanish. Raúl isn't sure what to do about it. His teacher seems nice, but he doesn't know what will happen if he tells him, so he just suffers through the bad treatment.

Raúl's last class is music. Students are working in small groups to write lyrics for a melody given to them by the teacher. Each group will present their songs to the whole class in either a live or a pre-recorded performance. Together Raúl's group has come up with the topic for their song "Day and Night." The teacher has organized the groups to include students with different language profiles. Other students in Raúl's group speak Somali, a local Native American language, and different varieties of English. The music teacher encourages students to collaborate and be as creative as possible with the lyrics. The class will vote for the best song in each of three award categories they came up with: "Most relatable topic," "Best use of multiple languages," and "Most inspiring." Raúl is anxious to win the multiple languages award and pushes his group to share ideas about how to use their different languages. At first, it was hard for them to communicate and work together as a group. But over time, with the help of the teacher, they have found their groove and are excited about how they each can contribute to the lyrics.

In this scenario, over the course of the day, Raúl's teachers provide varying opportunities for student interaction and engagement as well as possibilities for students to use their whole linguistic repertoire. In science, he is in a large monotasking group with no differentiation or student choice. His English-speaking peers do not see it as their role to help him, and some appear to be making fun of him. In ELD, where all the students are new to English, they work in whole and small monotasking groups using scaffolding tools provided by the teacher. They are encouraged to collaborate and compare their experiences, but the use of home languages is discouraged as they work together to improve their English abilities. In social studies, students work in small multitasking groups that are organized so students can use their home languages for learning. Raúl is glad to be able to use Spanish, but one of his peers is unkind and makes him feel uncomfortable. The music teacher also uses small multitasking groups composed of students with varying language profiles (multilingual learners learning English, monolingual English speakers, and multilingual learners confident in English). She provides a great deal of student choice and affirms students' individual language practices and wishes.

What happens across the four classes reveals some of the complexities we need to consider as we plan for how students will be grouped and regrouped, including some of the issues around meaningful collaboration discussed in Module 7 (e.g., communicating across difference). Across the day, when language and identity profiles are thoughtfully considered, even when the content is distant from his current understandings, Raúl is better able to participate as he has the scaffolds and supports to be successful on his learning journey. However, even in the context of grouping students together with the same language background, work needs to be done to ensure meaningful collaboration and respectful engagement as students work together. The least effective environment for Raúl is whole-group instruction through lecture and independent seat work, yet this is the setting that multilingual learners most often find themselves in during content instruction, especially at the secondary level.

## Providing Support for Home Languages Through Strategic Grouping

A major reason we advocate that students be able to use their home languages in school is so they can interact with concepts at higher levels of abstraction than they might be able to do only through English. Using home languages in schools also deepens students' multilingualism and expands the authentic ways they can exist in the world multilingually. Precisely because these opportunities are the least available to most multilingual students, we need to pay special attention to what we can do to provide them. Thoughtful grouping and regrouping practices are possible in a variety of ways, as suggested in the scenario below.

*Teachers at Miramontes K-8 School have all agreed to incorporate languages other than English in their instruction. In Ms. M's fourth grade, two small groups of students review websites she has identified in Ukrainian and Spanish related to weather, the current topic in science. In Ms. L's third grade, multilingual learners are paired with sixth graders from the same language background who come weekly to read, discuss, and create story books in their home languages. In a kindergarten, several parents are working with individual and small groups of children who are counting in their home languages and matching numerals from 1 to 20 to quantities of blocks. In a seventh-grade Health class, several newcomers are working independently on the computer doing multilingual webquests, exploring websites in both English and their home languages. In Mr. G's eighth-grade class, a small group of Arabic-speaking students is discussing Math concepts with a community member who works with them every week. The P.E. teacher is sharing a poster she created with the key vocabulary for the health unit translated into the four most represented languages in the school. Some students are adding visuals to the poster, and those from low-incidence languages are encouraged to contribute additional terms if they know them. The music teacher is reviewing a homework assignment with fourth graders. They were asked to bring in the words in their language(s) to the song "Are You Sleeping Brother John / Frère Jacques," which they will later learn and compare. The librarian is pointing out to a group of fifth graders where they can find resources (print, online, and local community members) in languages other than English related to the social studies unit they are studying.*

Every teacher at this school has found some way for students to use their home language to go deeper into concepts, access information, share their ideas, and tap into their funds of knowledge. The message is transparent that languages other than English are valued and play a role in students' learning at school. Students work on their own as well as with peers and with adults who speaks their language. They are introduced to new ideas, engage with text, create demonstrations of their learning, and clarify their understandings. These opportunities are made possible by incorporating flexible grouping and multitasking into our instruction.

There are many complexities to consider as we form home language groups. While students may fluently speak their home language, it doesn't necessarily mean they have the literacy skills needed to investigate written materials on their own. This is why it is important to get to know our students' skills in their various languages and how to best scaffold their use of their entire linguistic repertoire in our classes. Starting with strategies like read-alouds, conversation, and dialogue so students can discuss and clarify concepts orally can be helpful.

We also cannot assume that students and adults who speak the same language or have a similar heritage will automatically share an affinity. They may share certain cultural understandings, experiences, and practices, but regional differences within and across countries, class status, and colorism will also affect how they receive and act toward each other. They may be from ethnic groups currently in conflict or have a history of strife or oppression. There are sometimes tensions between newer and more established immigrants from the same country and region. We can anticipate and even avoid problems that might arise among students when we have gotten to know the current and historical contexts that surround them.

When we use home languages in school, we need to pay attention to how students respond academically and affectively. We have found that most often our students are excited and grateful when we affirm the importance of their languages and cultural practices. When that isn't the case, we need to be open to understanding their hesitation. Even when we affirm and promote multilingualism, students and their families may initially be reluctant (or outright resistant) to engage multilingually.

For too long, multilingual learners have received the message that only English counts. Many have experienced linguistic discrimination and fear that using home languages at school and even at home will lessen students' chances for academic success. Some families start using only English at home, even if it isn't the parents/caregivers' strongest language, cutting off deep communication. To ease their fears, we discuss the importance of multilingualism and often share the notion of the conceptual reservoir (see Module 10) to demonstrate why their role using their family language(s) is so important to students' academic success. We want families to interact using their strongest language, and they are more likely to do so when they see home languages playing a meaningful role in classroom learning.

Making space for languages other than English can be tricky when we are unfamiliar with students' languages. In the past, we were both reluctant for students to use languages we didn't know in our classrooms. We wondered how we could monitor student work or ensure that they were remaining on task. Over time, we were able to let go of those concerns. We realized that we don't always know what students are saying in English and that their body language typically tells us if they are on task.

Sometimes teachers push back, saying "It's not fair if I can't do it for everyone, so I won't do it for anyone." This most often occurs when there are language resources available to support one group of students but not another (e.g., Spanish textbooks are available, but nothing is in Arabic or Chinese). Our response is that we maximize the opportunities we have while we are transparent with students and families, seeking collaboratively constructed solutions. We explain to students that supports will be different due to a variety of factors. For example, in the school cafeteria, we wouldn't withhold wheat bread from all students because some can't tolerate gluten. We would feed all children by finding gluten-free food for those who need it or non-dairy milk for those who are lactose-intolerant. There may be more resources available for some language groups to have more supports for their home language uses in schools or even fully developed bilingual programs, but that doesn't mean that other language groups can't also have home language supports at school.

Unless students have opportunities to talk about content concepts in their home languages, they may never grow that aspect of their multilingualism. Building relationships with adults who speak the language(s) of our students and positioning them in the classroom as knowledgeable is a valuable practice on multiple levels for all students to learn from. Otherwise, students can get the message that English is the only language for schooling and that only English speakers have important knowledge. The more we bring different people, languages, and ideas into our classroom and normalize the value of all of them for understanding the world and growing our abilities as learners, the more we can disrupt messages about what languages matter, in which circumstances. Multitasking classrooms are especially useful for this because community volunteers can work with small groups of students as collaborators in their shared languages.

## Supporting English Language Development

The practice of grouping and regrouping students is informed by the learning goals of various lessons and units. When students are grouped intentionally to work with peers who are also new to English, it can offer a brave place for students to practice their new language with others at a similar place in their language learning trajectory. Students learning English need to interact with all of their peers for various learning opportunities and targets. The intent of grouping students with similar proficiencies in English is to provide a lower stress setting and create opportunities to review and pronounce new vocabulary, try out a new sentence structure, or practice a presentation. Ideally, these connections to the content classroom would happen in ELD classes, but that is seldom the case. Therefore, providing even short times for multilingual students to connect and learn together in our general education classes can be deeply impactful. However, as with every grouping configuration, we would not want this to be a permanent grouping for students.

When a collaborative community exists, multilingual students learning English grouped together can feel more confident about their contributions because they don't have to compete with students who are already fluent in the language of instruction. Multilingual learners can more easily shine among their peers, something not always possible in groups dominated by confident English speakers. This can reduce the psychological stress experienced when learners have to try to make sense of and communicate through a language they are still learning. Further, students from varying language backgrounds can support one another in learning about the codes and uses of English as well as engage in communicative practices that both are accessible in terms of language demand and create the context for ongoing language growth. We've often seen students from different language backgrounds explain features of English to their peers in ways that we couldn't.

When multilingual students learning English work together, they can pre-read a text (in English or another language) or engage in other activities that will prepare them for upcoming activities. Such work can be guided by the question: What language practices do students need to be familiar with to participate in the main activities of the content unit? For example, if the content unit will require students to participate in a debate, we can prepare students for both how debates work and the content of what they will say in their contributions to the debate. Our role is to ensure that they have supports for the kinds of language practices they will be expected to engage in. These can include sentence stems, an outline of how the debate should unfold, and key phrases that will help the students express their ideas.

Living museums, debates, and science fairs—just about all learning activities—are perfectly appropriate for multilingual learners still in the process of acquiring English. We just need to provide students with time to prepare, to practice, and to receive guidance on how to express their ideas effectively in English or even in multiple languages, all of which is made possible through multitasking.

## From Monotasking to Multilingual Multitasking

In this book, we emphasize the importance of creating a multitasking classroom, where a variety of different learning activities are occurring at the same time. To be clear, we are not saying that whole-group instruction or small-group monotasking is never appropriate. We are saying that their frequent and almost exclusive use makes it nearly impossible to fully support multilingual learners.

Typically, in whole-group monotasking approaches, monolingual students and multilingual learners confident in English sit alongside students new to English. If we gear instruction to the language levels of confident or monolingual English speakers, aspects of the instruction may be beyond the grasp of even advanced English-speaking multilingual learners. We may be reluctant (or not even realize that we need) to slow down or stop to explain concepts and vocabulary in depth to just a few students.

Whole-group instruction also leaves little room for students to be able to use their entire linguistic repertoire or receive needed support in English so that they can better comprehend the instruction. When students work in smaller groups, it is easier to facilitate discussion and dialogue to support students' learning. But just having students seated in small groups doesn't guarantee things will improve. Consider the contrast between classrooms A and B, described below.

*In classroom A, there are 28 students in a sixth-grade math class. Students represent different language profiles, from monolingual English speakers to multilingual speakers from three distinct language backgrounds: Spanish, Hmong, and Ukrainian. Some of the multilingual learners have been attending the school since kindergarten and have been bureaucratically reclassified as fluent in English. Others have arrived in the past six months. Students have been randomly assigned to sit at small tables of five or six. When we enter the classroom, Teacher A is reviewing the previous day's homework assignment and asking the whole class for volunteers to answer different problems. In response to every question, about ten students raise their hands and three students at different tables sometimes shout out the answers. More than half the class never raises their hand, though a glance at their papers indicates that most have done the problems correctly. Students newest to English just stare at their mostly blank homework papers.*

*In the classroom next door (classroom B) is a class with similar student demographics. Students are also reviewing homework at their* tables, but the process is much different. Students have been strategically assigned to the tables and have had several opportunities to practice different collaboration protocols. At each table, there are students with a range of language and identity profiles. Where possible, students newest to English are seated with a peer from the same language group who is more comfortable in English. As they go through the problems, students at each table share their answers. If their responses differ, they talk and agree on the correct answer, making sure everyone knows what they decided on. The students at each table have been given a number (from 1 to 6), and the teacher uses a spinner to see who will answer the question aloud. Nearly every student is participating at their tables.

Both classrooms described above have students sitting in groups composed of students who are extremely confident in their English use with those still developing their English abilities and fluency. This is the setting in which most multilingual students in US schools find themselves throughout the school day. The difference is that, in classroom B, the students have been strategically grouped and provided structured ways to cooperate and help each other.

A one-size-fits-all or a sit-and-get approach will never be sufficient for multilingual students and many other learners in our classrooms. Working in smaller groups provides (but doesn't guarantee) opportunities to build authentic relationships among students. We discuss with our students that we intentionally plan different opportunities so they can expand their facility with language and learn the content as well as hone their abilities to work with people across differences. We want to provide concrete ways that students can support their peers. We especially want students who are newer to English to be able to express their thinking via multiple modalities (auditory, visual, and kinesthetic) and/or languages. The most successful multilingual classrooms are centered on interactive, hands-on, inquiry-oriented learning. They allow us to embrace the unique linguistic and cultural assets the student brings to the learning. Multitasking classrooms give flexibility and more opportunities for this kind of active engagement.

Through our words, actions, and pedagogical practices, the message we try to communicate is the following: *In our multilingual classroom, we each bring different positionalities, strengths, and abilities with us. All our languages and dialects are vehicles for learning, and we will do everything we can to promote multilingualism. We will form working groups in many ways—sometimes by language background or proficiencies, other times with students from across languages and cultural backgrounds. Each way of grouping students in this class provides opportunities for learning that are different than in others. But no matter who is working together or what the task, we are guided by our shared agreements about how we treat each other to honor our shared humanity and disrupt inequities.*

 **Make It Work**

In the Explore section, we discussed possibilities for different kinds of groupings with multilingual students' language profiles in mind and suggested why each is important to advance equity, justice, and diversity in our classrooms. Now is your chance to play with these ideas and make them work in your practice! Below we have provided some options of how you can do that, thinking about the intrapersonal, interpersonal, and systemic levels of engagement. Any of these could (and potentially should) be done just by yourself but also could be accomplished through learning activities with your students. As you choose an option, keep in mind the module's critical reflection and complexity thinking questions: *Whom do students typically get to work with in my classroom? Across their whole school day? What markers of identity get attended to in determining such grouping? How can I group and regroup with multilingualism in mind? What other factors need attention to ensure that inequities are not perpetuated as my students work together in different groups?* We encourage you to revisit the components of humanizing pedagogies from the introduction and think about the implications of what you learned from engaging in this module in relation to context, orientations, and pedagogy. When you have completed your Make It Work activity, reflect on your findings to share them with your colleagues.

### Intrapersonal: My Views of Multilingualism

Purpose: Critically reflect on your own stances toward multilingualism and notice where biases may impact your judgments, impressions, and work with multilingual people, taking into consideration their home language background as well as race, class, and other identity factors.

For this option, we ask you to engage in a self-study of how you encounter multilingualism and how you and others respond to it. This could happen over the course of a day, a week, or even a month. Take note every time you encounter multilingualism in any form. Notice: how do you feel about the person speaking and their multilingualism? Do you feel impressed? Why? Do you feel frustrated? Why? What do you notice about your response to their multilingualism? What does it illustrate to you about your attitudes toward multilingualism? Be sure to attend to how factors like race, class, language background, or gender affect your responses. For instance, do you see the neighborhood grandma who takes daily walks from India differently than the construction worker from Mexico building a fence at your neighbor's house? Why? What differences, if any, are there in how you view their multilingualism? From this critical reflection and self-study, consider whether and how you need to expand your openness to multilingualism. Plan for how you can work against any biases that you have uncovered to increase an appreciation for multilingualism in all its forms.

### Interpersonal: Multilingual Multitasking Grouping

Purpose: Plan for and, if possible, implement multilingual multitasking grouping.

Pick an upcoming lesson or unit and reflect on the learning goals. Then consider how students could be grouped and regrouped to organize multitasking opportunities to maximize the learning opportunities for all students. When and for what purpose might you group students together who speak the same language? How could community volunteers assist you to work with students in their home languages? What resources might help you support students working together in their home languages? When might it be useful to group multilingual learners learning English together? How could you use that grouping to support their English development in the context of this lesson or unit? Building off of the ideas from Modules 6 and 7, strive to implement meaningful collaboration and multitasking with students' language profiles and learning targets in mind. Be sure to reflect on how it goes and think about ways to grow these approaches in your practice and continue to improve them.

**Systemic: A Day in the Life**
Purpose: Explore how multilingual students experience their entire day at your school with a focus on grouping. Use this information to advocate for any needed changes within your school building.

Many decisions that affect how we group students have been made before we even meet them. Looking beyond your own classroom can help you fine-tune your own practice and be the impetus for discussion among the faculty about what you discover. In addition, students' experiences in other settings affect how they respond to what we attempt in our own classrooms. Shadowing multilingual students helps discover how they experience their learning in a wider context and what the whole school day experience looks like, as described in the scenario above about Raúl. In his case, we uncovered both different grouping strategies and views on supporting students' multilingualism, some more successful than others.

As you shadow students, you can look for the kinds of languaging practices they engage in, who they work with, and what kinds of learning activities they are offered. For this reason, we recommend organizing opportunities for you and your colleagues to do this work together. After everyone has had a chance to shadow multilingual students, you can think together about what you can do as a school community to ensure that multilingual learners can grow their multilingualism and participate in engaging, impactful learning across the whole school day.

**You Make It Work!**
Purpose: To make the ideas from Explore work in your own practice.

Design your own activity (or tweak one of ours) to ensure that you are spending your time doing work that is most useful and relevant to you and your students. We recommend starting with the critical reflection and complexity thinking questions. Then clarify for yourself which level you are working at (intrapersonal, interpersonal, or systemic) and build your effort to make this module's learning work for you from there!

## Share

Share is your opportunity to engage with your peers and receive feedback about the work you have done and what you have learned in this module. Begin by revisiting the reflection you wrote at the beginning of the module and revise it to include your thinking now, noting any changes and what they might mean for your practice. Be sure to attend to opportunities to strive for justice and equity and to potential barriers to achieving it. Don't shy away from the complexities that come up—embrace them. Think about different ways of being and doing in your classroom that could address those complexities. Once you have completed your reflection, be prepared to share it with your colleagues along with a description of the work you did in the Make it Work section. By sharing what you have learned, you have the chance to both solidify your own learning and thinking and expand it by learning from your colleagues.

# 9

# Authentic Language Practices

Many books and resources have been created for teachers of multilingual learners about the discrete aspects of language, literacy, and specific strategies for teaching language and literacy in the classroom. This is not the purpose of our book generally or this module specifically. Rather, here we build on ideas from previous modules, especially Module 3 (*Toward a Multilingual Classroom Ecology*), about expecting and accepting multiple language practices as valid and valuable and moving away from dictating and policing language practices. If you have not already completed Module 3, we recommend doing so before beginning this one. If you have, take time to revisit your reflections and Make It Work efforts to remind yourself of the ideas and content. Then, as you approach this module, think about your current stance toward varying language practices. Consider these questions: *What do I currently do to promote student agency, meaning-making, and a commitment to equity in the use of different language practices? How can I address the complexities of using a variety of language practices to humanize the languaging in my classroom?* Be sure to keep your initial reflection, notes, and ideas so you can revisit them during the Make It Work and Share sections of the module.

## 💡 Explore

We once participated in a professional development for teachers of multilingual learners where the facilitator taught us strategies to help students "talk like a book." She insisted that as we use the strategies with students, we should also police their language practices to ensure that they were talking like a book. For us, this felt so inauthentic and contrived. It seemed ridiculous to expect students to be creative and curious about content and language while having to rigidly control their oral language practices and speak in such formal ways. As academics and published authors, we don't always speak like books in our oral academic discourse. In fact, it's not rare to hear us use curse words, slang, and colloquialisms even as we have collaborated to write this book!

As teachers and academics who are committed to great learning and teaching for multilingual students, we have spent a lot of time thinking about, researching, reading, and experimenting as we collaborate to discover the best ways to support multilingual student learning. Various discrete strategies can be quite useful and are widely available from other highly respected authors for both teachers and multilingual students seeking to support multilingual language development, improved content learning, and equity and justice. What we have found to be most important is quite simple: create the space and provide useful scaffolds for students to successfully engage in authentic, meaningful, and purposeful language practices. In this way, students learn by doing and grow expansive, complex, and multifaceted linguistic repertoires.

Communicating across language barriers is anything but simple. But we can help our students and ourselves develop skill sets to expand our communicative abilities and grow our facilities with different language practices. We want to develop skillful communicators, students who can effectively language and translanguage to get their meaning across. Creating collaborative, multitasking, inquiry-oriented classroom contexts sets the stage for authentic languaging and translanguaging to occur.

When students work as language detectives and architects, they can use their curiosity and creativity to develop meaningful communication skills that attend to issues of power and facilitate sharing their own ideas and perspectives.

## Openness to Varying Language Practices

In order to create the kind of classroom where authentic languaging and translanguaging can thrive, we need to orient our pedagogical practices toward openness. The varying ways we use language—our language practices—are at the center of most human interactions, among them teaching and learning. Our language practices are so much part of us that unless we have a specific interest in studying languages, we seldom stop to think much about them.

As teachers of multilingual learners, we must all pay attention to the powerful, deficit messages that exist in society that privilege some ways of using language and denigrate others. The more we attend to the different language practices we and others use at work, at home, and at play, the more open we can become to the multiple legitimate ways that people express themselves.

Many factors influence our choices about which language practices to use, among them the social roles and relative power of each participant. One of the complexities in teaching multilingual learners is the tension between language practices that are valued in school versus other ways of communicating. Further, there are issues of power and privilege in play across varying languaging contexts and practices. For instance, when we view some practices as wrong or "less than" rather than just different, we can discriminate against the language users. Through our language detective work, we can grow with our students to recognize these issues and disrupt them in our personal and professional life.

Students need tools to successfully navigate all the communicative contexts they find themselves in. We can help all students expand their linguistic repertoires so they can communicate their ideas and perspectives not just in schools but across the various contexts of their daily lives. This necessitates students becoming familiar with and, when they choose, also being able to use the language of power in varying situations. For us, this is an important shift from privileging and focusing only on so-called academic language. Rather, we can craft an effort to help students maintain their authenticity through their languaging and translanguaging practices as they expand the communicative skills they have across all language domains: reading, writing, listening, and speaking.

As teachers of multilingual learners, we are responsible for much more than making sure students learn English. And as we support multilingual language development, because differing language practices are viewed through the lenses of race, class, gender, ability, and nationality, we need to be careful not to perpetuate inequitable social hierarchies that have tangible negative impacts on multilingual students and families. Through curiosity, we can deepen our understandings of language itself and the language practices of our students. We can then affirm the variety of language practices that our multilingual students and their families utilize inside and outside of school. Additionally, we can provide space and time for students to become creative language architects who can express their ideas and interests in multiples ways. A brave space for multilingual language development to occur is fostered not by overly correcting or policing our students' language but by focusing on effective communication and creating learning opportunities for students to expand their current practices.

Our understandings of language development are informed by a variety of perspectives. One in particular is Systemic Functional Linguistics (Halliday, 1993) which examines *language as meaning-making* and *language use in context*. In this view, no matter the topic or content, every interaction is affected by the relationships among the users and the channels used to communicate (e.g., orally, in writing, or through multiple modalities). Communication rests on the vocabulary we choose (general, specific, or technical), the forms and grammatical conventions we use to put the words together (syntax), and the discourse style or ways we get our meaning across.

Effective communication is always a negotiation between the participants in an interaction grounded in their positionality in the larger society. It is one thing to negotiate communication when you are a Black teenage girl talking to a White male school principal who sees you in the hall during class time. It is another to negotiate communication when you are a female Teacher of Color leading a class where a White male student just hurled a racist slur at you. We can make visible to our students, and explicitly explore, the role that social power and privilege play in these kinds of negotiations.

We often do this by bringing in examples—from books, movies, our real life, or the internet—of language exchanges which we analyze together to notice how different social positions of power affect the ways people communicate. We examine what was communicated both explicitly and implicitly and discuss how students knew who had power in the exchange. We encourage students to expand this language detective work to notice, record, and bring their own examples of language practices so the class can examine and explore them together.

The way that language is taught in schools usually doesn't account for or embrace varying language practices nor attend to the role that power plays in languaging decisions. Of course, students should learn about and be able to use the various language practices that are typical in formal and informal school spaces. Making these complexities visible is a critical part of teaching in multilingual settings. Students need to understand that whether they realize it or not, they are always making choices about how they express themselves. We can foster student agency by helping them evaluate a situation and be more intentional about choosing which language practices will further their desired communication goals. We don't want to censor students. We must refrain from policing practices and controlling too tightly what students say and how they say it, so as not to stifle their creativity. At the same time, students need to be cognizant of the varied impacts and consequences of choosing different language practices. They also may benefit from some supports and scaffolds as they grow their linguistic repertoire.

We can point out how each discipline has different ways of using all four language domains as well as the similar ways language is used across content areas. For example, in all content areas, students are often asked to compare and contrast ideas or situations. We can give students sentence frames to help them communicate their ideas like "X and Y are the same because_____" or "X and Y are different because _____." The purpose, however, is to provide a starting point and not trap students into a controlled effort that communicates "this is the one right way to compare and contrast." There are multiple variations in every language for how things can be compared. Students can and should be encouraged to try on new ones so they can choose among them. Unfortunately, we often hear teachers insist that students have to use the language models that students have been given. Instead of controlling or monitoring student language use, we should be encouraging the exploration and construction of language practices so students can develop their own authentic voices. We can help students self-evaluate the impact of their language choices by having them self-reflect: Was I able to communicate my ideas? Why or why not? When we focus on meaning-making as the purpose of our communications, we can move away from policing and controlling students' language practices.

There are many complexities involved in engaging in linguistic accountability work through our language practices. Just because we want to open up opportunities for authentic expression of ideas and avoid prescribing or policing the ways that students use language doesn't mean anything goes. As communicators, we still have to be accountable to ourselves and others regarding the impact of our language practices. It is important to explore with students the tension between all language practices being legitimate, acknowledging that some of them are problematic for the harm they cause.

We can explore public examples of this from social media or movies while we ask students to find examples. For instance, the artist Lizzo once released a song with an ableist word in it. This happened on a Friday and she immediately received feedback about the problematic nature of using that word. By Monday, she re-released the song without it. She also apologized for not knowing about the history and impact of the word and committed to learning more. Exploring this example with students can help them see the value of accountable language practices and working to minimize the harm we cause through our languaging.

Often as teachers we are concerned how students might be negatively judged or viewed by others due to their choices around language practices. But we also do not want to prevent students from authentically developing their identities and ways of communicating for fear of how biases grounded in racism, sexism, xenophobia, ableism, and other oppressive forces will impact them. Students need to have both an awareness of these issues and the strong language skills that will allow them to make careful choices for themselves about how and when to communicate their ideas in a variety of contexts.

For example, it is common in Black English to pronounce the word "asked" as "axed." This is neither wrong nor a mistake, it is simply part of the dialect. Instead of correcting this usage, we have the opportunity to legitimize a dialect that many people in the US use regularly to communicate effectively in a variety of contexts. We can point out how racism and anti-blackness are linked to perceptions of this as a mispronunciation versus a dialect-specific language practice. When students have this awareness, they can make decisions for themselves about when and how they want to use this language practice and how they will respond to others who use it. We can also talk about code-switching and how many people do so extensively, saving their use of home language practices for their more intimate and connected spaces like with family and friends.

For example, there are many videos on social media by content creators from Black, Latine, and other racial/ethnic/language groups explaining how they choose to use the more standardized and expected forms of English in predominantly White spaces as a way to reduce the amount of energy they have to expend to exist in those spaces. At the same time, they illustrate how this often limits their ability to be authentic. These are the very real kinds of tensions and choices that people who use language practices that are not imbued with high levels of social, political, or economic power have to grapple with. Our students need to have a clear awareness of this reality, tools to navigate it, and opportunities to disrupt it and create a different kind of inclusive reality. When we interrogate linguistic hierarchies and how power operates in social contexts around language, our students can decide how to navigate or disrupt the inequities they face. It's an ongoing tension we all have to grapple with: the reality of the world as it is while we strive to create the world that should be.

We often focus on language practices in schools in terms of the languaging that students produce (either orally or in print). However, we also need to focus on the role of the person consuming or receiving the communication and the ways our social positioning and identities influence how we interpret the language practices of others. Starting with ourselves, do we use our power and privilege as teachers to delegitimize students' authentic language practices? Or do we see their languaging as capable and effective for communication, even when it is different from our own or the expected uses of language in school? We also need to help students to do this work—are they open to the language practices of their peers? Or do they make fun of students for pronouncing words differently? Multilingual learners are often the target of jokes and bullying as they learn English and fumble around with grammar and vocabulary. It is imperative that we help students develop an openness to varieties of language practices and a willingness to negotiate meaning with people who use language differently than them.

## Multiliteracies

Around the world, print-based language practices are privileged over other ways of learning and demonstrating knowledge in schools. The current emphasis on literacy and mathematics in the US is reflected in and driven by accountability testing. Students who don't yet have strong literacy skills or proficiency in the sanctioned dialects of English used in the test are penalized. We too want students to become highly literate mathematical and scientific thinkers. But we also want teachers of multilingual learners to expand the ways that can happen and embrace the notion of multiliteracies.

Far beyond the simplistic notion that literacy is decoding what is on the page and writing down words, it is a politically contextualized and multimodal process that is developed through all the languages and dialects that students speak. Embracing multiliteracies in our content classrooms is part of helping students claim their voices and deepen their academic and linguistic repertoires to fully express themselves and solve problems in their own lives.

Learning to read and write is a political act. The work of Paolo Freire (1975), who sought to bring literacy to Brazilian campesinos in the '60s and '70s, is particularly relevant here. He maintained that educators must do more than teach people how to read and write words but also to read the world around them. He saw literacy development as an active, revolutionary, liberatory process that includes the written word or a single language. Freire argues that by reading not just the word but also the world, we open the possibility for a participatory pedagogy that blurs the lines between teacher and student—a pedagogy where the ultimate goal is ending oppression and, importantly, preventing the oppressed, as they seek liberation, from becoming the new oppressors.

Content classrooms are spaces where students can learn to multilingually read the word and the world as well as develop the skills to positively impact it. All students need access to and an understanding of the discourses and literacy practices that maintain structures of power. Together we can explore who has access to what information and for what purposes. We can examine our content and consider the ways the materials we use promote certain political perspectives, hide issues of inequity or limit students' engagement with and critique of issues of power and privilege. We can invite our students to analyze materials to uncover the context within which they were written and for whose benefit. Questions we might consider include the following: Who builds knowledge? What counts as knowledge? How is knowledge constructed? Which languages count as languages for learning? We can disrupt inequities by reimagining the who, the what, and the why in our content areas. Consider, for example, how understandings might shift if we talk about American history in terms of Eastern Encroachment rather than Western Expansion.

It may seem easier for teachers of English Language Arts or Social Studies to adopt this stance, but Mathematics, Science, Art, PE, Health, World Languages, and indeed every school subject are shaped by the external context and how knowledge is used and valued for different purposes in different communities. While understanding chemical bonding or algebraic equations may seem like pure content unadulterated by politics, the way these understandings are applied in the real world matters. We can investigate whose communities are polluted and who has access to the knowledge needed to mitigate the pollution. What is the difference to the community in real dollars when costs are considered relative to the profits generated by the polluters? Where else in the world and through which languages are other communities addressing these issues? Orienting toward curiosity when reading and exploring different contexts, especially as they relate to power and privilege, helps answer such questions as students learn to read the world and the word.

## Multilingualism and Multiliteracies

Developing multiliteracies in content classrooms means attending to opportunities and complexities. Despite assertions to the contrary, there is no single best approach to literacy instruction for students with diverse backgrounds and language profiles. Nothing about literacy development, including (or especially) the methods we use to teach our students, is neutral. Print-based language practices in multilingual classrooms are surrounded by unique complexities. Policies and practices crafted by districts and states in the US are nearly always guided solely by research on monolingual English speakers, even though the public school population is far more diverse.

One-size-fits-all methods make it less likely that multilingual learners will receive instruction that will advance their intellectual and academic progress. This is a major critique of the current conversations around the so-called "science of reading" in the US. The scientific research of multilingual education scholars, which is rarely cited or considered part of the science of reading in these discussions, illustrates the variety and complexity of the processes of learning to read while multilingual. Many current approaches to literacy instruction run directly counter to their perspectives, narrowly focusing on teaching students to decode words on a predetermined page. A major focus is on teaching phonemic awareness and phonics but without accounting for the different sound systems across dialects and languages that students know and use in their daily lives. Such one-size-fits-all approaches divert us from attending to other facets of good literacy pedagogy, including oral language development and building background knowledge. It leaves out connecting to students' communities, home languages, and cultural practices, which is integral to humanizing literacy instruction.

Decades of research from around the world shows that reading and writing skills are best initially developed in the language in which children have the strongest proficiencies. Once a child has strong understandings of print-based language practices, they can apply them to other languages. Learning to read in a language a student doesn't yet speak or understand is much more difficult than in one they already know. For students reading through a language that they know well, text opens doorways to new ideas, conceptualizations, and ways of understanding the world. However, the text itself—that is, the words on the page—are often barriers to accessing ideas if students don't already have the requisite literacy skills or sufficient knowledge of the language the words are written in.

An orientation toward openness and curiosity prompts us to investigate what multilingual students already bring to literacy learning. We want to ensure that students can work at their cognitive level and not be trapped into being provided information solely through simplistic texts. For students new to English, text should not be used to introduce new information; rather, text should be used to confirm, deepen, and extend understandings that students develop through multiple modalities first. For example, before students read about a new topic, we can introduce them to the big ideas by modeling an experiment or via a movie, a virtual tour of museums or historical sites, or other kinds of visual and interactive presentations. When we use multiple modes and languages to convey conceptual information, multilingual students' can focus on underlying concepts and draw on their background knowledge. In the process, they can develop vocabulary, predict and analyze information, and anticipate ideas as they build conceptual understandings.

In classrooms where textbooks are either required or the main resource provided to teachers, it is even more important that our planning centers on creating meaning and building students' schema around the topics of our instruction. One way is to supplement textbooks with materials in students' home languages even if we don't know those languages ourselves. Using multilingual multitasking orientations and pedagogies from Modules 6, 7, and 8 can be particularly helpful.

## Multilingual Oracy

Schools typically privilege reading and writing and focus extensively on helping students develop their language skills around print. However, it's also important for us to support students' development of expansive speaking and listening skills, or oracy.

Currently in England, a major push for oracy is happening from policy-makers and educators to mixed effect. One of the most impressive schools we have ever visited, a multilingual school in which over 90% of the student population are multilingual learners, is in England, not far from London. The educators at that school have devoted a great deal of attention to developing oracy skills with their students. We've seen students talk confidently across difference, ask poignant questions, and effectively communicate their own ideas. However, we've also read about schools in England where a push for oracy has become another lever for language policing in schools (Cushing, 2024). This must be avoided and we can do so by orienting ourselves toward openness, curiosity, and creativity in our language detective and architecture work related to supporting students' expansion of their oracy skills.

A place to start is consistently encouraging students to use their entire linguistic repertoire to deepen their understandings, thereby counteracting and disrupting the idea that only English counts for learning. Building multilingual students' linguistic flexibility can increase their confidence in using all of their linguistic resources—named languages, as well as different dialects, and registers—to deepen their understandings and expand their tools for meaning-making.

Through dialogues where students work within and across all their linguistic resources (translanguaging), they can explore how concepts exist in human experience, not just within the confines of a single language. Beyond allowing or encouraging them to do so, we can also explore with students the myriad ways that different languages and cultures have impacted and created the world we live in. For instance, we can investigate the accomplishments of scientists, historians, mathematicians, or representatives of other disciplines from a variety of cultural and linguistic backgrounds who contribute to the knowledge base of our content areas. In these explorations, we should identify the languages these people used and the variety of cultural backgrounds and perspectives they came from.

Another approach is to compare how different languages express concepts or how some words or ways of phrasing can be more useful in one setting over another. Preview/review is another beneficial strategy that brings languages other than English into building oracy and authentic talk. In this process, students' home languages are used to preview the main ideas and activities of a lesson or a unit and to debrief their understandings afterwards. These oral discussions do not require that students have literacy skills in those languages and can vary from listening to a formal presentation by someone fluent in the language, to a small-group discussion among students from the same language group or an individual listening to or watching something online. Depending on the resources and personnel in the languages of our students, formal preview/review lessons can happen daily, weekly, or at intermittent times during the duration of a unit.

## Promoting Talking and Listening

Many content teachers rely solely on textbooks in English to disseminate information and written tests in English to assess student knowledge. This severely limits the possibilities for many multilingual learners to access and demonstrate their understanding of the content. Oral interactions provide students with opportunities to learn content through dialogue and conversation without the barrier of text. Researchers have also illustrated how multilingual students can often express their learning more effectively orally than in writing or through multiple modalities (Grapin, 2022).

In addition, when content instruction is delivered only through lectures and text materials, the learners remain mostly silent. In too many classrooms, students have few opportunities for productive back-and-forth conversations with either their peers or the teacher, resulting in many missed opportunities in content lessons for students to build or communicate ideas or to develop their language and literacy facilities. With the support of scaffolds such as images, models, and other tools that organize information, students can engage with and act on concepts in conversation and through their actions. This allows students the flexibility and permission to access and represent their understandings through multiple linguistic channels. Scaffolds such as visual images play a particular role in this work by providing a focus for discussion and setting the stage for students to access the ideas through multiple linguistic channels.

While students may talk endlessly with their peers, they often grow silent or reply to our questions with minimal responses even when invited to express themselves. To understand what is happening, we have benefitted greatly from recording a lesson segment and noting who is talking, about what, and for how long (even though it can be painful to watch ourselves on video). Just counting how many minutes different people speak reveals if one voice dominates and too often, we learn it is ours. We have been able to notice whom we call on, whom we don't, where we look, our facial expressions, and tone of voice. Taking a close look at a lesson allows us to observe which students are engaged, using which kinds of language practices and with whom. The point is not to judge the situation as good or bad but to consider what is happening and establish a baseline for encouraging students to do more of the talking with more people, in ways that honor their identities. We've also been able to create a classroom with more authentic talk by designing learning activities grounded in joint productive activity and instructional conversations (see Module 7).

As we share our hopes and expectations about talking and listening as central to our classroom community, we must also invite students to contribute their ideas. We can let them know that, over time, we expect every individual will interact with every other individual in the classroom and discuss together how we can hold each other accountable for participation. We can make a real difference for our multilingual learners by providing opportunities that extend beyond a narrow prescriptivist approach that focuses on "saying things correctly" and instead building students' confidence that not only do they have something to say but they can express their understandings and ideas using multiple modalities and languages. We need to be patient and become comfortable with extending student talk by modeling different ways to acknowledge, restate, disagree, expand, clarify, or challenge each other's thinking.

Strategies like using a talking piece (only the person with the piece/object talks), giving each student three talking chips (each time they talk, they have to give up a chip helping ensure that more students get a chance to talk), numbered heads together (students in groups each get a number and the teacher calls out a number to indicate who should talk in the group), or randomly pulling names from a box are aimed at equalizing the participation and increasing the likelihood that all students have a chance and are expected to contribute. We also want to develop our listening skills so we can hear what students are saying without passing judgment and as a way to learn more about who each person is.

As we've discussed in previous modules, dialogue does not develop by simply putting students into small groups and telling them to talk to each other. Talk increases when students are regularly and actively engaged in situations where they *need* to get their ideas across to each other. The goal is not to get students locked in the one right way to say something or interact. Rather than conducting language drills, we should provide spaces for authentic talk and oral rehearsal.

Using discussion protocols that structure talk, with assigned roles that distribute responsibilities and opportunities among all the learners, provides a way to scaffold students' skill development around small-group dialogues. Protocols like *Final Word*, *Block Party*, or *4 A's Text* from the National School Reform Faculty (nsrfharmony.org) and many others describe guidelines, step-by-step processes, and time limitations that allow students to participate equitably in the task. These structured conversations can help students to formulate and synthesize ideas and internalize their learning. Importantly, they can also be enacted in any language. Students who might normally hold back have a defined place to talk which makes it easier to contribute their ideas.

Protocols do need to be modeled and practiced, but the goal is not to enact the protocol itself (thus perhaps over-scaffolding or limiting student creativity with language) as much as creating a predictable and framed way to engage in a discussion. The protocols are simply scaffolds to help students develop their talking and listening skills. The efforts we make up front to introduce and practice each new protocol will lead to deeper participation over time as students become familiar with the expectations of the different assigned roles. Student creativity with the protocols can also increase as they are more comfortable learning together and have built the trust necessary for collaborative work. We can introduce a new protocol first by using familiar topics drawn from students' lives and interests. In this way, they can increase their agency in directing the conversation and build on their everyday modes of communication using all their linguistic resources.

Protocol guidelines also provide structures that can make it safer for students to ask challenging questions of each other. Because listening is valued just as much as speaking, students who tend to dominate a discussion can learn how to step back and let their peers participate. Protocols are especially well suited to groups where students from varying language backgrounds are working together with ample opportunities for interaction, modeling, and building cross-cultural understanding. We can also create spaces for students to work in home language groups or provide extra scaffolding for those students at the earlier stages of developing English in order to build their confidence in participating in classroom discourse.

Other activities that promote talking and listening among students often contain what are called information gaps where participants in an activity have different parts of the information that they can fill in for each other to build shared understandings. For example, in a science lab, instead of all students doing the same experiment, small groups can conduct related experiments with somewhat different variables, so that there is an authentic purpose for reporting out and sharing information. Barrier games are activities where two students can complete a task only by describing orally what their partner should do or request the information they have. These might include using shapes and directions to recreate a drawing, finding similarities and differences in a picture or text passage, or solving a content-based crossword puzzle when each partner has only some of the clues and answers related to the content. Jigsaw activities are also effective as students get information in their expert groups to complete the activity in their home groups. Strategies such as Socratic Seminars or creating and performing a script for Reader's Theater, also center speaking and listening as essential to accomplishing the task while focusing on deepening understandings. Other ideas include doing role-plays in social studies or language arts where students are tasked with explaining what is happening from different points of view or taking on the perspective of different sides in a conflict or story. In science, students can practice how they might explain findings from their investigations on water pollution to persuade different audiences such as members of the school board, a community organization, or younger children to take action.

## Linking Talking and Writing

A final benefit of a focus on oracy is the role it can play in strengthening multilingual students' writing. Through guided conversations, we can show students how talk can help them to put their ideas into writing. For most of us, having the opportunity to verbalize ideas makes it easier to put our thoughts into writing, even if we just do so internally. Especially for younger learners, if they can't yet express their ideas out loud, it is unlikely they will be able to represent them or recognize them in print. In addition, the conventions of written language, especially in academic settings, vary from the ways we typically express ourselves orally. As an example, we have observed teachers incorporate song lyrics as a means to connect words and print. Having students listen to and/or sing lyrics while they see them represented in print can help them make connections between oral expression and writing on the page. We and they can also create new lyrics to familiar tunes on the basis of whatever content we are engaging with.

An excellent way to make the link between talk and text is through discussion of ideas around a concrete experience orally and then co-construct text based on it. It could be about a science demonstration, watching a play, a field trip, or discussing visual images that represent the essential understandings of a unit. Following extended oral discussion, we use students' contributions to co-construct a written text in a small group which can be used in a variety of ways. This cycle of interaction provides ways for students' ideas to be valued while helping them see how their talk can be transformed to text on the page.

We are always more effective using new approaches when we have had opportunities to try them out ourselves. All of the suggestions included in this module will be easier to implement in the classroom if we have practiced with our colleagues. For example, we can use a checklist to document who talks for how long in staff meetings. We have found that many of the same individuals who teach primarily through lecture resent the principal for taking up a whole staff meeting talking at them. We can discuss as a faculty that if we don't think "sit and listen" professional development is a good use of our time, then what does this mean when we use it in our teaching? We can also examine what we think respectful interactions look like to us. We may find that there is not a universal definition.

A schoolwide approach to growing students' oracy skills makes all our individual efforts more effective. We can practice using discussion protocols with our colleagues as part of staff meetings and professional development or try out different ways of extending oral production to become adept at automatically using them with students. We can plan together with our peers to share the protocols we are working on and which ones we need help with and then incorporate them intentionally into our lessons. Especially at the secondary level, students tend to be more willing to try out new approaches when they encounter them across several classrooms. When there is consistency among the faculty, students can become more comfortable and confident in taking part. We have found that, for many teachers, these become ingrained habits of interaction over time.

## Make It Work

In the Explore section, we discussed how language practices are complex and varied and the need to move beyond binary thinking of language as correct or incorrect. We addressed how language and power are intertwined and ways to attend to effective communication while addressing issues of justice and equity. We also explored a variety of ways to grow students' skills with language practices across all language domains: reading, writing, listening, and speaking. Now is your chance to play with these ideas and make them work in your practice! Below we have provided some options of how you can do that, thinking about the intrapersonal, interpersonal, and systemic levels of engagement. Any of these could (and potentially should) be done just by yourself but also could be accomplished through learning activities with your students. As you choose an option, keep in mind the module's critical reflection and complexity thinking questions: *What do I currently do to promote student agency, meaning-making, and a commitment to equity in the use of different language practices? How can I address the complexities of using a variety of language practices to humanize the languaging in my classroom?* We encourage you to revisit the components of humanizing pedagogies from the introduction and think about the implications of what you learned from engaging in this module in relation to context, orientations, and pedagogy. When you have completed your Make It Work activity, reflect on your findings to share them with your colleagues.

## Make It Work Options

### Intrapersonal: Examine Your Own Language Practices

Purpose: Uncover what makes it possible and what blocks your being able to use your own authentic language practices.

Engage in a self-study of your own language practices. We recommend spending a day (or more) documenting your languaging across all four language domains (listening, speaking, writing, and reading). For instance, perhaps in the morning you speak with your family members over breakfast and coffee. Then you listen to the news or music as you prepare for the day. Then when you get to school, you read your lesson plans and review the text as you prepare for class, and so forth. What additional practices do you engage in after work or over the weekend? After documenting your language practices, reflect on what you uncovered. Consider the purpose for each language practice and how power dynamics were at work (e.g., who had the power, how did you make decisions about which practices to use, where the expectations about "appropriate" language practices come from, and anything else you noticed). How authentic was your communication in different settings and domains? What might account for any differences (e.g., did you have power in certain situations and not others)? What allows you to engage in authentic language practices? What are the barriers? How can this self-study and reflection inform your work with students to support their development of authentic language practices?

### Interpersonal: Attending to the Impact of our Language Practices

Purpose: Assist students in developing a critical awareness of the impact of their language practices and a willingness to language in ways that are humanizing for all.

Plan and, if possible, teach a lesson or unit that includes explicit attention to the impact of our language practices. The goal is to explore language uses that communicate harm and creating ways to avoid them. For example, ableist language is very common in everyday uses of English. You could plan for how students will learn about ableist language (ideally through their own language detective work) and for how students could translate that learning into their language architecture work. As a class, you could co-construct shared agreements around humanizing language practices that expand as understandings around such issues grow. You can also apply this process to language practices that are racist, sexist, or homophobic or that denigrate a particular religion. In the process, you will need to plan how you can support students in developing a sense of how their use of language can thoughtfully attend to the human dignity of all rather than participate in perpetuating oppressive behaviors.

## Systemic: Disrupt Language Policing

Purpose: Explore policies and practices in your school and/or district that serve as language policing and advocate for their change.

Begin by exploring and documenting the policies and practices in your classroom, school, or district regarding language use. If possible, involve your colleagues in these investigations. Notice both their intent and impact and whether there are spaces that legitimize language variety or if they privilege or accept only particular language practices. Is there explicit mention of using (or not) languages other than English? Are there unstated or implicit messages in these policies? For example, your district's assessment policy may dictate evaluating the reading abilities of students only in English, regardless of their multilingual literacy skills and background. In this situation, student language practices are being curtailed by not allowing their full linguistic repertoire to be part of their literacy development and demonstrations of abilities. Where very specific language practices are expected, how are students, families, and community members treated when they do not meet those expectations? Where you uncover language policing that limits the ability for authentic language practices for all, what changes should you and your colleagues advocate for?

### You Make It Work!

Purpose: To make the ideas from Explore work in your own practice.

Design your own activity (or tweak one of ours) to ensure that you are spending your time doing work that is most useful and relevant to you and your students. We recommend starting with the critical reflection and complexity thinking questions. Then clarify for yourself which level you are working at (intrapersonal, interpersonal, or systemic) and build your effort to make this module's learning work for you from there!

 **Share**

Share is your opportunity to engage with your peers and receive feedback about the work you have done and what you have learned in this module. Begin by revisiting the reflection you wrote at the beginning of the module and revise it to include your thinking now, noting any changes and what they might mean for your practice. Be sure to attend to opportunities to strive for justice and equity and to potential barriers to achieving it. Don't shy away from the complexities that come up—embrace them. Think about different ways of being and doing in your classroom that could address those complexities. Once you have completed your reflection, be prepared to share it with your colleagues along with a description of the work you did in the Make It Work section. By sharing what you have learned, you have the chance to both solidify your own learning and thinking and expand it by learning from your colleagues.

# 10

# Deepening Conceptual Understandings

The education of multilingual students is often focused solely on their need to learn English. However, we've also seen educators and administrators overlook the complex ways that language and content learning are intertwined in classrooms when they suggest that students who are learning English should have no trouble with grade-level mathematics. The reality is that language and content learning are deeply intertwined. We can do a great deal as educators to create humanizing pedagogies that embrace these complexities. Integral to this work is how we can bring the life experiences and perspectives of multilingual students into our classrooms.

In this module, we seek to orient ourselves toward openness and generate a pedagogy that is learning-centric to deepen students' conceptual understandings, building on their cultural backgrounds, languages, and life experiences. In this way, we can sustain the cultural ideas and understandings that students bring to learning and provide the kind of loving, supportive instruction that enables them to grow from a place a strength, embracing who they are and how they would like to live in the world.

To begin, consider the following questions for complexity thinking and critical reflection: *Do I treat students as complex multiplicities with a variety of important life experiences that can inform their growth and development? Do I do so even if those perspectives and experiences are different from my own or the knowledge that is valued at school? Is there space in my curriculum and instruction for ideas, perspectives, and life experiences that students bring from a variety of cultural and linguistic backgrounds? Do I sufficiently decenter whiteness and monolingualism to make space for different ways of knowing and being in my classroom?* Be sure to preserve your initial reflection, notes, and ideas so you can revisit them during the Make It Work and Share sections of this module, paying attention to your growth and keeping track of your learning.

## Explore

US schools have long been criticized for implementing a factory model of teaching and learning. Many graphics exist of students as products on an assembly line and teachers lined up to dump knowledge in their brains. When we show and discuss these images with teachers and teacher candidates, they never feel like they are that kind of educator, nor do they aspire to be. We and they know that students are not empty vessels and that for authentic learning to occur, students cannot simply be passive recipients of ideas.

Yet we often still resort to simplistic approaches to teaching and learning that mirror the factory model despite knowing what great teaching and learning look like. This includes substituting telling for teaching, or accepting that knowledge only counts when expressed in written or spoken dominant standard English (rather than in other languages, mediums, or dialects) or that only certain ways of knowing and being are valuable for school learning and knowledge (such as grade-level content based on standards or "academic language"). It's important that we look at our actual practice and see if it matches our intent. We need to examine our orientations and perceptions for any deficit mindsets toward students. Might we be overlooking the knowledge and life experience that students already have because it doesn't match what we are familiar with or value in our curriculum?

Sometimes, we assume that multilingual students don't know something because they can't express that knowledge in English. We see teachers use language barriers to justify not engaging students in meaningful content learning or critical discussion. Once we observed a class where, in a unit on butterflies, most students were exploring metamorphosis in a variety of ways. The sole multilingual learner was sitting in the corner, just coloring images of a butterfly. There was nothing in the picture to represent the stages of the butterfly life cycle or to suggest them as a metaphor for migration. In other cases, we've seen multilingual students who understand the math concepts but are unable to show their knowledge because of the language of the test, leading teachers to decide that students require remedial instruction. To avoid these situations and proactively create meaningful learning for all our multilingual learners, we must expand our ways of thinking about conceptual understandings and their relationship to language.

## The Conceptual Reservoir: A Useful Metaphor

In many classrooms, content learning consists of students reading information and listening to lectures. Instruction is often decontextualized or includes limited perspectives and typically occurs only in English. In the US, ideas are typically Eurocentric and mostly aligned with the perspectives and values of able-bodied, White, middle- to upper-class, monolingual English-speaking Americans. Students are expected to assimilate to the ideas and show what they know by taking written tests only in English. We control which knowledges and language practices are positioned as valuable in the classroom, especially when we don't view what students bring with them as meaningful sources of ideas and tools for learning. If we stick to these routines, we perpetuate inequity on various levels by limiting the information that students can access and their opportunities to demonstrate their understandings. We can instead provide all students, and especially multilingual learners, numerous entry points to access important concepts as well as engage with ideas through multilingual, multicultural approaches. We want to ensure that students can use all their linguistic and cultural resources to deepen knowledge, interrogate ideas, and expand their understandings of the world.

Students are learning all the time and have been since birth. No matter their background, economic circumstance, or language uses, all students can think and have acquired many perspectives about the world that may or may not coincide with what schools deem important to know. The knowledge gained from their homes and communities is important in their identity development and enhances learning opportunities at school. Our task is to tap into, learn from, and build on the knowledge and experiences that all students bring to the learning community. To do so, it can be helpful to think of our brains as a conceptual reservoir that can be accessed and added to through all languages and dialects as well as through a variety of experiences and resources (Figure 10.1).

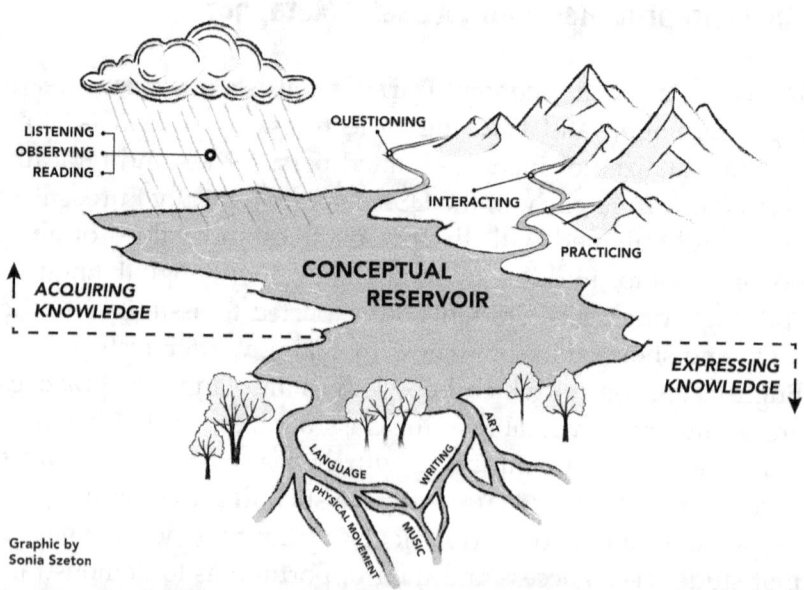

**FIGURE 10.1** Conceptual reservoir.

The water in the reservoir represents concepts, knowledge, and understandings of everything from how people are treated in the world around us, to how to nourish plants in a garden, to ways to show respect, fix a bicycle, build a rocket, or find one's way home from the store. Much of the knowledge that students have in their conceptual reservoir initially comes from their experiences at home and with their families. Therefore, that knowledge is also often connected to powerful emotions like love and belonging.

Researchers refer to what students bring as their Funds of Knowledge (Moll et al., 1992). These funds represent the wealth of knowledge, practices, and networks that students, families, and communities engage with. They are often overlooked or invisible to teachers simply because they are different from the ones the teacher has themself. Getting to know and honoring the expansive existing resources students have in their conceptual reservoirs from their lives outside of school are deeply important for engaging in humanizing teaching and learning that centers who students are and would like to be.

Language practices are also embedded in the conceptual reservoir. We add to our reservoir and represent what we know from birth onward, through every language we know or learn. Knowing something is different from being able to talk about it in any particular language or dialect. As illustrated above, we can add to our conceptual reservoir through observation, interactions, and practices that do not have to be language-based. It is important that we, our students, and their families understand that already-acquired information, knowledge, and concepts can be accessed through any language or dialect we speak or understand. No matter how information got into the reservoir, it can be made use of through any language or dialect as well as through other communicative tools like music, art, and physical movement.

The languages and dialects in our linguistic repertoires flow along multiple channels and throughout the reservoir, threading together and separating as the context demands. As we interact with others, we all selectively draw from our linguistic repertoire to communicate using skills from one named language (or dialect) over another to share and add to what we already know and can do. In some situations, we may even choose to utilize a variety of codes and linguistic practices (i.e., translanguage) to most authentically express our ideas and feelings.

Learning is a natural and ongoing process for all humans that occurs through these various channels all day, every day. A key distinction we make is that the reservoir of knowledge itself is different from the process we use to add to and take from it. The channels going in and out of the reservoir represent the different means we have for acquiring and expressing knowledge and are constantly in use, both at school and at home. The channels that add to reservoir include listening, reading, observing, viewing, questioning, interacting, and practicing. The channels coming out are how we use and show what we know, through speaking, writing, artistic representations, physical movement, and any other expressive skills. As we learn more, the channels grow deeper and flow more freely, making it easier to fill the reservoir and to represent what is known more precisely. The more we know (the deeper the conceptual reservoir), the easier it will be to learn more about and interrogate school topics.

We want to emphasize that, while important in school, reading and writing are too often singled out as the most important (or only) tools for learning, neglecting the various other channels in and out of the reservoir. This generates inequity for those students who don't yet speak the language of instruction or who are still refining their literacy skills.

While reading and writing are privileged in schools, literacy skills in and of themselves are not the ultimate goal of education. Rather, deepening conceptual development is. Of course, learning new information is greatly facilitated by language and literacy skills, but important learning also happens when we interact with people and concepts orally and through visual images, models, diagrams, charts, songs, art, and pictures as well. Too many multilingual students are denied access to ideas while they work on rote memorization of sound–symbol relationships or mathematical algorithms. We can help all students deepen and expand their understandings by attending to both the channels in and out of the reservoir and the reservoir itself.

The conceptual reservoir metaphor also opens the door to valuing students' background knowledge even if it was gained through languages other than English or cultural experiences that differ from majoritarian cultural practices. Too often, we pay limited attention to the issues of injustice that certain topics and points of view may perpetuate. We can counteract this by instead incorporating multiple perspectives and ideas regarding our content of study. One way is to support students in having conversations with their families about the topics of instruction and sharing those ideas in the class. For instance, in a unit on supply and demand, students could talk with immediate and extended family members to understand their lived experiences in relationship to this economic concept. Through those conversations, students' conceptual reservoir can deepen as they contextualize an otherwise somewhat abstract concept. Students might hear stories of drought or famine, of abundance, of creatively meeting needs, or of government corruption or failures. The act of collecting these stories can strengthen the channels into the reservoir while the stories themselves deepen and expand the reservoir itself. Students can then creatively choose how to represent what they learned, perhaps through visual images that represent supply and demand as told through their families' stories, or through musical expression, or by dramatizing them via live action or video. In doing so, they strengthen the channels extending out of the reservoir.

Students who are learning content through a new language may be able to think more deeply about their learning in their more proficient language(s). This is facilitated when teachers and schools support learning vocabulary associated with new ideas by providing access to resources in multiple languages. What is referred to as multidirectional transfer doesn't just happen. It is not automatic that students will know the words for measurement, the principles of democracy, or the life cycle of plants in their home language if they have learned about those topics in school in English. But they need to know that those words exist and that people who speak their languages also discuss these topics and contribute to the world's knowledge about them. Further, we can encourage their exploration of the varying cultural perspectives in their family and communities around these ideas. In this way, we can legitimize that any concept presented at school is also understood, explored, and valued in different cultural groups. Such learning might also lead to important collaborative actions to combat inequity and injustice locally.

We can and must let multilingual learners know that we value their home languages, dialects, and community knowledge. We can show students different ways they can take advantage of their multilingualism and multiculturalism as they continue to grow it in school. Further, we can help students seize on opportunities to utilize their learning to strive for equity and justice. These understandings underpin what is termed translanguaging, an asset-based view of multilingualism (see Module 3) and culturally sustaining pedagogies (Alim et al., 2020).

## Identifying Essential Concepts, Multiple Perspectives, and Language Pathways

Rather than telling learners what to think, we want to create avenues for questioning, examining, and making meaning from the learning activities in our classrooms. We can stimulate students' curiosity and expose learners to things they might not have noticed on their own, even when they are still early on in their English-learning journey. Further, we can support students' development as creative problem-solvers and future worldbuilders, using their unique knowledges and perspectives.

To prepare for such explorations and creative engagements with learners, we need to identify the essential concepts of our instruction as well as think through the implications of those concepts related to issues of justice and equity. There is significant complexity here to grapple with: some of the expected learning and essential concepts from our content and grade levels are problematic as they often provide only part of the truth. For example, a current literacy program includes a picture of George Washington accompanied by text that describes his jobs as measuring land, leading an army, and becoming the first president of the US. What is not stated is that the land being measured had been taken from Native American communities or that throughout his personal and professional life he benefitted from the labor of enslaved people because he was a slave owner. We need to develop ways to help students learn essential ideas *as well as* how to interrogate those ideas for their complexities and impacts while growing multilingually and multiculturally.

Planning should begin with clear answers to the questions: What concepts must students learn and understand to meaningfully think through and engage with increasingly complex ideas and content? How can we connect the often-abstract essential concepts of instruction to students' already-developed understandings and background knowledge? What different perspectives and ways of understanding these concepts need to be explored? How can students' understanding of these concepts lead to increased student agency and creativity in building the world they would like to live in? The answers to these questions are fundamental in creating meaningful learning opportunities for all our students that embrace their varied strengths and learning assets.

A graphic organizer called a concept ladder is a useful tool in clarifying our focus as we plan instruction. We have used it on our own and with colleagues to deconstruct the content we are planning to investigate with students. Each rung of the ladder prompts thinking that can generate synonyms, examples, definitions, and essential aspects of any concept. The prompts (words in bold in Figure 10.2) are both abstract and somewhat redundant. Others can be added and there are no right or wrong answers. The example below is taken from a brainstorming session among sixth-grade teachers about predator–prey relationships. The ideas that repeatedly emerged became the essential concepts to further interrogate and plan instruction around.

This activity deconstructs content ideas and defines an instructional path forward that is responsive, interesting, critical, and clear. For instance, sixth-grade science lessons around predator–prey relationships could focus on adaptation, interdependence, and ecological balance. By identifying these core concepts, we can also identify how those concepts relate to students' daily lived realities and what is already in their conceptual reservoirs. For instance, interdependence can be explored

**Looks like:** Chasing. Lying in wait. One animal eating another. Some animals trying to hide or remain invisible.

**Made (Used) for:** Keeping animals alive, keeping the ecosystem in balance, providing food for carnivores.

**Parts are:** Animals eating other animals. Adaptations to be able to catch and eat prey and to avoid being eaten - sharp claws, fast running, camouflage, protection. Life and death.

**Made of:** Carnivores and the things they eat. Different animals with different roles, different places in the food chain or web of life

**Replaces:** Some animals eat other animals to stay alive. Some animals are eaten by others

**Kinds of:** Fox/Rabbit, Bear/Fish, Hawk/Chipmunk, Human/Cow, Snake/Mouse, Frog/Fly

**A kind of:** Biological relationship, interdependence

**Also called:** Parts of food chain, food

**Predator/Prey Relationships are...**

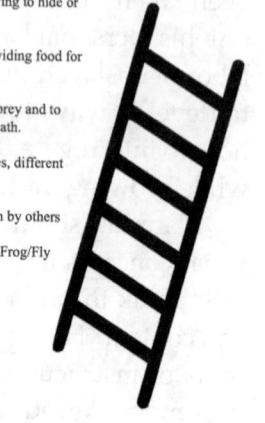

**FIGURE 10.2** Concept Ladder Example - Predator–Prey Relationships.

through a global or systemic lens where students can see that what they do right here today has an impact on people, animals, and land not just in our local community but across the globe. By learning about various systems and tracing the flow of information or commodities, students can grow their understandings of interdependence and its impact on issues like poverty, climate change, and immigration. As students deepen their understandings around these issues, they can then engage in problem-solving efforts to address them.

Part of deepening our conceptual reservoirs is considering varying perspectives that might be overlooked. We can do this by examining the curricula we are given and finding ways to engage with the topic multilingually and multiculturally. The example in Table 10.1 related to *adaptation* offers additional questions to consider once the essential concepts for planning have been identified.

As we plan for instruction, we need to distinguish between the conceptual understandings of our teaching/learning and the ways students will interact with those ideas. It can be helpful to think of teaching/learning activities as being comprised of different aspects or dimensions, including the conceptual knowledge itself (what students must learn or the essential concepts), the ways students and teachers speak and listen (oral communication), and the text materials that will be used and produced by

**TABLE 10.1** Exploring Varying Perspectives Example – Adaptation

| Standard topic | Whose perspective, knowledge(s), and/or ways of being are represented? | Whose perspective, knowledge(s), and/or ways of being are not represented? | How can we explore this topic to include varying ideas, beliefs, and ways of being in the world? | How can we explore this topic from perspectives relevant to students' lives outside of school? | How can we explore this topic from a multilingual perspective and include languages other than English as an integral part of the learning? |
|---|---|---|---|---|---|
| Adaptation | Adaptation as natural, normal evolutionary process. There is a relationship between these ideas and assimilation. | The difficulties of adaptation, what is lost, who is impacted. The impacts of when adaptation is similar to assimilation. | We can look at adaptation in the animal world as well as the human world and from the perspectives of those adapting as well as those who don't change but are part of the adaptation process. | Students can capture information from family members and friends about their experiences with adaptation. They could also look for examples of it in the natural world in their home and community. For example, is a plant growing through a crack in the sidewalk an adaptation? | Students will be encouraged to have conversations with their families in their language of choice regarding their perspective of adaptation in the animal and human worlds. We will use multilingual texts and websites to explore the topic in class. Students will work in home language groups at times to deepen ideas and make plans. Students can also represent learning in their language of choice. |

reading and writing (interaction with text). We recommend taking time to map out these aspects of lessons during planning to ensure that we create useful and relevant supports for students in growing their language and content knowledge and skills. This can be done using a simple matrix to map our activities.

## Deepening Conceptual Understandings Through Contextualization

We often visit classrooms where instruction is in a language we don't know. We are always impressed by how much we understand when teachers use visuals and manipulatives to contextualize their instruction and connect it to students' lives outside of school. One such lesson was in an eighth-grade mathematics class in Finland where students were learning about percentages and ratios. The teacher brought pictures of items that students could buy and sell in shops around the room. Students took turns in the role of consumer or seller and together negotiated discounted prices for the products. Students figured out the prices for various items on the basis of different discounts (e.g., 50%, 80%, or 25% off). The students were very engaged as they walked around the room, figuring out the different possible costs of sale items. For the Finnish learners in her class, the teacher provided sentence stems and key vocabulary to assist them in having the language tools they needed to fully participate in the task. We marveled at how much we could follow from the lesson despite not knowing any Finnish.

We later talked about how this kind of lesson could help students see how the cost of the items affected people in various occupations and with different income levels. Students could calculate percentages to determine how much of a person's income would have to go to housing, transportation, and food and how that varied depending on how much they earned. To take their learning further, they could advocate for solutions to issues they uncover like the need for more affordable housing and reliable public transportation to ease the burden on lower-income residents. This kind of contextualization allows students to connect school learning to their lives outside of school and sets the stage for collaborative work in a learning community invested in equity and justice.

Deepening conceptual understandings is also furthered when we become familiar with students' lives outside of school, so our efforts don't miss the mark or replicate prejudicial stereotypes. It can feel overwhelming to try to make links to each student's life outside of school. Know that it is a process that develops over time and is easier to accomplish when we work with our colleagues and students. Together, we can explore their context and uncover connections to the concepts we are studying. It is particularly useful to help students discover those connections themselves as they read the word and the world.

As we seek to contextualize learning, we need to evaluate our curriculum and the associated materials for their authenticity and accuracy. While we may not have the freedom to radically change the resources we are given, we can try to supplement them in class. We can also be thoughtful about what we share with families. It's important to examine the messages in the resources that students are given to ensure that they have opportunities to see themselves and their life reflected (sometimes called "mirrors"). We also want them to be able to explore the life experiences and perspectives of others (sometimes called "windows"). One approach often used by teachers of multilingual learners is to share folk or fairy tales from the students' family's country of origin. This is not inherently a bad practice. However, it also isn't necessarily the mirror for students that the educators intend it to be. In this case, we would want to draw on the growing body of diverse stories from children's and young adult literature about being multilingual or belonging to various racial and ethnic groups in the US today. Such stories are important for how they are more genuine mirrors of students' lives—focusing on everyday and relatable experiences like cooking with family members, creating cultural artifacts with grandparents, and exploring new cities with new friends. All students need to have access to these kinds of stories in their education, ones where they can truly see themselves and their own lives reflected.

## Using the Physical Environment to Deepen Conceptual Understandings

The physical environment of the classroom is also an instructional tool that can act as a resource for students in their independent or collaborative work to deepen conceptual understandings. Treating the classroom space and the shared physical environment as a collaboratively owned space is a great place to start. With student collaboration and leadership, we can create a learning environment full of supports that students can reference, visit, and return to on their own to continue to work on the ideas and concepts we are exploring.

Students should always know how to successfully work within the community agreements and where to find information that supports their learning. We can intentionally organize the physical space to make visible to students the connections between what they are doing at any given moment and the overall big ideas or essential learning concepts without their having to rely on oral instructions or their memory. We can also make visible how the topic relates to their lives outside of school.

Visual images play a vital role in contextualizing learning and can serve as ongoing supports or scaffolds around the classroom. Visual images, graphic organizers, and three-dimensional models are particularly important in helping multilingual students take what they know or have learned in one language or dialect and express it through another. The best visuals go beyond simple pictures of individual vocabulary words and instead represent the larger concepts of the unit. We can then help students connect ideas and images to how they are represented in print, even multilingually. In Figure 10.3a, a poster from a second-grade class summarizes the needs of plants and animals. It is an example of representing overarching ideas and not just a list of vocabulary words. It connects the ideas of the unit with concepts and images that students understand and value from their lives outside of school. It also shows how it may take more than one picture to embody a concept, especially for more abstract notions.

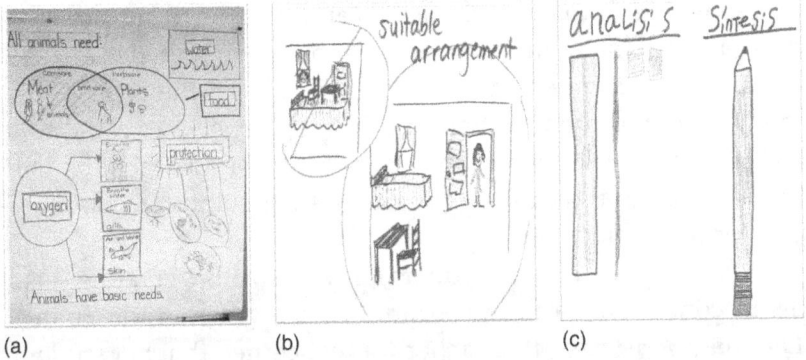

**FIGURE 10.3** Visualizing abstract concepts. (a) Needs of plants and animals, (b) suitable arrangement, (c) analysis and synthesis.

Figure 10.3b is an example of visual imagery that demonstrates a concept by contrasting it with its opposite. A group of teachers wanted their students to understand that a habitat was more than water, space, food, and shelter and get at the more abstract concept that the components need to be in a suitable arrangement. Students created drawings of places they were familiar with (classroom, bedroom, kitchen, etc.) and illustrated them both suitably and unsuitably arranged. This helped them to clarify the understanding that it wasn't sufficient to just have the components, they all had to be within reach. The images that students created became tools for them to understand a complex concept. They were also able to connect to real-world issues of justice and equity as they discussed what happens to animals and humans when they do not have access to one or more of those components. What might need to change so that living things can survive and thrive in their habitats?

Visual scaffolds that support conceptual development include different types of graphic organizers or thinking maps. Some are created with multilingual learners specifically in mind, such as picture dictionaries and bilingual glossaries. Others are more generally conceived. For example, the Frayer Model organizes information using definitions, examples, non-examples, and pictures. It has been adapted by many teachers to include space for words and information in students' home languages, something that benefits multilingual learners at all levels of language performance.

As we work to develop visuals and models to support conceptual understandings, we must remember that there is not an automatic connection between a visual and the concept it is intended to represent. Differing cultural perspectives can lead to varying interpretations of images. It is in the interactions with our students that we can agree what visuals stand for, communicate, or represent.

It is helpful when students play a role in creating visuals to contextualize their learning. In a seventh-grade Spanish Language Arts class, the teacher was concerned that her students didn't understand the difference between analyzing a text and synthesizing information, activities she was always asking students to do as part of reading and writing. She brought in a set of everyday objects as shown in Figure 10.3c, and she had students create two drawings in which they deconstructed an object and then put it back together—in other words, to analyze and then synthesize the object. All the students created their own visual images and then chose several exemplars to put together in a display on the wall of the classroom. To connect the visuals to the concepts they represented, she added labels as well as an explanation of synthesis versus analysis in relation to language arts. From then on, when students were unsure of what they were supposed to do in a particular assignment that asked for analyzing or synthesizing their readings, she would refer to the visuals and ask students to decide with their peers, based on the visuals, what they were supposed to do: take things apart (analyze) or put ideas together (synthesize).

Classroom walls can also be a place for students to pose questions and share ideas that they generate through their work. Some teachers have blank posters or shared files where students can jot down their ideas and questions for later discussion without disrupting the instructional flow. Setting time aside to explore student-generated questions and ideas as a learning community allows for additional insights and perspectives to become part of the collaborative learning. Further, it generates a space for students to question each other's ideas and have more agency and leadership over their learning.

As another example, we can ask students to co-plan a word wall so that it supports their multilingual language development. One strategy we've seen in multilingual classrooms is to post quotes from students' home language. We can't assume, however, that if we choose the quotes, they will automatically make students feel seen and at home in our classrooms. Instead, we could ask students and their families to share a favorite quote from their heroes or community leaders. Students can create the posters themselves and decide where they should be displayed and which language(s) to use. These displays can and should change from time to time—perhaps on a regular basis so that each student has the opportunity to share important people and ideas in the language(s) of their choosing with the class.

We visited a school that took a community approach to classroom organization that made it easier for all students to act independently and autonomously as well as collaboratively. They committed to instituting certain classroom routines (e.g., note-taking protocols or formatting guidelines) in very similar ways across the whole school so that students didn't have to learn a new organization system each time they entered a new classroom. This is in contrast to treating the classroom like it is ours alone rather than ours as a whole community of learners.

## Teaching Complex Thinking

An inquiry-oriented, collaborative, multilingual, and multitasking classroom provides multiple possibilities for students to engage in higher-order thinking. Students need strong supports to confidently engage in this kind of complex thinking. Research from the CREDE Center (Tharp et al., 2000) is also quite useful here. It illuminated some simple steps that help students develop their higher-order thinking abilities and apply them in classroom learning: set a clear, high standard for students to work toward; give them meaningful assistance; and provide ongoing feedback to ensure that they achieve it. As teachers of multilingual learners, we need to do this for both content and language development.

To set high standards for student learning, we need clarity around what the essential learning is for each lesson or unit, so we can ensure that all students are working toward it. Students who are just learning the language of instruction can engage in complex cognitive work and have many strong conceptual resources to draw from to do so (their conceptual reservoir). They may need to take different pathways to get there, but with thoughtful support, especially in multitasking classrooms, high levels of cognitively complex learning are indeed possible.

In addition to setting rigorous learning goals, we need to ensure that students have a clear understanding of what they are working toward. A very successful fifth-grade writing teacher we observed consistently worked with students to co-construct shared understandings about "proficient" writing. At the beginning of the year, the whole class reviewed the indicators the district used to evaluate writing as below, at, or above proficiency. Students concurred that they all wanted their writing to be judged as at least proficient.

To get a better sense of what proficient writing in fifth-grade could look like, the class analyzed multiple writing samples, synthesizing what they noticed. At times, they focused on writing conventions (punctuation, spelling, and grammar). At others, they talked about how writers communicated their ideas and brought readers along with them. They co-constructed texts and reviewed them for whether they met their shared conceptualization of proficiency. Knowing that writing proficiency grows over time, they spent several months doing this work to collaboratively clarify and expand their notions of writing proficiency. Simultaneously, they worked on developing those skills themselves.

Even when students had a clear sense of where their learning was heading, they needed assistance to get there. A key part of their success was the targeted, thoughtful feedback they received. Ongoing and productive feedback loops provide students with information they can use to adjust and refine their work. In turn, this builds confidence in their strengths and growth.

The most impactful feedback is sincere and grounded in truth. It focuses on strengths as well as opportunities for growth and leads students where to go next. Too often, multilingual learners working on their English just have their language corrected as they use it across the day, which can be defeating as well as feel like language policing. Instead, we recommend helping students see the patterns in their languaging that limit communication and shared meaning-making, so they can develop strategies for improvement. For instance, we might notice students struggling to conjugate verbs to match the subject or tense of their sentence. This can create confusion regarding who is doing whatever action is being described. Or maybe some students are using articles "a" or "the" in ways that cause confusion for the listener/reader. Noticing this can help us provide feedback through mini-lessons and supportive learning activities so that students will understand the issue, its relationship to meaning-making and communication, and how to improve. Our ability to notice these patterns grows as we work as language detectives ourselves, perhaps even noticing things about how English works that we may haven't thought about before. By connecting our feedback around language practices to how such practices may limit or impede meaning-making or clear communication, we can move away from focusing on 'correcting' students and instead help them grow as creative, authentic communicators of their ideas and perspectives.

Giving meaningful feedback is facilitated when we orchestrate joint productive activities and instructional conversations where we are full-fledged collaborators with a small group of students (see Module 7). Here, we can act as the more-knowledgeable-other assisting students in accomplishing something together that they would not be able to accomplish on their own. This kind of collaboration is an important scaffold for students as they build more independence in approaching complex tasks. Assistance can also come in the form of multilingual print resources, classroom volunteers, or digital tools.

A multitasking learning environment allows us to set up regular learning dialogues with individual students. We've worked with teachers who did this every week. Others plan for monthly learning dialogues or during each unit or each quarter/trimester/semester. We've also worked with teachers who have created data collection strategies to inform their feedback to students like charts where they can quickly note strengths and opportunities for next steps as they observe or collaborate with students. With that data, teachers then pop into conversations with students organically during class to tell them what they are doing well and suggest where they might have a chance for improvement. We worked with one elementary teacher who used data she collected during regular observations to provide written feedback to both students and their families about their accomplishments and next steps.

Teachers are not the only ones with useful ideas and feedback for students' growth which is important since in busy classrooms we can't be everywhere all at once. Other feedback loops include the following: students own self-reflection, especially using co-constructed rubrics; peer assessments; and inviting families to give feedback in conversations at home around the learning topic. We can deliberately build in these feedback loops that will help students grow in their complex thinking as well as recognize that everyone around them, including themselves, is an important contributor, collaborator, and leader in their learning.

## Make It Work

In the Explore, we explored the conceptual reservoir metaphor and discussed how it can help us think about the important knowledge and skills that students bring to the classroom as well as how to deepen those skills through the pathways in and out of the reservoir. We examined the possibilities of using visuals to support learning as well as the necessity to have a clear sense of the essential concepts being taught along with their implications for equity and justice inside and outside the classroom. Finally, we discussed the affordances of contextualization and teaching complex thinking. Now is your chance to play with these ideas and make them work in your practice! Below we have provided some options for how you can do that, thinking about the intrapersonal, interpersonal, and systemic levels of engagement. Any of these could (and potentially should) be done just by yourself but also could be accomplished through learning activities with your students. As you choose an option, keep in mind the module's critical reflection and complexity thinking questions: *Do I treat students as complex multiplicities with a variety of important life experiences that can inform their growth and development? Do I do so even if those perspectives and experiences are different from my own or the knowledge that is valued at school? Is there space in my curriculum and instruction for ideas, perspectives, and life experiences that students bring from a variety of cultural and linguistic backgrounds? Do I sufficiently decenter whiteness and monolingualism to make space for different ways of knowing and being in my classroom?* We encourage you to revisit the components of humanizing pedagogies from the introduction and think about the implications of what you learned from engaging in this module in relation to context, orientations, and pedagogy. When you have completed your Make It Work activity, reflect on your findings to share them with your colleagues.

## Make It Work Options

### Intrapersonal: Perceptions of the Conceptual Reservoir

Purpose: Deepen your understanding of the conceptual reservoir as it relates to your own educational experiences as well as how it positions multilingual students as fully capable learners, regardless of their cultural or linguistic background.

Step 1. Reflect on the idea of our brains as a conceptual reservoir and how it relates to your views regarding multilingual learners. Begin by thinking about the funds of knowledge, including language(s), that you brought to school. Were they recognized, valued, and expanded upon, or were they overlooked, devalued, or not taken into account in your instruction? How did it make you feel? What might your teachers have done differently?

Step 2. Consider the assertion that reading and writing are not ends in themselves, and our primary goal should be deepening students' conceptual reservoir through multiple channels. Does it affirm or contradict how you currently approach instruction? What does it mean for what you might do next?

Step 3. Pick a student you want to better understand, focusing on their background, strengths, or interests. You can talk with the student, visit their neighborhood, or find other ways to learn about their life outside of school. If possible, talk with their family to learn about their experiences, goals, and wishes. Use what you find to uncover any biases or misperceptions you might have had. Then reanalyze some of their work, keeping in mind the difference between the reservoir itself and the channels to get information in and out. How does what you learned about this student apply to how you might (mis)perceive and treat others in your classroom? How do your thoughts, words, and actions help or hinder you in supporting multilingual learners? An important internal check is whether you focus on students' strengths and abilities rather than perceived deficits.

Step 4. Consider the implications of this investigation for how you will plan instruction to expand conceptual development rather than completing assignments or doing well on the accountability assessments.

### Interpersonal: Contextualize Learning and/or Teach Complex Thinking

Purpose: Plan and, if possible, implement a lesson or unit that contextualizes learning and/or teaches complex thinking with multilingual learners.

Use the ideas in Explore (conceptual reservoir metaphor, conceptual ladder, and examining different perspectives) to guide you in crafting an instructional plan that contextualizes students learning and/or teaches complex thinking. Identify the concepts and key understandings of the lesson/unit. Some questions to consider: What are some of the complexities that students need to attend to? What are ways you can connect the content to students' lives outside of school? How will you incorporate students' multilingualism into the process? What different modalities/ channels will you use to add to students' conceptual reservoirs and have students demonstrate their understandings? Be sure to consider the distinction between conceptual knowledge itself (what students must learn), the ways that students and teachers speak and listen (oral communication), and the text materials that will be read and produced (interaction with text). If you can't teach the lesson, share your ideas with a colleague who is teaching the same or similar topics to solicit feedback and ideas for fine-tuning your plan. If you get to teach the lesson, use critical reflection to determine how the work went and how you might grow and improve as you continue to contextualize students' learning or teach complex thinking.

### Systemic: Analyze Students' Opportunities to Deepen Conceptual Understandings Across the School Day

Purpose: At the school level, examine and evaluate opportunities for multilingual students to engage in learning set to high standards that build on their linguistic resources and funds of knowledge.

A major theme of this book is that what happens in our classroom is embedded in a larger context. In order to advocate for systemic change, we need to understand the policies, practices, and dominant cultural narratives that affect students' learning. In this option, you will analyze the opportunities that multilingual learners have to deepen their conceptual understandings and engage in complex thinking across their whole school day. How do school and district policies and practices facilitate or hinder their potential? If possible, work with colleagues to uncover information.

Questions to keep in mind include the following: What kinds of classes and learning opportunities do your multilingual students currently have? Are multilingual learners tracked into basic skills classes where they do below-grade-level, rote memorization and boring and uninspiring work? Are there beacons of hope where they are challenged and pushed to reach higher? Where are their conceptual understandings being deepened?

Does this happen in every subject, in most, or hardly ever? How often do students simply pass the time or do work that is decontextualized from their lives outside of school? Where might they be denied strong learning opportunities because of perceptions of their abilities based on their level of English proficiency?

Based on your findings, make a plan for how you can advocate for more justice and equity for multilingual students so they can fully develop their conceptual understandings using all their resources at your school. What are some small and big steps that could be taken schoolwide to do this? Identify any systemic barriers to making change (language policies and mandated assessment practices) and what the staff might do to overcome them.

**You Make It Work!**
Purpose: Make the ideas from Explore work in your own practice.

Design your own activity (or tweak one of ours) to ensure that you are spending your time doing work that is most useful and relevant to you and your students. We recommend starting with the critical reflection and complexity thinking questions. Then clarify for yourself which level you are working at (intrapersonal, interpersonal, or systemic) and build your effort to make this module's learning work for you from there!

 **Share**

Share is your opportunity to engage with your peers and receive feedback about the work you have done and what you have learned in this module. Begin by revisiting the reflection you wrote at the beginning of the module and revise it to include your thinking now, noting any changes and what they might mean for your practice. Be sure to attend to opportunities to strive for justice and equity and to potential barriers to achieving it. Don't shy away from the complexities that come up—embrace them. Think about different ways of being and doing in your classroom that could address those complexities. Once you have completed your reflection, be prepared to share it with your colleagues along with a description of the work you did in the Make It Work section. By sharing what you have learned, you have the chance to both solidify your own learning and thinking and expand it by learning from your colleagues.

# References

Aguirre, S., & Chou, A. (2024). *The Seal of Biliteracy 2023 National Report, for the 2021-2022 School Year*. SealofBiliteracy.org

Alim, H. S., Paris, D., & Wong, C. P. (2020). Culturally sustaining pedagogy: A critical framework for centering communities. In N. S. Nasir, C. D. Lee, R. Pea, & M. M. de Royston (Eds.) *Handbook of the cultural foundations of learning* (pp. 261–276). Routledge.

Bartolomé, L. I. (1994). Beyond the methods fetish: Toward a humanizing pedagogy. *Harvard Educational Review, 64*(2), 173–194.

Birman, D., & Addae, D. (2015). Acculturation. In C. Suárez-Orozco, M. M. Abo-Zena, & A. K. Marks (Eds.) *Transitions: The development of children of immigrants* (pp. 122–141). New York University Press.

Braidotti, R. (2022). *Posthuman feminism*. Wiley.

Brisk, M. (2022). *Engaging students in academic literacies: Genre-based pedagogy for K-5 classrooms* (2nd Ed). Routledge.

Brooks, M. D. (2020). *Transforming literacy education for long-term English learners: Recognizing brilliance in the undervalued*. Routledge.

Cullors, P. (2022). *An abolitionist handbook: 12 steps to changing yourself and the world*. Macmillan.

Cushing, I. (2024). Social in/justice and the deficit foundations of oracy. *Oxford Review of Education*, 1–18, doi:10.1080/03054985.2024.2311134

Delavan, M. G., Morita-Mullaney, T., & Freire, J. A. (2024). Demographic silencing, ableism, and racialization in dual language bilingual education: A call for intersectional and program-level data reporting to assess gentrification. *Linguistics and Education, 83*. doi:10.1016/j.linged.2024.101330

Donald, D. (2021). We need a new story: Walking and the wâhkôhtowin imagination. *Journal of the Canadian Association for Curriculum Studies, 18*(2).

Dudley-Marling, C., & Gurn, A. (Eds.) (2010). *The myth of the normal curve.* Peter Lang.

Flores, N. (2020). From academic language to language architecture: Challenging raciolinguistic ideologies in research and practice. *Theory Into Practice, 59*(1), 22–31, doi:10.1080/00405841.2019.1665411

Flores, N., & Schissel, J. L. (2014). Dynamic bilingualism as the norm: Envisioning a heteroglossic approach to standards-based reform. *TESOL Quarterly, 48*(3), 454–479. doi:10.1002/tesq.182

Freire, P. (1975). *Pedagogy of the oppressed.* The Seabury Press.

Freire, P. (1994). *Pedagogy of the oppressed.* Continuum.

García, O. (2009). *Bilingual education in the 21st century: A global perspective.* Wiley-Blackwell.

Genesee, Fred, Lindholm-Leary, Kathryn, Saunders, William, & Christian, Donna (2005). English language learners in U.S. schools: An overview of research findings. *Journal of Education for Students Placed at Risk* 10 (4): 363–385.

Gorski, P., & Swalwell, K. (2023). *Fix injustice, not kids and other principles for transformative equity leadership.* ASCD.

Gottlieb, M. (2023). *Assessing multilingual learners: Bridges to empowerment.* Corwin.

Gould, S. J. (1981). *The mismeasure of man.* Norton & Company.

Grapin, S. E. (2022). Assessment of English learners and their peers in the content areas: Expanding what "counts" as evidence of content learning. *Language Assessment Quarterly, 20*(2), 215–234. doi:10.1080/15434303.2022.2147072

Halliday, M. A. K. (1993). Towards a language-based theory of learning. *Linguistics and Education, 5,* 93–116.

Hayes, K., & Kaba, M. (2023). *Let this radicalize you: Organizing and the revolution of reciprocal care.* Haymarket Books.

Hilberg, R. S., Chang, J. M., & Epaloose, G. (2003). *Designing effective activity centers for diverse learners: A guide for teachers at all grade levels and for all subject areas.* CREDE Center for Research on Education, Diversity & Excellence. https://manoa.hawaii.edu/coe/crede/wp-content/uploads/Hilberg_et_al_20031.pdf

Kaba, M. (2021). *We do this til we free us: Abolitionist organizing and transforming justice.* Haymarket Books.

Kang, O., & Rubin, D. L. (2009). Reverse linguistic stereotyping: Measuring the effect of listener expectations on speech evaluation. *Journal of Language and Social Psychology, 28*(4), 441–459.

Kendi, I. X. (2017). *Stamped from the beginning: The definitive history of racist ideas in America*. Bold Type Books.

Kimmerer, R. (2013). *Braiding sweetgrass: Indigenous wisdom, scientific knowledge and the teachings of plants*. Milkweed Editions.

Lee, S. (2009). *Unraveling the "model minority" stereotype: Listening to Asian American youth* (2nd Ed.). Teachers College Press.

Menken, K. (2010. NCLB and English language learners: Challenges and consequences. *Theory Into Practice, 49*(2), 121–128. doi:10.1080/00405841003626619

Menyuk, P., & Brisk, M. E. (2005). *Language development and education: Children with varying language experience*. Palgrave Macmillan.

Miller, S. J., Burns, L. D., & Johnson, T. S. (Eds.). (2013). *Generation BULLIED 2.0: Prevention and intervention strategies for our most vulnerable students*. Peter Lang.

Moll, L.C., Amanti, C., Neff, D., & Gonzalez, N. (1992). Funds of knowledge for teaching: Using a qualitative approach to connect homes and classrooms. *Theory into Practice, 31*(2), 132–141.

Morita-Mullaney, T., Renn, J., & Chiu, M. (2020). Obscuring equity in dual language bilingual education: A longitudinal study of emergent bilingual achievement, school course placements and grades. *TESOL Quarterly, 54*(3), 685–718. doi:10.1002/tesq.592

Morita-Mullaney, T., Renn, J., & Chiu, M. M. (2022). Spanish language proficiency in dual language and English as a second language models: The impact of model, time, teacher, and student on Spanish language development. *International Journal for Bilingual Education and Bilingualism, 25*, 3888–3906.

Portes, A., & Hao, L. (1998). E Pluribus Unum: Bilingualism and the loss of language in the second generation, *Sociology of Education, 71*, 269–294.

Prasad, G., & Lory, M.P. (2020) Linguistic and cultural collaboration in schools: Reconciling majority and minorities language users. *TESOL Quarterly, 54*(4). 797–822 doi:10.1002/tesq.560

Salazar, M. (2013). A humanizing pedagogy: Reinventing the principles and practices of education as a journal toward liberation. *Review of Research in Education, 37,* 121–148.

Shuster, K. (2007). Civil discourse in the classroom. *Teaching Tolerance.* https://www.learningforjustice.org/sites/default/files/2017-07/Civil_Discourse_in_the_Classroom_0.pdf

Simpson, L. B. (2017). *As we have always done: Indigenous freedom through radical resistance.* University of Minnesota Press.

Strom, K., & Viesca, K. M., (2021). Toward a complex framework of teacher learning practice. *Professional Development in Education, 47*(2–3), 209–224. doi:10.1080/19415257.2020.1827449

Subtirelu, N. C., Borowczky, M., Hernández, R. T., & Venezia, F. (2019). Recognizing whose bilingualism? A critical policy analysis of the Seal of Biliteracy. *The Modern Language Journal, 103*(2), 371–390.

Tatum, B. (1997). *Why are all the Black kids sitting together in the cafeteria?* (1st Ed.). Basic Books.

Teemant, A. (2024). *Enduring principles of learning: Theory to practice instructional guide* (3rd edition). Teemant & Associates, LLC.

Teemant, A., & Hausman, C. S. (2013). The relationship of teacher use of critical sociocultural practices with student achievement. *Critical Education, 4*(4). Retrieved from http://ojs.library.ubc.ca/index.php/criticaled/article/view/182434

Tharp, R. G., Estrada, P., Dalton, S. S., & Yamauchi, L. (2000). *Teaching transformed: Achieving excellence, fairness, inclusion, and harmony.* Westview Press.

Thompson, K. D., Umansky, I. M., & Rew, W. J. (2023). Improving understanding of English learner education through an expanded analytic framework, *Educational Policy, 37*(5), 1315–1348. doi:10.1177/08959048221087214

Umansky, I. M. & Reardon, S. F. (2014). Reclassification patterns among Latino English learner students in bilingual, dual immersion, and English immersion classrooms. *American Educational Research Journal, 51*(5), 879–912.

UNHCR. (2024, October 8). *Refugee data finder.* https://www.unhcr.org/refugee-statistics

Venet, A. S. (2024). *Equity-centered trauma-informed education*. Routledge.

Viesca, K. M., Alisaari, J., Flynn, N., Hammer, S., Lemmrich, S., Routarinne, S., & Teemant, A. (2024). Orientations for co-constructing a positive climate for diversity in teaching and learning. Invited manuscript published in *Teacher Education in (Post-) Pandemic Times: International Perspectives on Intercultural Learning, Diversity and Equity*. Peter Lang.

Viesca, K. M., & Hutchison, K. (2014). Reflections on effective writing instruction: The value of engagement, expectations, feedback, data, and sociocultural instructional practices. *Writing and Pedagogy, 6*(3), 681–696. doi:10.1558/wap.v6i3.681

Viesca, K. M., Strom, K., Hammer, S., Masterson, J., Linzell C. H., Mitchell-McCollough, J., & Flynn, N. (2019). Developing a complex portrait of content teaching for multilingual learners via nonlinear theoretical understandings. *Review of Research in Education, 43*, 304–335. doi:10.3102/0091732X18820910

Wiley, T. G. (2004). Language planning, language policy, and the English-only movement. In E. Finegan & J. R. Rickford (Eds.) *Language in the USA: Themes for the 21st Century*. Cambridge University Press.

For Product Safety Concerns and Information please contact our EU
representative  GPSR@taylorandfrancis.com
Taylor & Francis Verlag GmbH, Kaufingerstraße 24, 80331 München, Germany

www.ingramcontent.com/pod-product-compliance
Lightning Source LLC
Chambersburg PA
CBHW070758230426
43665CB00017B/2405